THE BEST

Books and CD-ROMs by Drs. Ron and Caryl Krannich

THE BEST JOBS FOR THE 21ST CENTURY

Third Edition

Ronald L. Krannich, Ph.D.
Caryl Rae Krannich, Ph.D.

IMPACT PUBLICATIONS
Manassas Park, VA

THE BEST JOBS FOR THE 21ST CENTURY

Third Edition

Library of Congress Cataloguing-in-Publication Data

Krannich, Ronald L.
    Best jobs for the 21st century / Ronald L. Krannich, Caryl Rae Krannich.
        p. cm.
    Rev. ed. of: The best jobs for the 1990s & into the 21st century / Ronald L. Krannich, Caryl Rae Krannich, c1995
    Includes bibliographical references and index.
    ISBN 1-57023-091-9 (alk.paper)
    1. Job hunting. 2. Vocational guidance. 3. Occupations.
I. Krannich, Caryl Rae. II. Krannich, Ronald L. Best jobs for the 1990s & into the 21st century. III. Title.
HF5382.K68   1998   98-16137
331.7'02—dc21   CIP

For information on distribution or quantity discount rates, Telephone (703/361-7300), Fax (703/335-9486), E-mail (*impactp@erols.com*), or write to: Sales Department, IMPACT PUBLICATIONS, 9104-N Manassas Drive, Manassas Park, VA 20111-5211. Distributed to the trade by National Book Network, 15200 NBN Way, Blue Ridge Summit, PA 17214, Tel. 1-800-462-6420.

Contents

Preface X

CHAPTER 1: Are You Ready For the 21st Century? 1

- Sailing Through a Downsized and Uncertain Future 1
- Your Mother and Teachers Were Right! 2
- Key Success Factors 2
- Welcome to the New Talent-Driven Economy 3
- What We Know and Don't Know 4
- Good Guesses and Feeling Good 4
- Welcome to the Revolution 7
- Think About Your Future 8
- Take Charge 9
- Test Your Future Careering Capabilities 9
- Prepare For Uncertainty 11
- Forecast the Future 12
- Tomorrow's Economy 13
- The Coming Job Transformation 14
- You in Tomorrow's World of Work 15
- Choose the Right Resources 15
- Empower Yourself 17

PART I
Consider Your Future

Chapter 2: Prepare For Turbulence and New Opportunities .. 21

- Dream Your Possible Dream   21
- Work and Meaningful Lifestyles   22
- Prepare For Life in a Boom and Bust Economy   23
- Understand Employment Dynamics in a Dual Society   28
- Face Increased Structural Unemployment   31
- Take Initiative in a Fundamentally Flawed System   32
- Predict and Prepare For an Uncertain Future   34
- Beware of Incomplete Approaches   37
- Career and Re-Career For Today and Tomorrow   40

CHAPTER 3: Prepare For 33 Coming Changes 42

- Images of the Future   42
- Turn Turbulence Into New Opportunities   43
- Face New Demographics   44
- Experience the Impact of New Technologies   49
- 33 Coming Changes   52
- Be Realistic   68

CHAPTER 4: Identify the Best Jobs For Tomorrow 71

- What Are the Jobs?   71
- Beware of Changing Occupational Profiles   72
- Expect Job Growth in Most Occupations   74
- Examine Growing and Declining Occupations   80
- Determine "The Best" Job For You   87
- 100 "Best" Careers For the 21st Century   88
- Similarities and Differences   93
- Look For Exciting New Occupations in the 21st Century   94
- Consider the Implications of Future Trends For You   95

CHAPTER 5: Best Paying Jobs and Salary Ranges 98

- Variable Compensation 98
- Salary Ranges For 229 Occupations 99
- Pursuing a $100,000+ Job 106

CHAPTER 6: The Best Places to Live and Work 107

- Relocate For New Opportunities 108
- Target Communities 109
- Know the Growing States and Communities 111
- Consider the Best Places to Work 113
- Find the Best Place to Live 114
- Seek Out the Best Employers 116
- Look For Solid Metro Areas 121
- Select a Location Properly 121
- Consider Your Financial Costs 123
- Conduct a Long-Distance Community Search 125
- Penetrate the Local Job Market 127
- Identify Opportunity Structures 129
- Your Ideal Marriage 130

PART II

The Best Jobs

CHAPTER 7: Medical and Health Care Careers 135

- Chiropractors 137
- Clinical Laboratory Technologists and Technicians 139
- Dental Assistants 140
- Dental Hygienists 142
- Dentists 143
- Dietitians and Nutritionists 145
- Electroneurodiagnostic Technologists 146
- Emergency Medical Technicians 147
- Homemaker—Home Health Aides 148
- Licensed Practical Nurses 150
- Medical Assistants 151
- Medical Record Technicians 152
- Nursing Aides and Psychiatric Aides 153

- Optometrists 155
- Pharmacists 156
- Physical Therapists 157
- Physicians 158
- Podiatrists 160
- Occupational Therapists 161
- Radiologic Technologists 162
- Recreational Therapists 163
- Registered Nurses (R.N.) 165
- Respiratory Therapists 166
- Speech-Language Pathologists/Audiologists 167
- Veterinarians 169

CHAPTER 8: Computer and Internet Careers 171

- Computer and Office Machine Repairers 173
- Computer Programmers 174
- Computer Scientists, Computer Engineers, and Systems Analysts 176
- Operations Research Analysts 178
- Webmaster 179

CHAPTER 9: Science and Engineering Careers 181

- Biological and Medical Scientists 182
- Chemical Engineers 183
- Chemists 184
- Civil Engineers 185
- Electrical and Electronics Engineers 186
- Geologists and Geophysicists 187
- Industrial Engineers 188
- Mechanical Engineers 189
- Meteorologists 190
- Science Technicians 192

CHAPTER 10: Business and Financial Careers 194

- Accountants and Auditors 195
- Actuaries 196
- Cashiers 198
- Counter and Rental Clerks 199

- Financial Managers   200
- Human Resources, Training, and Labor Relations
  Specialists and Managers   201
- Information Clerks   203
- Management Analysts and Consultants   204
- Marketing, Advertising, and Public Relations Managers   206
- Property and Real Estate Managers   207
- Underwriters   209

CHAPTER 11: Education, Government, and Legal Careers 211

- Adult Education Teachers   212
- Correctional Officers   213
- Counselors   214
- Education Administrators   216
- Guards   218
- Inspectors and Compliance Officers   219
- Lawyers and Judges   221
- Paralegals   223
- Police, Detectives, and Special Agents   224
- Psychologists   226
- School Teachers   228
- Social and Human Service Assistants   229
- Social Workers   231

CHAPTER 12: Art, Media, and Entertainment Careers 233

- Actors, Directors, and Producers   234
- Dancers and Choreographers   236
- Designers   237
- Photographers and Camera Operators   239
- Radio and TV News Announcers and Newscasters   240
- Visual Artists   242
- Writers and Editors   244

CHAPTER 13: Travel and Hospitality Careers 246

- Aircraft Pilots   247
- Chefs, Cooks, and Other Kitchen Workers   248
- Flight Attendants   250

- Food and Beverage Service Workers   251
- Hotel and Motel Desk Clerks   253
- Hotel Managers and Assistants   255
- Reservation and Transportation
  Ticket Agents and Travel Clerks   256
- Restaurant and Food Service Managers   258
- Travel Agents   260

CHAPTER 14: Resolution, Personal Services, and Transportation Careers 262

- Adjusters, Investigators, and Collectors   263
- Electricians   265
- Services Sales Representatives   266
- Truck Drivers   267
- Veterinary Assistants and Nonfarm Animal Caretakers   267

PART III

Resources For the 21st Century

CHAPTER 15: Finding Your Best Job For the Future 273

- Key Directories   273
- Annual Surveys   276
- Future Jobs   276
- Alternative Jobs and Careers   278
- Community Opportunities   282
- Electronic Job Resources   284

INDEX   289

THE AUTHORS 293

CAREER RESOURCES 295

Preface

Get ready to sail into an exciting 21st century job market! Whatever you're doing today will most likely be history ten years from now. During the next ten years you will probably have three different jobs with three different employers. You'll change careers at least once and probably move twice; one move may be to a new community. You may even get fired or "downsized."

But are you planning to sail into the 21st century like an inexperienced sailor, buffeted by the winds of change, with little control over your career future? Or do you know how and where you are going?

Many individuals are unprepared for the future. They acquire jobs but lack vision about their career future. They fail to plan and invest in their future. While they have skills for today's jobs, they may be ill-prepared for the turbulent changes in the job market that will require new education and training for the jobs of tomorrow. Many are shocked to discover the job they had yesterday disappeared today; they may not find a similar one tomorrow nor in the coming decade. They are tomorrow's potentially displaced workers.

This should not happen to you. If you understand the dynamics of today's rapidly changing economy and job market, you should be in a good position to prepare for tomorrow's most rewarding jobs. You'll formulate a vision that will help guide you in acquiring the necessary skills and abilities to land one of tomorrow's best jobs.

In the following pages we examine the changing nature of the economy and its implications for both the job market and your career choices in the decade ahead. We also outline nearly 100 of the fastest growing jobs between now and the year 2006. These are some of the best jobs in terms of overall job growth. They will employ a large number of individuals in the decade ahead. Many of these jobs pay well and offer excellent opportunities for career advancement. Others are low paying jobs that provide entry into growing career fields.

This edition includes a new chapter on salary ranges for 229 major occupations. We believe this information will be useful in evaluating the long-term financial potential of various jobs and careers. If you want to make a lot more money in the future and you want to do so working for others rather than starting your own business, then you should consider jobs that can be financially rewarding in the long term. As you can quickly see from examining salary ranges, many jobs are not very financially rewarding; they may be unfair in terms of their financial rewards. Indeed, some of our best jobs for the 21st century are abundant and may be personally rewarding, but they pay poorly and will continue to do so in the future. If you pursue one of these jobs, you may discover that your salary quickly plateaus at a low level. Consequently, you may want to look at salary ranges *before* you select a particular job or career. Deciding to pursue a career in finance, for example, will have very different long-term financial consequences than selecting a career as an animal caretaker. Ten years from now you may work just as hard making $25,000 as a zookeeper as you would be making $500,000 as a stockbroker. While you may be happier working with animals, you might also be happier making $500,000! Chapter 5 should help you consider the long-term financial implications of your career choices.

The following chapters should help you develop a vision of your career future. For we believe a vision may well be the most important ingredient for preparing for the future. With a clear vision of what you want to do, you'll know what you need to do to get the job you want. Your vision will motivate you to take charge of your career. You'll sail into the 21st century knowing exactly where you are going. Best of all, those seemingly unpredictable winds of change will become your ticket to career success as you take charge of your career future!

Ron and Caryl Krannich

THE BEST JOBS FOR THE 21ST CENTURY

1

Are You Ready For the 21st Century?

W hat are the best jobs for the 21st century and how can you get one? Are you afraid of making bad career choices? Do you feel you're in a deadend job and would like to do something more rewarding? Have you already been a victim of downsizing and would like to avoid repeating this experience in the future? Are there other job and career possibilities that look promising for someone with your particular interests, skills, and abilities? Are you prepared for a volatile 21st century job market with the right skills and mindset for taking control of your future? Will you be a major player in the new talent-driven, entrepreneurial economy of the 21st century or will you be content working on the periphery of this highly competitive economy?

Sailing Through a Downsized and Uncertain Future

The 1990s have been both a rocky and exhilarating road for many individuals who have experienced a combination of downsizing and tremendous growth in their careers. It has almost become a cliche that you should expect to have several jobs and careers throughout your worklife; that the job you have today may disappear tomorrow; that you must constantly acquire new skills in order to survive and prosper in

1

today's volatile job market; that you must think like an entrepreneur; and that you must take charge of your own career future. In other words, education and hard work, along with a keen sense of new opportunities, entrepreneurship, and drive, should serve you well in the coming decade.

Your Mother and Teachers Were Right!

Yes, it's true what your mother and teachers told you long ago—the best jobs go to those who get a good education and work hard! That's the basic message we've learned in our examination of the best jobs for the 21st century. Underlying the many lists of the 10, 25, 50, or 100 "best" or "top" jobs for the future are two common themes—education and hard work. While serendipity and luck play roles in getting ahead, education and hard work tend to predominate.

However, underlying these individual-level success factors is the single most important element determining whether or not education and hard work will result in rewarding jobs

> **Education, hard work, and luck are constant themes for getting the best jobs for the future.**

—an expanding economy that continues to generate jobs requiring education and hard work. Without such a dynamic economy, all the talk about a continuing job or work revolution is nonsense. As we have witnessed in the latter half of the 1990s, a rapidly expanding service economy driven by a dual high-tech and managerial revolution results in generating thousands of jobs requiring education and hard work. Whether or not this fast growing economy will continue to transform the job market in the foreseeable future is uncertain. The cyclical boom-bust American economy of the past 25 years often resulted in periods of high employment followed by recessions and high unemployment. It's uncertain if this pattern has ended for good.

Key Success Factors

Whether you define the "best" as the top paying, fastest growing, most secure, or most satisfying, these two themes remain the same. Over and over we find education and hard work at the center of the best jobs for the future. We also see two additional "success factors" that appear again and again when examining the best jobs for the coming decade:

1. **You must be fast on your feet and entrepreneurial** in today's and tomorrow's job markets by frequently acquiring new skills, keeping yourself marketable, being flexible, and changing jobs and careers when necessary.

2. **You should do what you really love** rather than chase after dreams not of your own making. In the end, the best job for you is one you really love doing rather than one that temporarily ranks at the top of someone's list or one purported to be "the best" based on some so-called objective criteria and analyses.

If you only get one message from this book, let it be this: The best jobs of the future will go to those who empower themselves with a capacity to shape their future. Understanding the dynamics of both the economy and job market, they take responsibility for their own employability. They dream possible dreams because they are well educated, work hard, and know they must be prepared for handling constant change in the economy, the job market, and their worklife. They prepare for uncertainty with more of the same—education, hard work, and realistic dreams. They are positive thinkers, but they do more than periodically get "pumped up" on positive thinking. They focus on the nuts and bolts of success in a talent-driven economy— they acquire skills through training and retraining and know when and where to apply those skills in the rapidly changing world of work.

> The best jobs of the future will go to those who empower themselves with a capacity to shape their future.

Welcome to the New Talent-Driven Economy

America's post-industrial economy has essentially become a talent-driven economy. Highly entrepreneurial and competitive, this economy's leading industries require more and more individuals skilled in today's latest technologies as well as capable of learning new technologies. In such a talent-driven economy, employers:

- face intense competition for their products and services
- need to constantly innovate and out-position their competition

- carefully watch their bottomline
- focus on productivity and profits
- recruit or partner with top talent
- willingly pay top dollar and extend the most generous benefits to those who demonstrate talent

It's a booming economy for individuals who are well educated and work hard at their jobs. It's a bust economy for those who lack appropriate education, workplace skills, and job search savvy.

At least for the next decade, the talent-driven economy will be the predominant model that defines the job market. The real winners in this job market will be highly talented and entrepreneurial individuals who know how to market their skills and accomplishments to employers who readily seek their talents and reward them accordingly.

What We Know and Don't Know

Let's talk truth about the future. No one really knows what the future will bring. Nor do we have a crystal ball or some magical formula that will reveal the best jobs of the future.

What we do know is very interesting and well worth your attention, consideration, and possible action. We do know about **job trends** based upon employment and census data compiled, analyzed, and disseminated by the U.S. Department of Labor. Economists, employment specialists, and career experts also tell us what they foresee as the future for jobs and careers based upon their familiarity with present trends, their interpretations of employment and labor market data, and, perhaps best of all, their intuition. Based on this information, we're willing to make some educated guesses, in the pages that follow, about future jobs.

What we do know is this: the future is very uncertain. In the world of work, we're probably in the midst of a profound revolution whose implications are still difficult to foresee. The volatile economy, with its dual technological and managerial revolutions, simultaneously destroys and creates jobs. Companies downsize, jobs disappear, and skills become obsolete at a breath-taking pace—so fast that it is difficult to prepare for the jobs of tomorrow when we don't know what they really look like today! It's a revolution that is transforming the way we both find and do work. Jobs we perform today may be radically transformed or disappear altogether within just a few years. One thing is certain—we're riding a revolution whose end is nowhere in sight.

Let's start by looking at the present, factor in uncertainty, project ourselves into the future, and make some realistic predictions based upon our intuition and best educated guesses.

Good Guesses and Feeling Good

As you will see in subsequent chapters, many individuals and institutions periodically attempt to predict the best jobs for the future. It's a popular topic for magazine and newspaper articles as well as for radio and television talk shows. Indeed, everyone seems to be interested in predicting the future, especially if it looks like tomorrow will be better than today! As we will see in Chapter 4, some of these predictions are good guesses; others may miss the mark altogether.

Examine for a moment one of the better and most recent "best" guesses—*U.S. News & World Report's* annual ranking of the 20 best jobs in America. Based on their own survey research, which included compiling data from numerous other studies conducted by the U.S. Department of Labor, private groups, and a variety of professional associations, their top 20 jobs consist of the following:

U.S. News & World Report's
20 Top Job Tracks, 1998

Career Field	Hot Job Track	Annual Salary Range
■ Account	Business Valuator	$30,000 - $200,000+
■ Arts/Entertainment	Animator	$800 - $6,000/week
■ Banking/Finance	Financial Planner	$20,000 - $175,000
■ Communications	Crisis Specialist	$23,000 - $76,000
■ Educator	Math/Science Teacher	$33,900 - $35,500
■ Engineering	Computer Engineer	$55,500 - $79,000+
■ Environment	Pollution Fighter	$30,000 - $76,000
■ Health Care	Physician Assistant	$52,750 - $89,900
■ Human Resources	Training Specialist	$31,400 - $73,900
■ Internet/New Media	Internet Executive	$175,000 - $300,000
■ Law	Business Expert	$82,900 - $381,650
■ Management	Supply Chain/Logistics	$50,000 - $150,000
■ Medicine	Cosmetic Dentist	$104,100 - $143,400
■ Personal Services	Professional Organizer	$25,000 - $100,000

▪ Public Services	Corrections Officer	$20,000 - $32,000
▪ Sales	Electronics Specialist	$38,400 - $108,400
▪ Social Work	Grief Therapist	$35,000 - $48,000+
▪ Telecommunications	Wireless Technician	$35,000 - $53,000
▪ Trades	Truckdriver	$25,000 - $80,000
▪ Travel/Hospitality	Inbound Tour Guide	$20,000 - $75,000

SOURCE: *U.S. News & Work Report*, October 27, 1997

While it is unclear how many jobs are currently available or will be generated in the future in these so-called "hot job tracks," several include thousands and even millions of jobs in 1998 and 2006:

Job	Number of jobs, 1998	Number of jobs, projected for 2006
▪ Truckdrivers	3,100,000	3,500,000
▪ Corrections Officer	335,000	450,000
▪ Computer Engineer	220,000	270,000
▪ Physician Assistant	65,000	80,000

SOURCE: U.S. Department of Labor, 1998

Others, such as animator, Internet executive, and cosmetic dentist, may be interesting new jobs but there are probably very few jobs available in these newly emerging occupations.

Not bad guesses, but maybe not good ones either. What are missing on this list are several other jobs that clearly are hot ones for the decade ahead. Most of these jobs are found in the rapidly growing fields of computers and medicine and include such occupations as dental hygienist, medical assistant, physical therapist, speech-language pathologist and audiologist, computer programmer, computer scientist, and webmaster. Other hot jobs for the future include management analysts and consultants, public relations managers, paralegals, and chefs. If you are in sales, marketing, engineering, travel, and elementary and secondary teaching, your job prospects look excellent in the decade ahead.

The future will eventually tell us whether or not these and other jobs were really the best ones. But for now, if you are already in one of these jobs, such a list will probably make you feel good, and especially good if you are near the top. As we will see later, these rankings are very similar to others' rankings and lists (Chapter 4), including our own in Chapters 6-14. But what do they suggest to you the curious reader or job seeker? Are these the types of jobs you want to pursue? Do they offer a bright career future in terms of earnings, security, job satisfaction, and location? Will many of these jobs undergo dramatic transformations in the decade ahead? What new skills, education, and training will you need to acquire in order to gain entry into and advance within these fields? Do you have the proper mix of interests, skills, and motivations to continue long-term in these jobs?

What is common about most of the top jobs on these and other lists is the fact that most such jobs require relatively high levels of education and training. High earnings and job security will go to those who are skilled in the job markets of today and tomorrow. Indeed, recent studies show a very clear relationship between education and earnings. For example, lifetime earnings of individuals with only a high school education are estimated to be about one-fourth of those with a professional degree, such as in medicine and law, and about one-half of those with a bachelor's degree. Individuals without a high school diploma make about one-third of those with a bachelor's degree. In addition, the U.S. Department of Labor's most recent job projections (1998)

> **18 of the 25 occupations with the largest and fastest employment growth, which also include high pay and low unemployment, require at least a bachelor's degree.**

for the year 2006 note that 18 of the 25 occupations with the largest and fastest employment growth, which also include high pay and low unemployment, require at least a bachelor's degree. These studies tend to confirm what we have known for a long time—education is closely related to earnings; the higher the educational level, the higher the earnings. Education and training also increase the career mobility of individuals—the higher the education level, the greater possibility of career advancement and the ability to successfully change jobs and careers.

Welcome to the Revolution

There's a revolution taking place in the world of work. It's more than just the latest management jargon, "reinvented" and "empowered" workplaces, new and transformed jobs, the rise of telecommuting and entre-preneurship, the role of the Internet, the impact of technology on jobs and the workplace, and "transparency." The revolution affects how you find jobs, plan careers, move on to other jobs throughout your worklife, and even retire and re-enter the job market. It's a revolution that is reshaping our notions of work. For some, it's a scary revolution that potentially threatens their job security and requires them to constantly train and retrain. For others, it's an exciting revolution of new opportunities. It's a revolution you should know more about as well as be prepared to participate in during the years ahead.

Make no mistake about it. The future is **now** in the world of work. A powerful combination of demographic, technological, economic, and political changes are fundamentally altering the way we both find and do work. These changes have important implications for you today, tomor-row, and in the decade ahead. They will affect what you will be doing and whom you will be working with throughout your worklife.

Think About and Take Charge of Your Future

While we would all like to better know and control our future, many people still believe they have little influence over their future. Living from day to day, they seldom dream about tomorrow. Going from job to job, few people think about planning and taking control of their career.

> **Those who fail to seriously think about their futures are likely to experience very disappointing futures.**

But those who fail to seriously think about their futures are likely to experi-ence very disappointing futures. Without dreams you will probably wander aim-lessly through life. You'll wonder why others are so lucky in finding interesting jobs and careers that seem to pay well and have a bright future.

It's time to stop thinking about others' "good luck" and begin dreaming about and shaping your own career future. Think about and plan your future now before today becomes tomorrow—and tomorrow becomes the 21st century!

You should take charge of your future rather than let others, or the whims of economic change, decide what you will be doing in the decade ahead. Begin by considering and planning for the kind of work you want to do over the next decade. Learn what skills are likely to be in demand for tomorrow's growing occupations. Most important, make sure you have the necessary skills and abilities to function in tomorrow's job markets.

Test Your Future Careering Capabilities

Let's begin by examining how well prepared you are for shaping your future in the world of work. You can easily identify your present level of capabilities to acquire the best jobs in the decade ahead by completing the following exercise:

INSTRUCTIONS: Respond to each statement by circling which number at the right best represents your situation:

SCALE: 1 = strongly agree   4 = disagree
                2 = agree   5 = strongly disagree
                3 = maybe, not certain

1. I can identify the 20 fastest growing jobs in the decade ahead.   1 2 3 4 5

2. I can identify the 20 fastest declining jobs in the decade ahead.   1 2 3 4 5

3. I know which jobs will offer the best salaries in the decade ahead.   1 2 3 4 5

4. I can identify the jobs that offer the most security in the decade ahead.   1 2 3 4 5

5. I know the education and skill requirements for the best jobs in the decade ahead.   1 2 3 4 5

6. I have a clear set of career goals I hope to achieve in the decade ahead.   1 2 3 4 5

7. I know which jobs are right for my interests, skills, and abilities.   1 2 3 4 5

8. I know where to find information
   on the jobs that interest me.   1 2 3 4 5

9. I know where I will be going in my
   current job during the next decade.   1 2 3 4 5

10. I know how to acquire the necessary
    skills for the jobs I want.   1 2 3 4 5

11. I have a five-year career plan that
    will put me into one of the best
    jobs for the decade ahead.   1 2 3 4 5

12. I can write my ideal job description
    for one of the best jobs in the decade
    ahead.   1 2 3 4 5

13. I usually keep focused on my goals.   1 2 3 4 5

14. I often dream of my ideal job.   1 2 3 4 5

15. I set high goals and am tenacious
    in achieving those goals.   1 2 3 4 5

16. I am highly motivated to acquire the
    necessary skills for getting a good job.   1 2 3 4 5

17. I can find both the time and money
    to achieve my career goals.   1 2 3 4 5

18. I've assessed my interests, skills, and
    abilities and can clearly communicate
    these to employers.   1 2 3 4 5

19. I know what I do well and enjoy
    doing in the world of work.   1 2 3 4 5

20. I can write a one to two-page resume
    that grabs the attention of employers
    and results in invitations to job
    interviews.   1 2 3 4 5

21. I know how to write at least five
    types of job search letters.   1 2 3 4 5

22. I'm good at small talk and networking
    both in face-to-face situations and on
    the telephone for developing job leads.   1 2 3 4 5

23. I know how to conduct informational
    interviews.   1 2 3 4 5

24. I know how to use electronic databases
    and the Internet for finding a job.   1 2 3 4 5

25. I know how to use online career services
    available on the Internet or through
    a commercial online service.   1 2 3 4 5

26. I can conduct an effective job interview.   1 2 3 4 5

27. I can negotiate a salary at least 10%
    higher than what an employer offers.   1 2 3 4 5

TOTAL _____

You can calculate your overall careering capabilities for the future by adding the numbers you circled to get a composite score. If your total is more than 75 points, this book should help you substantially increase your careering capabilities. If your score is under 50 points, you are well on your way to handling your career future. In either case, this book should help you better focus your career hopes and dreams on opportunities in the decade ahead.

Prepare For Uncertainty

This book is all about preparing for uncertainty in the world of work. It will help you create a vision of the future for making smart job and career choices. If you think and plan accordingly, you will shape your future in the direction of the best jobs for the 21st century.

For the job or career you are involved in today most likely will not be the same one you find yourself in a decade from now. Many skills you routinely use today will be obsolete ten years from now.

Twenty years from now you may look back at the late 1990s with fond memories and conclude that this was a major watershed period in your worklife. Hopefully, you and many others will remember this as a time in which you decided to prepare yourself for job and career uncertainty. You took charge of your career. You read the signs, acquired the necessary skills, and made strategic career choices that prepared you well for the best jobs of the 21st century.

If you plan and prepare today for the jobs of tomorrow, you will discover you put yourself on the right road to job and career success in the 21st century. But the choices are by no means obvious, especially given the turbulent nature of the economy as well as the demographic and technological changes taking place in the workplace. Like the fortune teller, you must first read the future before you can chart a path for securing your own future. And like the sailor, the exact course to your destination may vary depending on several variables; you may tack back and forth through turbulent waters.

Let's take a look into the future to see what lies ahead for you and millions of others who are concerned about the shape of their worklife in the years ahead. It's a fascinating picture of a work world that is coming faster than many people ever predicted.

Forecast the Future

The future is something we would all like to better understand, predict, and control. However, our best understanding of the future is based on analyzing past patterns and recent trends and then projecting them into the future. Such an approach assumes the future will largely be a replay of past trends. Forecasts based on this approach are often inaccurate, because they cannot foresee **unique events** that may significantly alter past patterns and trends. Consequently, important career decisions made on the basis of future forecasts may be subject to unexpected changes. For example, many engineers who pursued careers in the growing aerospace and defense industries of the 1960s, 1970s, and 1980s experienced career shock in the 1980s and 1990s; aerospace industries cutback in response to economic downturns, and defense industries began reeling from major downsizing attendant with the ending of the Cold War. Many talented workers experienced unemployment; they saw little likelihood of returning to their previous jobs or careers. The same unexpected shocks were experienced by thousands of students who pursued the highly touted MBA and law degrees of the 1980s. Many of these graduates experienced the "disappearing job phenomenon" when they entered a shrinking job market, due to economic changes, at the time when thousands of other new graduates were doing the same thing.

The latest casualties may be nurses. As nursing become a "hot" and increasingly well paid field in the early 1990s, enrollments in nursing schools increased accordingly and thousands of retired nurses reentered the job market. At the same time, the health care industry increasingly came under cost containment pressure by government and the insurance industry. More and more hospitals treated patients on an out-patient basis, thus freeing up more and more hospital beds normally serviced by nurses. By 1995 nursing appeared to have become another glutted field as fewer and fewer nurses were being hired. New nursing graduates who had entered this popular field just two or three years earlier were having difficulty finding jobs in the new and highly volatile health care economy. However, in 1998 nursing was beginning to turnaround again, but its future remained uncertain because of the uncertainty of America's highly volatile health care economy.

Tomorrow's Economy

Any discussion of jobs in the 21st century must be based on some assumptions about the future economy and its ability to generate jobs for specific industries. After all, regardless of your interests, skills, educational attainment, specialized training, and entrepreneurial talents, it is the larger domestic and international economies that generate jobs which, in turn, create career opportunities for individuals. For example, much of tomorrow's job growth will be dependent upon increased U.S. exports, rather than domestic consumption, which are projected to increase by 4.5 percent each year for the coming decade. Significant changes in U.S. economic performance abroad—in part dependent upon negotiating favorable trade agreements and in part due to a cheap U.S. dollar in relation to foreign currencies—will affect the overall domestic employment picture. Recent (1997-1998) economic downtowns in East and Southeast Asia will have an impact on the U.S. economy, especially on the states of California and Washington which in recent years have done a disproportionate amount of trade with the booming Asian economies.

Most realistic predictions of tomorrow's job generating economy are based upon analyses of past trends coupled with the realities of recent economic performance. It is these predictions that form the basis for identifying the fastest growing, hottest, or best jobs for the 21st century.

For example, most forecasters agree that the rate of economic growth for the coming decade will be much slower than during the 1970's and mid-1980's—the era of the baby-boom generation entering the workforce. Between 1990 and 2005, the annual growth in real GNP has been projected to be 2.3 percent—down from 2.9 percent in the 1975-90 period. This slower job growth rate is largely attributed to changing demographics—slow population growth rate. The labor force is expected to grow by 1.2 percent each year as compared to 1.9 percent in the 1975-90 period.

By the year 2005 the total labor force is projected to be 147.2 million, an increase of 24 million jobs since 1990 or a total labor force growth of 24 percent. Most of this job growth is expected to take place in the service-producing industries. Unfortunately, a large percentage of these jobs will be low paying, entry-level jobs which offer few opportunities for career advancement.

In predicting the future, the U.S. Department of Labor's Bureau of Labor Statistics forecasts three levels of economic performance in the decade ahead—low, medium, and high. In other words, their projections should be considered pessimistic, realistic, and optimistic. Each level of economic performance generates different rates of job growth. A lower than expected rate of economic growth, for example, could significantly alter the employment picture in the decade ahead. A recession, or even a depression, could result in turning these slow growth rates into new rates of employment decline.

The Coming Job Transformation

Growth in the labor force and jobs is only part of the employment picture in the decade ahead. Most important for individuals is that job opportunities will grow and decline at different rates for different occupations and industries, and the quality of jobs will change significantly. As we will see in subsequent chapters, job opportunities in several goods-producing industries will continue to decline while those in service-producing industries will continue to increase.

At the same time, the nature of many jobs will change within organizations. As more and more industries acquire advanced technology, automate operations, improve their managerial systems, and downsize, fewer high paying jobs will be available in the decade ahead. Indeed, a disproportionate number of jobs in tomorrow's economy will be low paying service jobs. Dubbed by some as the "coming job drought," this will be an important change for individuals who expect to advance far beyond basic entry-level positions and steadily increase their incomes in their later years. If current patterns are any indication of things to come, we can expect a high rate of employment accompanied by declining wages. Indeed, in March 1998 unemployment stood at a decade low 4.7 percent (6 percent unemployment is considered by most economists to be full employment in the U.S. economy), but real wages had fallen considerably during the past ten years. Wage erosion in a seemingly robust economy is directly attributable to the shedding of middle to high paying jobs which continues throughout the workplace. Employers, from large Fortune 500 to small businesses, continue to downsize their workforces in order to compete more effectively.

You in Tomorrow's World of Work

The pages that follow outline what we and others see as the best jobs for the 21st century. Given changing demographics, technological changes, slow economic growth, a projected job drought, wage erosion, and the continuing decline of jobs in the goods-producing industries, we believe you should be knowledgeable about your career future in this period of rapid and turbulent change. You should know what skills you will need for the jobs of tomorrow. You should be aware that if you are just entering the workforce, you will probably have four careers and more than fifteen jobs in your worklife. And you should be prepared to experience some wage erosion in the years ahead.

If you are to do well in the job markets of tomorrow, you must be prepared to make job and career changes, acquire appropriate job performance skills, and relocate to where the jobs are most plentiful. This means knowing how to contact employers for jobs, taking advantage of education and training opportunities, and being willing and able to move to new job sites when necessary.

Choose the Right Resources

We wish you well as you take this journey into the future world of work. We are primarily concerned with relating key job and career issues to your situations—from understanding the nature of the job market to developing job search skills, acquiring work-content skills, relocating to other communities, and translating this book into action. Many of these issues, which are also job search steps, are outlined in our other books: *Change Your Job Change Your Life, Discover the Best Jobs For You, High Impact Resumes and Letters, Dynamite Resumes, Dynamite Cover Letters, Dynamite Tele-Search, 201 Dynamite Job Search Letters, Interview For Success, 101 Dynamite Answers to Interview Questions, Dynamite Networking For Dynamite Jobs*, and *Dynamite Salary Negotiations*. We also address particular jobs and career fields in the following books: *The Complete Guide to Public Employment, The Directory of Federal Jobs and Employers, Find a Federal Job Fast, The Complete Guide to International Jobs and Careers, International Jobs Directory, The Educators Guide to Alternative Jobs and Careers,* and *Jobs For People Who Love Travel*. Many of these books are available in your local library and bookstore or they can be ordered directly from Impact Publications (see the "Career Resources" sections at the end of this book). Most of these resources, along with hundreds of others, are available through Impact's comprehensive "Career Warehouse and Superstore" on the World Wide Web:

http://www.impactpublications.com

Impact's site also includes new titles, specials, and job search tips for keeping you in touch with the latest in career information and resources. You also can request a free copy of their career catalog by sending a self-addressed stamped envelope (#10 business size) and it will be mailed to you:

IMPACT PUBLICATIONS
ATTN: Free Career Brochure
9104-N Manassas Drive
Manassas Park, VA 20111-5211

Empower Yourself

The chapters that follow are all about empowerment—you have within you the power to shape your own destiny. You can begin this process by creating a vision of your future worklife. If you clearly see your future and act upon your vision, you can shape your future in the direction of your interests, values, skills, and abilities. For seeing and believing in your future are the most important steps for shaping your future.

We wish you the very best as you sail into the 21st century with a clear vision of your future. May you see it, believe it, and shape it in the form of exciting jobs and careers for the 21st century. For if you grasp the importance of education and hard work in the new talent-driven economy, you will have within you the ability to turn uncertainty and turbulence into new and exciting opportunities in the world of work.

Part I

Consider Your Future

2

Prepare For Turbulence and New Opportunities

W hat exactly do you want to do with the rest of your life? Do you have a clear vision of what you want to do? Is it what you really want to do—something you do well and enjoy doing?

Perhaps you've not raised these questions recently. Let's do so for the next few hours as you browse through the remaining chapters of this book. These are questions that force you to deal with your future, with all its uncertainties and possibilities, rather than with your past or present. They requires you to come face-to-face with some of your very basic values, interests, skills, and abilities. At the very least these questions ask you to begin **dreaming** what may well become a possible dream as you create new realities for yourself into the 21st century.

Dream Your Possible Dream

If you've not thought about what you want to do in the future, it's time to start dreaming. If you don't ask this question of yourself, potential employers are likely to raise it when you interview for a job as they try to determine your goals. For if you don't answer it, others in your future will assume control by your default and your life will take the shape of their answers. We assume you want to empower yourself and provide your own answers for your life.

You can best answer the question we pose by analyzing your past experiences and projecting yourself into the future. Let's examine your future to better understand where you are going with your career and life. You have many work years ahead.

> ➤ What exactly are your goals?
> ➤ Where do you want to go with your life?
> ➤ Where do you see yourself 5, 10, or 20 years from now?
> ➤ Are your goals realistic given your interests, skills, motivations, and image of the future?
> ➤ What types of jobs and careers will you choose?
> ➤ Will these choices be the right ones for you?
> ➤ How will they affect your lifestyle?
> ➤ How much control do you want over your life?
> ➤ What are you willing to risk in the decade ahead?

Work and Meaningful Lifestyles

The beginnings and ends of decades are times for reflection, assessment, and redirection. The past decade and a half has been a turbulent period for jobs, careers, and lifestyles. The best laid plans were subjected to unprecedented changes as millions of Americans first entered the job market, experienced unemployment, or changed jobs and careers several times. Many people attempted to develop lifestyles in the face of a turbulent economic world where jobs and careers were as unpredictable as the economy.

The 1990s have been a turbulent period for jobs and careers. It began with a highly predictable recession which took a major toll on businesses and employees alike as more than 12 million Americans joined the unemployment rolls. Millions of others became discouraged and abandoned their job search altogether. A deficit ridden and anemic economy gradually turned around, and by 1997 it actually surpassed the go-go boom years of the 1980s. In the meantime, millions of jobs were lost forever as the economy underwent major restructuring. Accordingly, millions of individuals were learning to play a new employment game—they would need to career and re-career throughout the 1990s and into the 21st century.

Prepare For Life in a Boom and Bust Economy

The 1980s began with serious economic problems and ended with few promises of improved future performance. These were the best and worst of times, depending on where and how you lived. Unemployment soared to nearly 11% in 1982—the worst since the Great Depression. Yet it fell to less the 6% in 1988, the lowest in 15 years, settled in at a relatively persistent 7.7% in 1992, gradually leveled off to a nagging 6.8% in 1993, and further dipped to 4.7 percent by the beginning of 1998. Trendy theories about the end of inflation, recessions, and boom/bust cycles and the rise of full employment—reminiscent of 1965—began appearing in 1996 as a strong economy generated nearly 3 million new jobs each year. These and other new employment theories would most likely continue as long as the economy remained strong, which was most unlikely given the new and highly volatile international environment in which the U.S. economy functioned.

Economic problems in the 1980s baffled the best of minds as the economy underwent major restructuring, millions of individuals experienced unemployment, and the education and political systems remained inert. Inflation and high unemployment during the first half of the 1980s was blamed on a variety of evils, including excessive public spending, the Vietnam War, Wall Street, irresponsible labor unions and corporations, the rich and the poor, liberals, conservatives, Democrats, Republicans, FDR, and the Japanese. Huge deficit spending and major trade imbalances during the 1980s were blamed on similar culprits as trade protectionist sentiments misdiagnosed the long-term nature of America's economic and employment problems. The key problems were *productivity* and *investment in the future*—or the lack thereof—rather than the need to artificially limit competition in order to protect obsolete and inefficient jobs at home.

Although some thinking about employment began to change, most continued to be based upon outmoded theories, short-term approaches, and trendy thinking to stimulate the economy, create jobs, and find employment. A relatively uninnovative educational system, lagging a decade behind the times, remained mired in irrelevant debates about educational theories and approaches. It failed to provide individuals with the skills necessary to function in an emerging 21st century economy. The unemployment insurance system continued to provide short-term income support rather than to invest in the long-term employment future of the unemployed by providing support for relocation, retraining, and job search activities. An antiquated, nonportable insurance-based health care system was responsible for creating "job lock" amongst at least 20% of the workforce; over 25 million workers could not risk changing jobs because they would automatically lose their health benefits. Limited changes to this archaic system finally started in 1996. But the tax code continued to provide few incentives for employers to provide, or workers to seek, retraining. And relatively nonportable pension plans discouraged workers from relocating.

Unfortunately, the public policy system created many of the very evils it was supposed to correct. How could it encourage training, retraining, and job mobility when the education, unemployment compensation, tax, health care, and pension systems were designed for other purposes? No one seemed to understand how such policies continued to work against everyone's best interests except those who operated the current systems, especially educators and insurance companies. Low productivity, disinvestment in the workplace, and limited job mobility would most likely continue until major changes took place in these systems. In the end, many concerned people wondered how could so many smart people create such a dumb system and then blame the evils on others?

> **How could so many smart people create such a dumb system and then blame the evils on others?**

The public policy failures of America's checkerboard political system in the 1980s were enormous, and they would most likely continue to plague the economy and employment picture throughout the 1990s and into the 21st century. No one had the political will to substantially slash defense spending, restructure education and training programs, nor cut the great middle and upper-class subsidies, primarily affecting the elderly, that continued to bleed the federal budget—Social Security and Medicare entitlement programs. Rather than invest in building human capital, the government continued to cater to special interests and engage in politically symbolic, and safe, reforms—restructure welfare, dismantle affirmative action, and downsize the federal bureaucracy. Its "jobs" rhetoric would not be matched by new and costly policy initiatives for investing in the future.

Despite a great deal of tough public talk, leadership in the 1980s and 1990s failed to develop effective education and training programs to produce long-term employment results. In the meantime, educators continued to manage an education system of questionable quality. Others reconfirmed what they do best—debate educational theories and approaches in meaningless jargon. At the same time, politicians advanced another trendy theory and middle class subsidy—privatizing public education—and developed highly visible policies for the poor with few program successes. Somehow America's relatively nondirected, fragmented, and decentralized economic and political systems were supposed to simultaneously resolve education, employment, and economic problems. The results were otherwise: they wasted human capital rather than invest it for the future.

The end of the 1980s began to close with a booming economy experiencing unprecedented levels of employment. The economy had generated the largest number of new jobs ever in the history of the United States. Indeed, nearly 3 million new jobs were created each year. However, in 1990 it became increasingly evident that the boom of the 1980s was largely built on a highly volatile house of cards—junk bonds; massive government, corporate, and individual debt; and a highly inflated, nonproductive, and speculative real estate market. Accompanying this temporary flight into prosperity was the cumulative yearly litany of millions of unemployed, thousands of business failures, an incredible national deficit hobbled by expensive and nonproductive entitlement programs, and major international dislocations—all threatening to restructure the economic and employment pictures of the 1990s in the direction of the early 1980s, or even worse.

> **The public policy failures of America's checkerboard political system in the 1980s and 1990s were enormous, and they would most likely continue to plague the economy and employment picture in the decade ahead.**

The 1990s began with the unexpected collapse of the Russian Empire, the crumbling of communist regimes and nation-states in Eastern Europe, the ending of the Cold War, the emergence of new armed conflicts in the Middle East, and preparation for an economically unified Europe as the largest consumer market in the world. These changes promised a newly restructured political and economic world order where the U.S. would become the major force shaping the new post-Cold War international political and economic order. However, chaos rather than predictable change and prosperity reigned as the ex-communist states became economic basket cases, new armed conflicts centering on traditional ethnic rivalries emerged in Eastern Europe and Africa, and the economies of the Pacific Rim experienced the greatest growth and promise for the future. European economies within the much hyped new European Union—many with unemployment rates exceeding 11 percent— continued to be some of the world's most anemic. The U.S. economy became increasingly internationalized and job growth more dependent on U.S. exports to Asia. In fact, what economic growth took place in the U.S. in the 1990s was largely due to the export of U.S. products and services in a world where the U.S. dollar continued to be eroded in relation to the Japanese yen and the German mark. However, unexpected problems in the Middle East threatened the newly emerging world economic and political order. The U.S. and United Nations' response to continuing crises, coupled with a mounting national debt and the collapse of major financial institutions, helped trigger a recession and a new cycle of unemployment to mark the beginning of the decade. These "unique events" tested important institutions and relationships that would help shape the employment situation throughout the 1990s.

For many Americans, the 1990s were best approached as another turbulent decade punctuated by boom and bust cycles and a repeat performance of public policy failures in education and employment. But by 1997 some economists concluded, based on three years of low inflation and high employment, that the traditional boom/bust economy and its attendant recessions and unemployment cycles were over; the economy had now reached a new steady-state of growth characterized by full employment. However, only the naive and inexperienced could swallow such a theory. Recent experience with a turbulent international environment and "unique events" seemed to be a better guide to the future than this new trendy low inflation theory. Boom and bust seemed to be well and alive and shaping an uncertain future. Indeed, 1997 began with an extremely over-valued stock market that seemed to be on the verge of a major correction, if not a collapse. The 1994-1996 period had witnessed unprecedented speculation in the stock market; a major infusion of venture capital into start-up companies of marginal performance but which managed to quickly go public; and a great deal of hype about high tech industries and elusive business opportunities on the Internet. The bust side of another boom/bust cycle was fast approaching. Economists would soon have to compare this period with similar excesses of the

1980s and early 1990s, when real estate and junk bond speculation drove the memorable boom/bust cycles.

As we move into the 21st century, unemployment over the next decade is likely to fluctuate between five and eight percent. Millions of Americans will enter the job market for the first time; millions of others will experience unemployment; and millions more will change jobs and careers. Assuming continuing inertia in the public sector and political and economic turmoil in an international arena, individuals will face an uncertain future requiring greater initiative to regularly acquire new skills, change jobs and careers, develop greater financial security, and relocate to growing communities.

Public opinion polls toward the end of 1996 noted disturbing new perceptions arising during this decade of change and uncertainty: while unemployment was at an all-time low (5.2 percent) and job changing had not significantly increased during the past decade, perceptions of unemployment and individual job insecurity were at an all-time high. Indeed, millions of Americans actually perceived unemployment to be closer to 25 percent and believed they were very vulnerable to job loss. This gap between objective and subjective reality for individuals had continued to grow throughout the turbulent 1990s. It would likely continue in the decade ahead.

People's perceptions of reality **are** reality for them. If Americans learned anything about economics and employment in the during the past decade, it was this:

> We live in a highly complex society with an unpredictable and risky market place where even the best laid plans go awry due to numerous changes beyond one's control. Since economic and employment futures are unpredictable, one is well advised to develop flexible job and career strategies for dealing with uncertainty.

At the very least these strategies must address the issues of skills, lifestyles, opportunities, and risk-taking at the most significant level for both you and society—the individual. In other words, you are on your own in a sea of change, so you had better take initiative in shaping and securing your own economic and employment future. No one else, nor trendy theory, will do this for you. You simply must take charge of your career for a very different job market in the 21st century. If you don't, you may be heading for troubled waters.

Understand Employment Dynamics in a Dual Society

Employment in the United States is closely tied to an economic restructuring process taking place at the international, national, and local levels. During the past two decades the United States rapidly moved from a primarily industrial and technological society to one based on high technology, energy, services, and export-oriented manufacturing. It also moved from a credit nation to a debtor nation—fueling the international economy with its high level of spending and consumption but positioning itself for even more vulnerable economic times ahead.

The signs of an economy and job market undergoing major restructuring are especially apparent when examining the paradoxical unemployment/labor shortage problem: unemployment often persists at the same time major labor shortages exist. As millions of Americans become unemployed, millions of jobs also go unfilled at the two extreme ends of the job market: those requiring high level skills and those requiring low level skills. Many unemployed individuals lack the necessary skills to function in a newly emerging post-industrial, high-tech society; refuse to take low-paying service jobs; or do not know how to find a job appropriate for their level of skills and experience. Like the dual societies of many Third and Fourth World countries—one rural/agricultural and another urban/industrial—America is a dual society of a different type.

The dual society in America consists of two sectors. The first and most traditional sector is located mainly in the older urban centers of the Northeast and North Central regions. Known as America's "rust belt" and based largely on manufacturing and related service industries, this sector was characterized by stagnation, decline, and high levels of unemployment and underemployment in the early 1980s. A disproportionate number of poor, unskilled, and displaced people live in these aging communities which also have serious problems with deteriorating infrastructure, excessive welfare burdens, and high costs of living. The state of Michigan led this sector in 1983 with a depressing 18% unemployment rate. Ohio, Illinois, West Virginia, Indiana, and Pennsylvania were not far beyond.

The latter half of the 1980s witnessed a resurgent economy as some of the highest unemployment rates since the Great Depression were replaced by some of the lowest rates recorded in decades. Michigan's 18% unemployment rate, for example, fell below 8%; Illinois and Ohio managed to achieve 7.2% and 6.3% unemployment rates. And Massachusetts—once a troubled state with high unemployment—took the honors with one of the lowest unemployment rates in the country—2.9%—until this so-called "economic miracle" state slid back into high unemployment during the recession of 1990. But these unemployment figures were only low in comparison to historical highs. With more than 10 million Americans unemployed each day, the actual numbers of unemployed remained high. The goal of full employment remained elusive.

While unemployment in Michigan, Illinois, Ohio, West Virginia, and Pennsylvania decreased during the later half of the 1980s, many communities in these states, as well as throughout much of the Northeast, remained vulnerable in the boom and bust economy of the 1990s. Economic recovery in these states would take time given continuing plant closures, depressed real estate and financial markets, and the high costs of doing new business. By the mid-1990s, major bright spots were emerging among manufacturing industries in the Midwest, especially near Chicago, that benefitted from increased U.S. exports and the transformation of their "rust belt" industries.

> The emerging high-tech and service economy will require individuals with marketable skills who are willing to retrain and relocate when necessary.

The second sector points us toward a more promising yet unpredictable future. Located mainly in younger suburban areas and in the rapidly growing cities of the West and Southwest, as well as in a few cities in the East, Midwest, and Southeast, this sector is based on high-tech, communication, and service industries requiring a highly educated and skilled work force. In contrast to the first sector, this one is characterized by dynamic growth and relatively high employment. It is populated by a disproportionate number of well educated, skilled, and affluent people. Growth in these communities is mainly constrained by shortages of highly skilled workers and the overall boom and bust nature of the local economies. Communities heavily dependent on the energy and computer industries, such as Houston, Denver, and the Silicon Valley of California, witnessed both high employment and high unemployment in the 1980s as their local economies went bust due to major downturns in the energy and computer industries. Similar patterns have recently occurred in communities heavily dependent upon defense industries, especially in Texas and California, and may occur for so-called "hot" communities in the 1990s

—Seattle and Las Vegas. Other more economically diversified communities, such as metropolitan Washington DC, Atlanta, San Diego, and Los Angeles, led the way with strong economic performance throughout the 1980s. Except for temporary economic downturns in 1990-1995—due to a depressed housing market and major cutbacks in defense spending—suburban communities ringing these and many other metropolitan areas will most likely rebound in the near future. More and more individuals will relocate from the first sector into the second sector of America's dual society.

Similar to the 1980s, the most serious economic and employment problems in the 1990s and the beginning of the 21st century will be disproportionately felt by the unskilled poor who live in decaying central cities and rural areas. Lacking sufficient education, skills, and work experience as well as access to effective retraining programs and funding mechanisms for relocation and job search activities, the majority of these individuals will continue to live in and burden first sector communities. Their plight is further evidence of the inability and unwillingness of the political system to deal seriously with the pressing issues of productivity and income generation. Time-honored welfare and income support programs, scattered with a few train-the-poor initiatives, remain classic American subsidy approaches to the unemployed and poor. Such approaches have produced few cases of success. New welfare-to-work initiatives begun in 1996 are at best interesting political statements and photo opportunities about the state of America's troubled welfare system. While welfare rolls were substantially reduced by 1997, the reductions had little to do with skills training and retraining programs. Solutions to the hard-core unemployment problem remain elusive.

Lest we forget, America is an entrepreneurial skills-based society where individuals market their skills in exchange for money and position. Without the proper skills to function in such a society—or the means to acquire the necessary training, relocation, and job search assistance—many people will remain permanently displaced or take jobs which neither generate adequate income nor promote long-term skills development. The emerging high-tech and service economy in the decade ahead will require individuals with marketable skills who are willing to retrain and relocate when necessary.

Face Increased Structural Unemployment

Much of America's unemployment problem is structural in nature. The economy has entered into a major period of *structural unemployment.* While the normal pattern of unemployment is *cyclical*—people lose their jobs because of temporary business downtowns and then are rehired when business rebounds—structural unemployment has permanent features. Moreover, this type of unemployment has far reaching consequences for the economy, workers, and employment strategies into the 21st century. It's the type of unemployment associated with popular "downsizing" and "restructuring processes" taking place in both business and government in the 1990s. These processes are closely associated with the application of new technology to the workplace and increased emphasis on worker productivity, decentralized decision-making, and efficient management and networking systems.

Structural unemployment is caused when industries and skills become obsolete due to technological advances. In the past, street sweepers, buggy-whip makers, tailors, and shoemakers became victims of such unemployment. More recently, aerospace scientists and engineers, auto workers, tire makers, steel workers, farm laborers, slide-rule makers, and middle managers have experienced structural unemployment. Like yesterday's buggy-whip maker and shoemaker counterparts, the recent victims must acquire new skills and change careers to become gainfully employed.

Unfortunately, few people are prepared or willing to deal with the changing structure of employment in America. Many unemployed auto and textile workers, for example, still believe their condition is due to cyclical unemployment, with "unfair" Japanese, Taiwanese, Korean, Hong Kong, Chinese, and Mexican competition being the major culprits. They expect to be rehired when the business cycle improves—hopefully brought about through protectionist trade policies. While union leaders have begun to recognize the significance of structural unemployment by negotiating for more job security, give-backs, and retraining programs for their members, management introduces the latest industrial robot technology as well as total quality management (TQM) systems in a continuing effort to improve the productivity and competitiveness of the American auto industry. During the 1980s the major American auto-makers spent billions of dollars to modernize their production lines with robot technology as well as introduce new and more productive management systems. The end result of such modernization would be to permanently displace workers—from the assembly line to the board-room—throughout the 1990s. Such displaced workers must acquire new skills and find new jobs and careers if they are to survive and prosper in the job markets of tomorrow.

Following a pattern developing in the 1980s and 1990s, the early 21st century will be a period of accelerated structural unemployment. The dual issues of productivity and competitiveness tied to an increasingly internationalized economy and a newly shaping world political order are forcing corporate America to apply the latest cost-saving technology to the work place. Protectionist labor unions are correct in their analysis of the problem: increases in productivity displace high-cost labor which, in turn, erode union membership. But at the same time, more than 1.5 million new jobs are created each year to absorb many of the structurally unemployed. And without industry's ability to remain competitive in a global marketplace, those jobs and the businesses will both be lost.

The major issue for the 1990s and the beginning of the 21st century began in the 1980s: how to retrain and relocate an increasing number of structurally unemployed individuals in a relatively unplanned and unpredictable economy subject to a highly volatile international arena that is likely to make and break millions of jobs. Assuming continuing public policy failures to deal with economic and employment problems, individuals in the decade ahead must develop their own strategies for navigating their careers in the boom and bust economy of the early 21st century.

Take Initiative in a Fundamentally Flawed System

Some experts estimate that somewhere between 50 and 75 percent of American factory workers will be displaced by robots by the end of this century! Millions of others will be displaced by more efficient and effective management, networking, and communication systems. Contrary to popular perception of an American manufacturing sector in decline, manufacturing has strengthened itself through the application of new technology which displaces factory workers. Beginning in the 1950s and further accelerating today, the real source of new jobs is found in the rapidly growing service sector, especially in health care, food service, and retail sales.

But few people, especially displaced workers facing structural unemployment, are taking the initiative to provide or acquire the necessary skills training and retraining—and for good reasons. The tax, unemployment insurance, health care, and pension systems were designed for a different era when structural unemployment was not a major issue. Such systems have yet to adjust to the employment realities of a profoundly different society of the 1990s which is based upon high technology and service industries and which experiences a high level of structural unemployment.

The tax, unemployment insurance, health care, and pension systems provide few incentives for retraining, relocation, and job search. Few employers, for example, are given tax incentives to retrain or outplace displaced workers. The unemployment insurance system is designed to give temporary income support for individuals facing cyclical unemployment. It does little to encourage the structurally unemployed to seek retraining, develop job search skills, or relocate. And the limited portability of most health care and pension systems discourages individuals from changing jobs and relocating.

> **The tax, unemployment insurance, health care, and pension systems were designed for a different era when structural unemployment was not a major issue.**

As structural unemployment becomes more pervasive in the decade ahead, the problem of what to do with millions of unemployed workers with little education and obsolete skills may become a national crisis. Some analysts believe a major national training and retraining program, which goes far beyond the limited scope of the Jobs Training Partnership Act (JTPA), is desperately needed. Others see this as naive and nearly impossible to implement given the highly decentralized and fragmented nature of policy-making and implementation in America.

What will displaced workers do—many of whom are highly skilled in older technologies? What actions can be taken now, and by whom, to make a positive transition to the job market of the high-tech and service society?

We believe the answers to these questions primarily lie with the *individual* rather than with government or corporations. Indeed, one of our major purposes in writing this book is to urge you to become *self-reliant and effective* in dealing with the job markets of today and tomorrow. While government and the private sector may provide incentives and opportunities as well as a few limited-scale programs, the individual ultimately must be responsible for his or her own employment fate. We assume that both government and the private sector will be slow in responding to the obvious retraining, relocation, and job search needs of individuals and society. In the meantime, a serious national employment and economic development crisis is brewing, and many people are being hurt by public and private sector inaction. Individuals, therefore, must take their own initiative to acquire the necessary skills for success in the job markets of today and tomorrow.

Predict and Prepare For an Uncertain Future

We see seven major developments in the decade ahead which will have important implications for the employment futures of most Americans:

PREDICTION 1: **The restructuring of the world political and economic order creates new opportunities and challenges for jobs relating to a more export-oriented economy.**

IMPLICATION: While new international job and career opportunities will arise into the 21st century, domestic jobs will become increasingly dependent on U.S. trade abroad. Great job opportunities will be available with U.S. companies doing business in Asia, Europe, and Mexico.

PREDICTION 2: **Boom/bust cycles will continue into the 21st century as the economy experiences a combination of good times and bad times which, in turn, create a great deal of uncertainty for planning careers and lifestyles.**

IMPLICATION: You need to acquire the necessary work-content and job search skills for quickly changing jobs and careers. Also, be prepared to relocate to more prosperous communities as well as develop greater financial security to bridge the bust-boom cycles.

PREDICTION 3:   Millions of jobs will be created and eliminated. New jobs will be created at the rate of 1
to 2 million each year. At the same time,
nearly 1 million jobs will be eliminated each
year. In the midst of these changes nearly 20
million Americans will experience some
form of unemployment each year; between
6 and 12 million Americans will be unemployed each day.

IMPLICATION: While you have a high probability of experiencing some form of unemployment in the decade
ahead, new opportunities for careering and re-
careering will abound for those who know the
"what," "where," and "how" of finding jobs
and changing careers.

PREDICTION 4:   The rapidly expanding service sector will
create the largest number of new jobs. These
will be disproportionately found at the two
extreme ends of the job market—high paying jobs requiring high-level skills and low
paying jobs requiring few specialized skills.

IMPLICATION: You should focus on acquiring specialized
education and skills for the high-end of the job
market. Many of your skills also should be
sufficiently general and marketable so you can
easily make job and career transitions without
becoming a victim of structural unemployment
and boom-bust cycles.

PREDICTION 5:   Structural unemployment will accelerate
due to a combination of business failures in
the boom/bust economy and continuing
productivity improvements in both the
manufacturing and service sectors as new
technology and improved decision-making
and management systems are introduced to
the work place. Structural unemployment

also will be exacerbated by the increased movement of both manufacturing and service jobs off-shore to low-wage countries in Asia, the Caribbean, Central America, and Latin America.

IMPLICATION: You need to acquire the necessary skills to adjust to the coming changes in the work place and job market. Careering and re-careering should become your central focus in deciding which skills to acquire.

PREDICTION 6: **Thousands of stagnant communities and inner-city neighborhoods will generate too few jobs to provide sufficient careering and re-careering opportunities. "Rust belt" and "welfare-subsidy" communities, as well as those lacking a diversified service economy, will provide few job opportunities in the decade ahead.**

IMPLICATION: Individuals in stagnant communities must find ways to create their own employment or relocate to those communities offering long-term careering opportunities. The most likely candidates will be growing metropolitan areas with diversified suburban economies.

PREDICTION 7: **Public policy failures to resolve education, training, and unemployment problems—as well as initiate effective job generation, relocation, and job search approaches for promoting a more employable society—will continue throughout the 1990s and the early 21st century.**

IMPLICATION: Given the highly decentralized and fragmented governmental and policy systems in the United States, politicians and public policy relevant to

promoting full employment will remain relatively inert. Since most politicians will continue
to be preoccupied with form and style rather
than with substance and results in dealing with
pressing economic and employment issues,
individuals must take their own initiative in
acquiring skills, finding jobs, changing careers,
and relocating to communities offering better
job opportunities.

Whether our predictions turn out to be 30, 70, or 100 percent accurate
is beside the point. What is important is that you be aware, anticipate,
and prepare for change. In so doing, you will be ready to seize new
opportunities regardless of whatever direction the economy and employment situation takes in the decade ahead.

The changes taking place in the work place have important implications for individuals in planning their future. As more and more jobs
become obsolete and new opportunities arise in the high-tech and service
economy, workers must be better prepared to function in today's
evolving job market. At the very least, they must learn how to career and
re-career into the 21st century.

Beware of Incomplete Approaches

The nature of work and the process of finding employment have changed
dramatically during the past few decades. For those who lived through
the Great Depression, a job—indeed, any job—was something you were
lucky to have. A good job—one you enjoyed and earned a good living
from—was something only a few people were lucky enough to have.

As white-collar employment expanded in the 1950s and 1960s, a new
philosophy of work evolved. Work was to be enjoyed and based upon
one's strongest skills. Individuals also were advised to change jobs and
careers when they were no longer happy with their work.

Pioneered in the career planning methods of Bernard Haldane in the
1950s and 1960s and popularized in Richard Bolles' self-directed *What
Color Is Your Parachute?* in the 1970s and 1980s, job search was placed
on center stage as a skill that could be learned and applied with considerable success. Reflecting the do-your-own-thing philosophy of the 1960s
and primarily emphasizing the importance of self-assessment and self-

reliance, individuals were strongly advised to identify what they do well—their strengths—and enjoy doing. Based on this knowledge, they were further advised to take initiative in seeking employment outside the formal job market of classified ads and employment agencies by engaging in informational interviews, that is, asking people for information and advice about jobs and employment. The key principles for a successful job search were the familiar sales approaches of *prospecting and networking*—methods for developing job contacts and acquiring job information, advice, and referrals. Changing careers primarily involved a strategy of identifying and communicating transferable skills to employers rather than acquiring new job-related skills.

The process identified by Haldane, Bolles, and other career counselors for finding employment is what Adele Scheele (*Skills For Success*) calls "successful careering." It requires the use of certain marketing skills and strategies for selling yourself. According to Scheele, these skills consist of (1) self-presentation, (2) positioning, and (3) connecting. Other writers refer to these same skills as (1) role playing, (2) risk taking, and (3) networking—key skills, principles, or strategies applicable to most sales and marketing situations.

> Emphasizing process and form to the exclusion of such critical issues as job generation, relocation, and work-content skills, these approaches are at best incomplete.

The job search skills promoted during the past three decades are based on a business-sales analogy. According to many career advisors, finding a job is like selling—you sell yourself in exchange for status, position, and money. The emphases here are on the process of selling and the methods of self-presentation—not the substance of work-content skills. Seldom, if ever, does this group of career advisors address the equally critical issues of job generation and relocation nor advise individuals to acquire new work-content skills which are more responsive to the changing job market. Doing so requires more comprehensive approaches as well as a major investment of time and effort, especially in education and training, which may seem beyond the immediate employment needs of many individuals.

As more and more jobs require technical skills, and as the job market becomes restructured in response to the emerging high-tech and service economy, the career planning approaches of the past three decades need to be reoriented in light of new realities for the 21st century. Emphasizing process and form to the exclusion of such critical issues as job generation, relocation, and work-content skills, these approaches are at best incomplete in today's job market. Few individuals, for example, who use networking to market only such soft functional skills as reading, writing, and interpersonal communication will be successful in finding employment with a promising future. As many displaced homemakers and liberal arts students learned in the 1980s, such strategies have limitations in a job market requiring concrete technical skills applicable to specific work settings. Lacking an appropriate set of work-content skills, these individuals may become the new displaced, underemployed, and discontented workers of tomorrow.

The dual issues of job generation and relocation are critical in planning one's career future. We should never forget that people work in or from specific communities from which they rent or own property and develop particular lifestyles which may or may not be more important than their jobs or careers. If, for example, you live in an economically stagnant community that generates few job opportunities for someone with your interests and skills, using job search skills to find a great job in such a community would be frustrating, if not useless. Your options and approaches in such a situation come down to four:

1. Find a local job that may not fit well with your particular mix of interests and skills while hoping that more appropriate opportunities will eventually open for you in the future as this community generates more job and career options.

2. Commute to a job in another community within your region that offers opportunities appropriate for your interests and skills.

3. Start a business that is not dependent on local economic cycles —one that is broadly based with a diversified regional, national, or international clientele.

4. Relocate to a growing community that appears to be capable of generating many new jobs in the future. Such communities offer an ideal setting where job generation, relocation, and job search come together in providing individuals with numerous opportunities for careering and re-careering in the future.

Career and Re-Career For Today and Tomorrow

The processes we call "careering" and "re-careering" address present and future job realities and enable individuals to change their lives. Re-careering goes beyond the standard "careering" skills popularized during the past three decades, which were based upon an understanding of a job market in an industrial economy. As the job market becomes restructured in the direction of high technology and services, a new approach to job hunting, responsive to new economic realities, is required for the 21st century.

We anticipate a very different and intensely competitive job market in the future. The major dynamic for restructuring the job market is the emergence of a high-tech and service society, increasingly dependent upon international trade, requiring highly specialized and skilled workers who are prepared for job and career changes. These workers must not be overly specialized nor too narrow in their perception of the future demand for their present skills. Instead, tomorrow's workers must be flexible in learning new skills, for their specialized jobs may become obsolete with the continuing advancement and adaptation of technology to the work place and movement of both manufacturing and service jobs off-shore. Furthermore, tomorrow's workers must be adaptive to new jobs and careers. Overall, success in tomorrow's job market will require a new breed of worker who anticipates, prepares, and eagerly adapts to change. Such individuals prepare for career transitions by acquiring new skills and actively seeking new work environments through the use of effective job search strategies and relocating to new communities and work settings.

> **Success in tomorrow's job market will require a new breed of worker who anticipates, prepares, and eagerly adapts to change.**

Careering is the process of preparing to enter the job market with marketable skills to land the job you want. **Re-careering** is the process of repeatedly acquiring marketable skills and changing careers in response to a turbulent job market. The standard careering process of the past three decades, therefore, must be modified with four new re-careering emphases:

1. Acquire marketable skills through regular retraining.

2. Change careers several times based on a combination of job search skills, new work-content skills, and relocation actions.

3. Use more efficient communication networks for finding jobs, such as interpersonal networking and surfing the Internet.

4. Relocate to communities experiencing long-term job growth.

As you examine the best jobs for the 21st century, keep in mind that getting one of these jobs involves more than interest, education, training, and motivation. Landing and keeping a job with an excellent future will require that you career and re-career in the decade ahead. You must learn new skills, be willing to relocate if necessary, and market yourself through several job search channels, including the Internet.

While the following pages primarily identify the best jobs for the 21st century, you also need to know the best strategies for landing these jobs. If you are interested in identifying the best approaches to landing and keeping a job, see our *Change Your Job, Change Your Life: High Impact Strategies For Finding Great Jobs Into the 21st Century.* This comprehensive job search book will guide you through the processes of identifying skills, writing resumes, networking, interviewing for jobs, negotiating salaries, relocating to new communities, and even starting your own business.

3

Prepare For 33 Coming Changes

Whether or not we realize it, we all have some image of the future that influences important decisions in our lives. Assuming you are like most people, you would not, for example, purchase a new home, relocate to another community, or change jobs unless you first projected what the future might hold for you over the next three, five, or ten years. You want to predict your future to some degree.

Images of the Future

Individuals orient themselves to the future in different ways. Some people always view the future pessimistically. They find numerous reasons for doing what they always do—not taking risks. Others fantasize about the future and "hope" a prosperous future will come to them without taking action or risking the unknown. And others set goals and work toward achieving an image of a positive future.

Finding employment and charting careers in the job markets of today and tomorrow require strategies based on an understanding of new realities as well as a different image of the future. But few people know how to plan for uncertainty. Denying new realities, many continue to operate on old assumptions. Not surprising, their adjustment to change is at best difficult.

Turn Turbulence Into New Opportunities

How do you anticipate the future and plan accordingly? During relatively stable times, planning proceeds along a relatively predictable path: assume the future will be very similar to the past and present. Therefore, a good plan is one that is based on an analysis of historical patterns—you follow the lessons of the past in charting your future.

But during turbulent times, planning based on historical patterns is a problem. Peter Drucker's observations on planning for turbulent times are especially relevant for the decade ahead. Traditional planning:

> assumes a high degree of continuity. Planning starts out, as a rule, with the trends of yesterday and projects them into the future—using a different "mix" perhaps, but with very much the same elements and the same configuration. This is no longer going to work. The most probable assumption in a period of turbulence is the unique event, which changes the configuration—and unique events cannot, by definition, be "planned." But they can often be foreseen. This requires strategies for tomorrow, strategies that anticipate where the greatest changes are likely to occur and what they are likely to be, strategies that enable a business—or a hospital, a school, a university—to take advantage of new realities and to convert turbulence into opportunity. (from *Managing in Turbulent Times*)

Turbulent times can be dangerous times for people who fail to anticipate and adjust to new changes. Assuming continuity, or a return to previous times, they engage in wishful thinking. Many of these people are today's victims of structural unemployment. For others, who take action based upon an understanding of coming realities, turbulent times can offer new and exciting opportunities. These people anticipate where the greatest changes will take place and accordingly adapt to change as they advance with the new jobs and careers of tomorrow.

The economic transformation of American society has far reaching social and political implications which you should be aware of in planning your future. The projected changes are discussed at length by Toffler (*The Third Wave*), Naisbett (*Megatrends* and *Megatrends 2000*), Ferguson (*The Aquarian Conspiracy*), Cetron (*Jobs of the Future*), Feingold and Atwater (*New Emerging Careers*), Bridges (*Job Shift*), Dent (*The Great Jobs Ahead*), and Harkness (*The Career Chase*). Our major concern is not in predicting the future with precision. Rather, we are concerned with formulating an image of the future and outlining the implications of turbulent times for jobs, careers, and you.

The major question we need to address here is this:

What future should you prepare for in the world of work?

Based on an understanding of new trends in the work place and anticipat-
ing the impact of unique events on the economy, we believe you can
develop strategies for converting turbulence into new opportunities.

Two powerful currents—one demographic and another technical—are
converging at present in the work place and affecting the future of work
in America. These changes, in turn, are precipitating the emergence of 33
new trends for careering and re-careering into the 21st century.

Face New Demographics

The paradox of major labor shortages in the midst of high unemployment
is partly due to the impact of demographic changes on today's labor
market. For the American population is undergoing fundamental changes
at the same time the economy shifts from an industrial to a high-tech and
service base.

The major demographic changes characterizing today's labor force are
found at the entry-level: fewer young people are filling entry-level jobs
while more females, minorities, and immigrants are entering the job
market.

The major implication of these demographic changes for the coming
high-tech and service society will be continuing labor shortages for entry-
level jobs. However, the paradox of high unemployment may continue
if millions of displaced workers are not retrained for new jobs.

Forces

Two major demographic changes took place in the post-World War II
period to help shape the present labor force. The first change was the
baby-boom. As birth rates increased nearly 50 percent between 1947 and
1949, a new labor force was created for the latter part of the twentieth
century. American industry in the 1960s and 1970s absorbed some of this
new labor force, but the rapidly growing service sector absorbed most of
it. The U.S. economy, especially the service and high-tech sectors, was
able to provide employment for 10 million new workers between 1963

and 1980—a remarkable achievement for such a short time span. Between 1983 and 1988 the economy generated 16 million new jobs— the best performance in the history of the labor market. Between 1989 and 1996 the economy generated between 1 and 2 million new jobs each year. By 1998 the booming U.S. economy was generating nearly 3 million new jobs each year.

The second major demographic change has been the rapid increase of women, minorities, and immigrants entering the labor force. This demographic current continues. For example, in 1980 over 50 percent of women worked outside the home. By 1990 more than 60 percent of women were in the labor force. Today nearly 75 percent of women are in the workforce.

By the year 2000 the baby-boom generation will reach middle age. The number of traditional 16 to 21 year olds entering the labor market will fall dramatically. About 80 percent of all new labor force entrees will be women, minorities, and immigrants. These groups—as an aggregate— will be less educated and skilled than the new job entrees of previous decades. For example, despite the $400 billion spent each year on education in the United States, basic literacy and skill levels remain alarming for industries that must dip deeper into the entry-level labor pool. In a 1994 assessment of literacy among 21-to 25-year-olds, the Education Department found these alarming statistics:

- Only 60 percent of whites, 40 percent of Hispanics, 25 percent of blacks can find specific information in a news article or almanac.

- Only 25 percent of whites, 7 percent of Hispanics, and 3 percent of blacks can understand a bus schedule.

Furthermore, 63 percent of white and 14 percent of black high school graduates have only attained a "basic" skill level required by the armed forces for training.

The implications of these trends will be costly for industries in the coming decade. Paradoxically, they were at the forefront of a new talent-driven economy that lacked adequate talent to service its industries. Given rising skill requirements for entry-level jobs, coupled with the low skill levels of job applicants, many industries will experience severe labor shortages. They will most likely respond to this problem by cutting back on services and production and/or investing more resources on educating and training what is basically an entry-level labor force ill-prepared for the jobs of today and tomorrow. Indeed, by 1998, this reality had become very apparent for many companies. Several high-tech industries were recruiting and training entry-level workers for high-tech positions. Others were sponsoring public training programs from which they planned to recruit a new pool of skilled workers. Several state governments were developing special educational programs to meet the skilled labor needs of their growing business communities. Many industries were simply desperate for skilled workers. As the economy continued to boom, such labor shortages became more and more pronounced. The shortage of skills and talent would become a major impediment to the health and expansion of numerous industries in the decade ahead.

Implications

Declining birth rates between the 1960s and 1980s, with America now approaching a zero-population growth rate, have important implications for the future labor market. Assuming the American economy will continue to expand, despite temporary setbacks, stimulated by the high-tech and service industries, major labor shortages are likely to occur during the coming decade. The continuing entry of women, minorities, and immigrants into the labor force, as well as the expansion of automation and technology in the work place, will not significantly offset this labor deficiency.

Since birth rates declined in the 1960s and 1970s and immigration laws were changed in 1986, there are fewer young people and immigrants available for entry-level and low wage positions. In addition, women, who used to take part-time, low paying sales positions, are fast leaving this labor scene for better paying full-time positions. Teenagers, who make up a disproportionate share of the labor forces of fast-food restaurants, are scarcer because there are fewer teenagers in the population as a whole than during the previous 30 years.

Adjustments in the changing labor force have already begun. Fast-food restaurants employ older workers and introduce more self-service menus. Department stores recruit lower quality sales clerks—generally individuals who are less educated, skilled, stable, and responsible; training demands increase accordingly. Many small businesses, especially the "Mom and Pop" stores with fewer than five employees, experience difficulty recruiting and retaining the traditional young, low-salaried entry-level workers. Instead, many businesses cut back services and production as well as look toward the elderly, particularly retired individuals, for new recruits.

The changing population structure also has important implications for the quality of the labor force. While the private sector spends over $200 billion each year on training and retraining, much of this expenditure goes to training inexperienced entry-level personnel. Given the growing shortage of this traditional labor pool, high-tech industries will be forced to recruit and then retrain displaced workers. This will require a new emphasis on training—as well as a greater expenditure on retraining.

Other population dynamics have additional implications for the work force of tomorrow. Minorities, especially blacks and Hispanics, will enter the labor force at a faster rate because of their higher birth rates. As a result, minorities will disproportionately occupy entry-level positions. Furthermore, there will be greater pressure from minorities for advancement up the ranks, even though the upper ranks have become glutted with middle-age managers and executives who were rapidly promoted when they were young people during the 1970s and 1980s.

> **Mid-life crises may well disappear as more individuals experience re-careering transitions.**

With the entry of more women into the labor force and the concomitant emergence of the two-career family, individuals have greater freedom of choice to change jobs or careers, take part-time positions, retire, or drop out of the labor force altogether. Job-hopping may increase accordingly. In addition, employee benefit programs, many of which are still based on the model of the traditional male head of household supporting a family, will change in response to the two-career family with one, two, or no children.

Careering and re-careering are directly related to these changing demographics. As the work force ages, life expectancy lengthens, the social security system becomes modified, and labor shortages abound, fewer people will enter traditional retirement in their 60s or retire at all. An individual's work life may well become one's total adult life. Re-careering will become a standard way of functioning within tomorrow's labor markets. Thus, it will not be unusual for individuals to change careers in their 40s, 50s, and 60s. Mid-life crises may well disappear as more individuals experience re-careering transitions.

Responses

Population changes also will create a more heterogeneous work force. Along with increased minority representation in entry-level positions, more and more immigrants will come to the United States—both legally and illegally—to meet the expanding labor needs. Despite the 1986 changes in immigration laws to document illegal immigrants and stem the tide of illegal immigration into the United States—political efforts totally at odds with America's growing labor needs—nearly 600,000 immigrants enter the U.S. legally each year and another 600,000 immigrants, mainly from Mexico and the Caribbean, probably enter the U.S. illegally. Most of these people initially take low-paying, manual, and service jobs which non-minorities avoid. Hispanic-Americans are expected to constitute one-fifth of the population, or 50 million out of 250 million, in the year 2000.

Assuming continuing low birth rates among middle class white Americans which, in turn, may contribute to labor shortages in the future, the government may be forced into a major policy reversal: relax enforcement of the 1986 immigration laws as well as open the doors to immigrants in order to alleviate the coming labor shortages. If and when this happens, training and retraining programs will become more urgently needed for the future of the high-tech and service society.

Peter Drucker, however, outlines another scenario which is by far one of the most interesting organizational forms for coping with the coming labor shortages in developed countries and the explosive expansion of working-age people in the less developed countries. Under a production sharing system, less developed countries with surplus labor would be responsible for labor-intensive aspects of production. Developed countries, such as the United States, would provide the needed capital, technology, and managerial skills for operating transnational companies. Such an arrangement would fully employ the surplus educated and skilled people in the developed countries without experiencing the social, economic, and political dislocation attendant with large scale migration.

Production sharing forms of organization are already in place for various industries in the United States, Japan, Singapore, Hong Kong, Malaysia, Taiwan, Korea, and Brazil—the so-called First and Second World countries. They are likely to develop in many other countries, especially those in the Third World. As Drucker sees this system,

Production sharing is the best hope—perhaps the only hope—for most of the developing countries to survive without catastrophe the explosive expansion of working-age people in search of a job . . . for the standard of living of the developed world can also be maintained only if it succeeds in mobilizing the labor resources of the developing world. It has the technical resources, the entrepreneurial resources, the managerial resources—and the markets. But it lacks, and will increasingly lack, the labor resources to do the traditional stages of production.

Whether or not production sharing becomes a predominate organizational form, the changing population dynamics over the next two decades provide further evidence of the need for major skills training and retraining of the American labor force. Population dynamics undoubtedly will be a major force affecting the turbulent employment environment.

Experience the Impact of New Technologies

The second major current transforming the American work place is technical in nature. The electronics revolution began in 1948 in Western Electric Company's Allentown, Pennsylvania manufacturing plant. There, the transistor was produced, and it began an electronics revolution which has continued to evolve into even more revolutionary forms since the invention and application of the microprocessor in the 1970s. The end of this revolution is nowhere in sight. Many experts believe we are just at the initial stages of a profound transformation which will sweep across our society during the next two decades.

Evidence of a coming transformation began in the 1950s as white-collar workers began to outnumber blue-collar workers. The electronics revolution helped initiate an information and communication revolution. In 1950, for example, approximately 17 percent of the population worked in information-related jobs. Today this proportion has increased to over 50 percent. During the 1970s, when nearly 19 new jobs were created, only 16 percent were in the manufacturing and goods-producing sector.

As John Naisbett (*Megatrends*) and other futurists have noted, during the 1980s we began to move full-force into the second stage of technological development—the application of technology to old industrial tasks. Recognizing the urgent need to increase productivity in order to become more competitive in international markets, manufacturing industries have made major efforts to retool their plants with the latest labor-saving technologies and have thereby displaced workers skilled in the technologies of previous decades. Today, America's manufacturing plants are second to none in terms of technological adaptation. All evidence points to continuing productivity improvements and technological adaptation in the manufacturing sector in the coming decade. American manufacturing will be the envy of most countries as we move into the 21st century.

Movement into third stage technological development—innovation, making new discoveries with second stage technologies—should proceed into the 21st century. By the year 2000 many American manufacturing and service industries will be completely transformed by second and third stage technological developments. Entry into the labor market in the year 2000 will require a much higher level of education and skills than in the 1980s. Those who will be in the best position to advance into the best jobs for the year 2000 will be those who seriously focus on careering and re-careering issues by:

- acquiring new work-content skills through regular training and retraining

- developing effective job search skills

- relocating when necessary

The impact of the high-tech revolution is structural in nature. As computers, fiber optics, robotics, genetic engineering, and the Internet generate new businesses and integrate into everyday life, the economy and work place will be fundamentally altered. For example, fiber optics, which makes copper wire obsolete, will further revolutionize communication. Genetic engineering will create major changes in agriculture and medicine. The main-frame computer, which was developed for practical use in 1945, in the form of today's microcomputer is now a common tool in most work places. With the continuing impact of fiber optics and new generation microprocessing chips—not to mention some still unknown technological break-throughs—computers with vastly expanded capabilities will become common tools in the home over the next decade. Powerful laptop computers will increasingly displace standard desktop computers. And the continuing innovations and adaptation of the Internet may well transform the whole software industry within the next few years. Indeed, long-distance carriers such as AT&T and MCI, are in a race for survival as the Internet transforms long distance communications. Many in this industry predict that all long distance phone calls will be free in the not-too-distant future as telephone companies increasingly compete to become business service providers.

The microprocessor has dramatically altered the work place—from robots replacing assembly line workers to word processors displacing traditional typists. Office automation has transformed many secretaries into area managers, who are now in charge of coordinating work flows and managing equipment. Factory workers either become displaced or are retrained to deal with the new technology. Unfortunately, many displaced workers, who have not been retrained, have become permanently displaced or have moved into lower paying, high turnover, unskilled service jobs—the negative unemployment and underemployment consequences of structural changes.

Many futurists have predicted what seems to be an even more radical transformation of the work place—the emergence of the electronic cottage. According to these predictors, computers and word processors will create a decentralized work place where individuals can work from their homes on assignments received and processed via computer terminals. The electronic cottage, in turn, will alter family relationships, especially child rearing practices, and the structure of the traditional central business district. Many workers no longer will need to commute to the office, face traffic jams, and experience the accompanying office stress. Such changes, however, do not bode well for owners of downtown office buildings, parking lots, and businesses frequented by the noontime employee-shopper. The communication revolution may be the final death blow for some cities hoping to revitalize their downtown areas. In fact, the fastest growing business sector today is the home-based business which now employs over 25 million individuals. With the recent emergence of the Internet as a new business arena, these numbers will probably increase in the future. While only talked about as a future reality 10 or 15 years ago, today the electronic cottage has become a significant reality for millions of individuals in the space of only a decade.

These technological changes, coupled with the demographic currents, are transforming the nature of jobs. Yesterday's and today's workers are increasingly being displaced into an environment which is ill-equipped to help them gain advantages in tomorrow's high-tech society. Instead, a new class of individuals, skilled in the technology of previous decades, may become permanently displaced in the turbulent job market of tomorrow. Their major hope for career success is to become savvy in the technologies of today and tomorrow.

33 Coming Changes

Several additional trends are evident, and they will affect both the work force and the work place in years ahead. These trends are mainly stimulated by the larger demographic and technological changes taking place within society. We see 33 changes emerging in the areas of job creation, youth, elderly, minorities, women, immigrants, part-time employment, service jobs, education and training, unions and labor-management relations, urban-rural shifts, regionalism, small businesses and entrepreneurship, compensation, advancement opportunities, and relocation. Together these changes point to both dangers and new opportunities.

TREND 1:   **Shortage of competent workers, with basic literacy and learning skills, creates serious problems in developing an economy with an adequate work force for the jobs of the 21st century.**

Given the double-whammy of over 20 million functionally illiterate adults—or 1/6 of the potential labor force unable to read, write, or perform simple computations—and the availability of fewer easily trainable young entry-level workers, a large portion of the work force is destined to remain at the lowest end of the job market despite the fact that over 15 million new jobs will be created in the decade ahead. Most of these adults will remain permanently unemployed or underemployed while major labor shortages exist. As skill requirements rise rapidly for both entering and advancing within the work force, the nation's economic development will slow due to the lack of skilled workers. Both public and private sector worker literacy, basic education, and training programs will continue to expand, but their contribution to improving the overall skill levels of the work force will be minimal. The American economy and work force begin showing classic signs of Second and Third World economies—potential economic performance out-strips the availability of a skilled work force.

TREND 2:　　**A renewed and strong U.S. manufacturing sector will create few new jobs; service industries will be responsible for most job growth in the decade ahead.**

　　　　　　　Despite popular notions of the "decline" of American manufacturing industries, these industries are following the model of America agriculture—increased productivity accompanied by the increased displacement of workers. The American manufacturing industry is becoming one of the strongest economic sectors in terms of production output but the weakest sector in terms of its contribution to job growth and job creation. At the same time, American manufacturing is moving in the direction of Drucker's "production sharing system" by exporting the remaining high-cost, labor intensive aspects of the industries. As large manufacturing companies rebounded in the 1990s by becoming productive with smaller and more highly skilled workforces, many new manufacturing jobs developed among small manufacturing "job shops" employing fewer than 50 workers. The service industries, especially those in finance, retail, food, and healthcare, expanded their work forces during the 1990s. The second half of the 1990s witnessed major "productivity" and "management" improvement movements among service industries that developed among large manufacturing industries in the 1980s—a push for greater productivity because of (1) major labor shortages, and (2) the adaptation of new technology to increasingly inefficient, high-cost, labor intensive service industries, especially in the retail and healthcare industries.

TREND 3:　　**Unemployment remains cyclical, fluctuating between a low of 4 percent and a high of 9 percent.**

　　　　　　　These fluctuations are attributed to a combination of boom and bust cycles in the economy as well as the persistence of structural unemployment exacerbated by millions of functionally illiterate adults on the periphery of the economy. In addition, millions of other Americans will be underemployed in low paying entry-level positions which offer little or no career advancement.

TREND 4:
Most government efforts to stimulate employment growth will continue to be concentrated at the periphery of the job market.

Most government programs aimed at generating jobs and resolving unemployment problems will be aimed at the poor and unskilled. These groups also are the least· likely to relocate, use job search skills, develop standard work habits, or be trained in skills for tomorrow's job market. Given the mixed results from such programs and political pressures to experiment with some form of government-sponsored workfare programs, the government finally develops programs to directly employ the poor and unskilled on government programs as well as contract-out this class of unemployed to government contractors who will provide them with education and training along with work experience.

TREND 5:
After difficult economic times during the first half of the 1990s, the U.S. deficit significantly declines and trade becomes more balanced as the U.S. slowly regains a more competitive international trade and debt position due to improved productivity of U.S. manufacturing industries.

International and domestic issues become closely tied to employment issues. Emphasis shifts to issues of unemployment, productivity, population growth, consumption, and regional conflicts in Eastern Europe, the newly independent states of the former Soviet Union, the Middle East, and other Third and Fourth World countries that threaten the stability of international markets and thus long-term economic and employment growth in the U.S. New regional trading blocks play the most important role in redefining the post-Cold War era. Economic, trade, and employment issues take center

stage in defining a highly unstable yet emerging structure of a newly emerging post-Cold War order. Major
labor shortages in the U.S. become evident as a sluggish
economy turns around in the second half of the 1990s.
Another recession, reminiscent of the early 1990s,
begins in 1999 as a result of declining markets for U.S.
products in the economies of the Pacific Rim and the
melt-down of a highly speculative and over-valued stock
market. Unemployment increases accordingly.

TREND 6:   **A series of domestic and international crises—
shocks and "unique events," some that already
occurred in the 1980s—emerge at the end of the late
1990s and early 21st century to create new boom
and bust cycles contributing to unemployment.**

The most likely sources for the international crises will
be problems developing among former communist
regimes and poor Third and Fourth World nations: the
disintegration of the nation-states in the former Soviet
Union and a few former communist regimes in Eastern
Europe; energy and precious metals shortages due to a
depletion of current stocks and regional military conflicts; the collapse of financial markets due to default on
international debts; and dislocation of lucrative resource
and consumption markets due to continued wars in the
Middle East, Africa, and South Asia. The most likely
domestic crises center on financial markets, real estate,
energy, water, and the environment. Crises in the
banking and real estate markets continue to create major
debt, credit, and bankruptcy problems for the economy.
An energy crisis once again revitalizes the economies of
Texas, Colorado, and Alaska. A new crisis—water
shortages—in the rapidly developing Southwest, further
slows employment growth in the once booming economies of Southern California and Arizona. Environmental issues, such as acid rain and air and water pollution, emerge as important international and domestic
crises.

TREND 7:   **New jobs will be created at the rate of 1 to 2 million each year, with some boom years resulting in the creation of more than 3 million jobs each year.**

The good news is that employment will increase in most occupations throughout the 1990s and the early 21st century with export industries leading the way toward economic growth. Economic expansion in the service sector, coupled with the low productivity and low cost of labor in many parts of the service sector, contributes over 90 percent of all new jobs. Large scale manufacturing experiences labor declines while small scale manufacturing "job shops" contribute most of the minimal job growth in the manufacturing sector. The labor declines will be offset by increases in related service jobs, especially in manufacturing sales and marketing.

TREND 8:   **A major shortage of skilled craftspeople will create numerous production, distribution, and service problems throughout the coming decade.**

During the 1980s the number of apprenticeship programs declined significantly; fewer individuals received training in blue-collar occupations; and interest among the young in blue-collar trades declined markedly. The impact of these changes will be felt into the early 21st century as production and service industries requiring critically skilled craftspeople experience major labor shortages; distribution of products and services will be uneven. Despite government efforts to revitalize apprenticeship programs, expect to personally encounter the effects of such labor shortages—long waits for servicing your automobile and for repairing your home and major appliances as well as very expensive charges for such services.

TREND 9:   **As the baby-boomers reach middle age and birthrates continue at a near zero-population growth rate, fewer young people will be available for entry-level positions in the coming decade.**

Businesses will recruit and train more of the hard-core unemployed, unskilled, and the elderly; they will automate; and/or they will contract for cheap off-shore labor for everything from accounting and marketing to manufacturing jobs. As a result, more stopgap job opportunities will be available for individuals losing their jobs or wishing to change jobs or careers.

TREND 10: **Retirement practices undergo a major transformation. More job and career choices will be available for the elderly who are either dissatisfied with traditional retirement or who no longer can afford the high costs of retirement.**

As the work force increasingly ages, the trend toward early retirement will decrease. Many people will never retire, preferring instead part-time or self-employment in their later years. Others will retire from one job and then start new careers after age 50. A continuing financial crisis in the social security system results in declining social security benefits. Fewer social security benefits and higher costs of retirement will further transform retirement practices and systems into the 21st century. Expect to see more elderly working in the McDonald's and 7-Eleven stores of tomorrow.

TREND 11: **More minorities and immigrants—especially those with disproportionate high birth rates, low education and skill levels, and poor economic status—will enter the job market.**

A large proportion of minorities will occupy the less skilled entry-level, service positions where they will exhibit marked language, class, and cultural differences. Upwardly mobile minorities may find advancement opportunities blocked because of the glut of supervisors, managers, and executives already in most organizations.

TREND 12: **Women will continue to enter the labor market, accounting for nearly 80 percent female participa-**

tion in the labor force by the year 2000; their share
of the labor force will slowly increase from 46 to 47
percent from 1996 to 2006.

The entry of women into the work force will be due less
to the changing role of women than to the economic
necessity of women to generate family income in order
to survive in an expensive consumer-oriented society.
Women will account for two-thirds of the growth in all
occupations. They will continue to expand into nontraditional jobs, especially production and management
positions. Both men and women in a growing number of
two-career families will have greater flexibility to
change jobs and careers frequently.

TREND 13:   **More immigrants will enter the U.S.—both docu-
mented and undocumented—to meet labor short-
ages at all levels.**

Despite major efforts of the INS to stem the flow of
illegal immigrants, labor market demands will require
more immigrants to occupy low-paying, entry-level
service jobs in the decade ahead. The brain drain of
highly skilled scientific and technical workers from
developing countries to the U.S. will accelerate. Unskilled immigrants will move into service positions
vacated by upwardly mobile Americans.

TREND 14:   **Part-time and temporary employment opportunities
will increase.**

With the increase in two-career families, the emergence
of electronic cottages, and fewer retirees, part-time and
temporary employment will become a more normal
pattern of employment for millions of Americans. More
women, who wish to enter the job market but not as
full-time employees, will seek new part-time employment opportunities. Temporary employment services
will continue to experience a boom in business as more
and more companies attempt to lower personnel costs as

well as achieve greater personnel flexibility by hiring larger numbers of temporary employees.

TREND 15: **Part-time and contingency workers will constitute a new and desired class of workers.**

The number of contingency workers—part-time, temporary, or contract workers—will steadily increase in the decade ahead as more and more businesses cut back costly full-time employees, eliminate generous benefit packages, and seek greater flexibility in hiring and firing employees. Given economic uncertainties, the high costs of hiring, and the advantages of working with employment firms that field contingency workers, more and more employers will replace full-time employees with contingency workers. By the year 2000 many businesses employing 100 or fewer employees will routinely use contingency workers to staff at least 30 percent of their positions.

TREND 16: **White-collar employment will continue to expand in the fast growing service sector.**

Dramatic growth in clerical and service jobs will take place in response to new information technology. The classification of workers into blue and white-collar occupations, as well as into manufacturing and service jobs will become meaningless in a service economy dominated by white-collar workers.

TREND 17: **The need for a smarter work force with specific technical skills will continue to impact on the traditional American education system as both businesses and parents demand greater job and career relevance in educational curriculum.**

Four-year colleges and universities will face stable to declining enrollments as well as the flight of quality faculty to more challenging and lucrative jobs outside education. Declining enrollments will be due to the inability of these institutions to adjust to the educational and training skill requirements of the high-tech society as well as to the demographics of fewer numbers in the traditional 18-21 year-old student age population. The flight of quality faculty will be replaced by less qualified and inexpensive part-time faculty. Most community colleges, as well as specialized private vocational-technical institutions, will adapt to the changing demographics and labor market needs and flourish with programs most responsive to community employment needs. As declining enrollments, budgetary crises, and flight of quality faculty accelerates, many of the traditional four-year colleges and universities will attempt to shut down or limit the educational scope of community colleges in heated state political struggles for survival of traditional educational programs. More and more emphasis will be placed on providing efficient short-term, intensive skills training programs than on providing traditional degree programs—especially in the liberal arts. Career planning will become a major emphasis in education programs; a new emphasis will be placed on specialization and flexibility in career preparation.

TREND 18: **Union membership will continue to decline as more blue-collar manufacturing jobs disappear and interest in unions wanes among both blue and white-collar employees.**

As unions attempt to survive and adjust to the new society, labor-management relations will go through a turbulent period of conflict, co-optation, and cooperation. Given declining union membership and the threat to lay-off employees unless unions agree to give-back arrangements, unions will continue to find themselves on the defensive, with little choice other than to agree to management demands for greater worker productivity. In the long-run, labor-management relations will shift from the traditional adversarial relationship to one of greater cooperation and participation of labor and management in the decision-making process. Profit sharing, employee ownership, and quality circles will become prominent features of labor-management relations. These changes will contribute to the continuing decline of traditional unions in many industries. New organizational forms, such as private law firms specializing in the representation of employees' interests and the negotiation of employment contracts, will replace the traditional unions.

TREND 19:   **The population will continue to move into suburban and semi-rural communities as new high-tech industries and services move in this direction.**

The large, older central cities, especially in the Northeast and North Central regions, will continue to bear disproportionate welfare, tax, and criminal justice burdens due to their declining industrial bases, deteriorating infrastructures, relatively poor and unskilled populations, and high rates of crime. Cutbacks in their city government programs will require the retraining of public employees for private sector jobs. Urban populations will continue to move into suburban and semi-rural communities. Developing their own economic base, these communities will provide employment for the majority of local residents rather than serve as bedroom communities from which workers commute to the central city. With few exceptions, and despite noble attempts to "revitalize" downtown areas with new office, shopping, and entertainment complexes, most large central cities will continue to decline as their upwardly mobile residential populations move to the suburbs where they find good jobs, housing, and education; enjoy attractive lifestyles; and experience lower crime rates.

TREND 20:   **The population, as well as wealth and economic activity, will continue to shift into the Northwest, Southwest, and Florida at the expense of the Northeast and North Central regions.**

By the year 2000 the South and West will have about 60 percent of the U.S. population. These areas will also be the home for the nation's youngest population. Florida, Georgia, Texas, Colorado, Arizona, Nevada, Utah, and Washington will be the growth states for the decade ahead; construction and local government in these states will experience major employment increases. Many states in the Northeast and Midwest, and parts of the South, will be in for continuing difficult times due to their declining industrial base, excessive welfare burdens, older population, aging infrastructure, and shrinkage of non-cyclical economic sectors—services, retail trade, and public employment. However, some Midwest states (Ohio, Indiana, Illinois, Wisconsin) will experience strong growth—based on the Massachusetts model of the 1980s—due to important linkages developing between their exceptionally well developed higher educational institutions and high-tech industries which depend on such institutions. Many manufacturing industries in the Midwest, especially auto, will continue to expand as they play an increasingly important role in the expanding U.S. export economy. Some states in the Midwest and Northwest will out-perform the rest of the economy at the end of the 1990s.

The growth regions also will experience turbulence as they see-saw between shortages of skilled labor, surpluses of unskilled labor, and urban growth problems. A "unique event"—devastating earthquake in Southern California or major water shortages in California and Arizona—could result in a sudden reversal of rapid economic and employment growth in the Southwest region.

The problems of the declining regions are relatively predictable: they will become an economic drain on the nation's scarce resources; tax dollars from the growth areas will be increasingly transferred for nonproductive support payments. A new regionalism, characterized by numerous regional political conflicts, will likely arise centered around questions concerning the inequitable distribution of public costs and benefits.

TREND 21:   The number of small businesses will continue to increase as new opportunities for entrepreneurs arise in response to the high-tech and service revolutions and as more individuals find new opportunities to experiment with changing careers.

As during the past decade, over 700,000 new businesses will be started each year during the coming decade. These businesses will generate 90 percent of all new jobs created each year. The number of business failures will increase accordingly, especially during the bust cycles of the boom/bust economy. Increases in self-employment and small businesses will not provide many new opportunities for career advancement. The small promotion hierarchies of these businesses will help accelerate increased job-hopping and career changes. This new entrepreneurship is likely to breed greater innovation, competition, and productivity.

TREND 22:   As large companies continue to downsize, major job growth will take place among small companies and millions of new start-up businesses.

Between 1979 and 1993, Fortune 500 companies reduced their personnel by 4.8 million while firms with fewer than 500 employees generated 16 million new jobs. We expect this trend to continue in the foreseeable future. The best opportunities in terms of challenges, salaries, and opportunities will be with growing companies employing fewer than 50 employees. Large Fortune 500 companies, especially service industries, will continue to cut jobs as they attempt to survive intense competition by becoming more productive through the application of new technology to the work place and through

> **The best employment opportunities will be found among growing companies employing fewer than 50 employees.**

the introduction of more efficient management systems. Cutbacks will further lower the morale of remaining employees who will seek new job and career opportunities—and many will start their own businesses.

TREND 23:   **Opportunities for career advancement will be increasingly limited within most organizations.**

Organizations will have difficulty providing career advancement for employees due to (1) the growth of small businesses with short advancement hierarchies, (2) the postponement of retirement, (3) the continuing focus on nonhierarchical forms of organization, and (4) the already glutted managerial ranks. In the future, many of today's managers will have to find nonmanagerial positions. Job satisfaction will become less oriented toward advancement up the organizational ladder and more toward such organizational perks as club memberships, sabbaticals, vacations, retraining opportunities, flexible working hours, family services, and health care packages.

TREND 24:   **Job satisfaction will become a major problem as many organizations will experience difficulty in retaining highly qualified personnel.**

Greater competition, fewer promotions, frustrated expectations, greater discontent, and job-hopping will arise in executive ranks due to limited advancement opportunities. As middle-management positions continue to be eliminated as part of overall downsizing efforts, managerial and executive turnover will increase accordingly. The problem will be especially pronounced for many women and minorities who have traditional aspirations to advance to the top but will be blocked by the glut of managers and executives from the baby-boom generation who are trying to survive at both the middle and top of their organizations. Many of these frustrated individuals will initiate affirmative action cases to open the closed upper ranks as well as become entrepreneurs by starting their own businesses in competition with their former employers.

TREND 25:   **Many employers will resort to new and unorthodox hiring practices, improved working conditions, and flexible benefit packages in order to recruit and retain critical personnel.**

In an increasingly tight job market for skilled workers, employers will use new and more effective ways of finding and keeping personnel: job fair weekends; headhunters and executive search firms; temporary employment services; raids of competition's personnel; bonuses to present employees for finding needed personnel; entry-level hiring bonuses for new recruits; attractive profit-sharing packages for long-term commitments; vacation and travel packages; relocation and housing services; flex-time and job-sharing; home-based work; and day care services.

TREND 26:   **Job-hopping will increase as more and more individuals learn how to change careers.**

As more job and career opportunities become available for the skilled and savvy worker, as pension systems become more portable, and as job search and relocation techniques become more widely known, more and more individuals will change jobs and careers in the decade ahead. The typical employee will work in one job and organization for four years and then move on to a similar job in another organization. Within 12 years this individual will have acquired new interests and skills and thus decide to change to a new career. Similar four and 12-year cycles of job and career changes will be repeated by the same individual. Job-hopping will become an accepted and necessary way of getting ahead in the job and career markets of tomorrow.

TREND 27:   **Geographic relocation will accelerate as more and more individuals become drawn to growing com-**

munities offering attractive job opportunities in a wide variety of occupations.

As the real estate market slowly rebounds across the nation, individuals will have a greater incentive to pull up stakes in one community to relocate to another. More and more people will move into the southeast and west in pursuit of better job and career opportunities.

TREND 28:   **The hot jobs in the decade ahead—those offering excellent pay, advancement, and security—will be in healthcare and high-tech service industries.**

These jobs will require substantial amounts of education, training, and retraining. They also will command top salaries and benefits as well as offer attractive advancement opportunities and numerous career options for individuals interested in careering and re-careering.

TREND 29:   **Salaries will only incrementally increase in the coming decade. In many organizations, executive level compensation will actually decline as well as be more closely tied to productivity indicators.**

The large salary gains of the 1980s are all but over for most occupations in the 1990s, excepting those requiring high level skills which will be difficult to recruit, such as computer science and engineering. Indeed, many chemical engineering graduates in 1997 started at $43,000 a year! Salary increments will more and more be tied to annual performance evaluations which link pay raises to quantifiable performance indicators. More attractive and portable benefit packages will be offered by organizations seeking to recruit and retain highly skilled workers.

TREND 30:   **Benefit packages will undergo major changes.**

Health insurance and pensions will be targeted for cutbacks. More and more employers will require employees to make significant contributions to health insurance and retirement plans. While most employers will offer some form of health insurance, fewer employers will provide company-sponsored retirement plans. Workers can expect to contribute at least 20 percent to the cost of health insurance as well as develop their own retirement plans which will include little or no contribution from employers. More and more employers will opt to hire contingency workers whose benefits are handled by contractors.

TREND 31:   **Apprenticeship programs will increase in number as the nation attempts to train and retrain a skilled labor pool for high-demand service industries.**

The coming shortage of skilled labor to service everything, from air-conditioners to automobiles, is directly related to the decline of apprenticeship programs and the lack of interest in pursuing careers in the trades. The government in cooperation with industry will make a major effort to revitalize such programs. Individuals not pursuing higher education degrees will find excellent career opportunities available through such programs.

TREND 32:   **More and more skilled and high-tech service jobs will move off-shore as U.S. businesses take advantage of both cheap skilled labor and high-speed communications.**

The next decade will be the decade of the global job market for both skilled and unskilled labor. The stereotypical manufacturing sweat shops with cheap and relatively unskilled labor producing garments, footwear, and toys in China, Indonesia, and India will give way to more high-tech sweatshops in these and many other countries. However, the high-tech sweatshops will focus more and more on the service industries and use skilled labor in Third World countries. For example, given inexpensive high-speed communications, many businesses can now export their accounting, design, telemarketing, and data management functions to India, the Philippines, Mexico, and countries in the Caribbean via faxes, the Internet, and special two and three-day delivery services (DHL, UPS, Federal Express). Skilled cheap labor will pose a new challenge to the U.S. labor market. While it will help relieve some labor shortages, it also will compete directly with high wage skilled workers in the U.S.

TREND 33:   **Fewer people will be obsessed with chasing tradi- tional careers. More and more people want satisfy- ing jobs that enable them to pursue interesting lifestyle goals.**

The concept of a "career" is deeply rooted in the post-World War II era of big manufacturing corporations. Until the 1990s, many individuals pursued careers, often within a single organizational setting. Given the changing structure of the job market, the decline of traditional career paths, and the increased interest in pursuing satisfying lifestyles, the 1990s has witnessed the gradual erosion of careers. More and more individuals today and in the decade ahead will be interested in finding specific jobs which may or may not be related to careers.

Be Realistic

While many individuals look toward the future with unquestioned optimism, there are good reasons to be cautious and less than enthusiastic. The decade ahead may be the worst of times for many people. Take several examples which indicate a need to be cautiously optimistic. Factory workers who remain unemployed after five years will have received an industrial death sentence of continuing unemployment, underemployment, or socio-economic decline. Many of the nation's poor, with high birth rates, are destined to remain at the bottom of society; their children may fare no better. Large cities in the Northeast and North Central regions, and even small communities in these and other regions, will have difficult adjustment problems. And we should not forget that America has not solved its energy and environmental problems, and a boom/bust economy is well and alive.

The best of times are when you are gainfully employed, enjoy your work, and look to your future with optimism. In the turbulent society, people experience both the best and worst of times at the same time. Those who are unprepared for the growing uncertainty and instability of the turbulent society may get hurt.

We lack a healthy sense of reality in facing change. Indeed, the future is seldom what we think it is. Only recently have we begun to take a second look at the high-tech and service revolutions and raised some sobering questions about their impact on work and the work place. We have not fully explored unanticipated consequences of new structural changes on individuals and society.

The 33 changes we forecast will create dislocations for individuals, groups, organizations, communities, and regions. These dislocations will require some form of public-private intervention. For example, the question of renewable energy resources has not been adequately dealt with in relation to the high-tech revolution. Many of the key metals for fueling the high-tech economy are located in politically unstable regions of Africa and the former Soviet Union. Such resources must be secured or substitutions found in order for the revolution to proceed according to optimistic predictions. Capital formation, investment, and world markets must also be secure and stable. New management systems must evolve in response to the changes. In other words, these key factors are variables or "if's"—not the constants underlying most predictions of the future. As such, they are unpredictable.

> In the turbulent society, people experience both the best and worst of times at the same time.

The clearer picture of unanticipated consequences of technological changes are already evident on the changing assembly lines, in the automated offices, and in the electronic cottages of today. While automation often creates more jobs as it displaces workers—usually at higher skill levels—the jobs may be psychologically and financially less rewarding. Supervising robots eight hours a day can be tedious and boring work with few on-the-job rewards. The same is true for the much touted "office of the future." Interacting with a computer terminal eight hours a day is tedious, tiring, and boring work for many people; and job burnout may accelerate.

The electronic cottage has similar unanticipated consequences. Many people may miss the daily interaction with fellow workers—the gossip, the politics, the strokes. Instead of being rewarding, work at home can become drudgery and low paying work, a 21st century version of the sweat shop.

The optimists often neglect the fact that the nature of work itself provides rewards. Many people intrinsically enjoy the particular job they perform. Furthermore, many rewards are tied to the human dimension of work—the interaction with others. Thus, the high-tech and service society will have to deal with serious management and motivational problems arising from the changing nature of work and the work place.

Many workers may need to re-career in order to overcome the boredom and burnout accompanying many of the new jobs or work situations of tomorrow. And even if the high-tech and service society does not emerge in the form outlined by us and other forecasters, the need to re-career will become necessary given the job and career uncertainty of a turbulent society largely shaped by a cyclical boom/bust economy.

4

Identify the Best Jobs For Tomorrow

T he best jobs for you hopefully will also be amongst the 50 to 100 best jobs predicted for the coming decade. These are some of the fastest growing jobs that should generate a large number of job opportunities for millions of people. Best of all, many of these jobs also offer excellent salaries and opportunities for advancement. They will be some of the most sought-after jobs in the 21st century.

This chapter in no way should imply that the best jobs for you will be found amongst the so-called "hot" jobs for the coming decade. Indeed, the best jobs for you will most likely be discovered through an examination of your interests, values, skills, and abilities in relation to alternative jobs and careers.

What Are the Jobs?

Where are the jobs, and *how* do I get one? These are the first two questions most people ask when seeking employment. But one other equally important question should precede these traditional questions:

"*What* are the jobs of tomorrow?"

For the nature of jobs is changing rapidly in response to (1) technological innovations, (2) the development and application of technology to the work place, and (3) the demand for a greater variety of consumer services. Today's job seeker needs answers to the "what," "where," and "how" of jobs for the coming decade.

Many jobs in the year 2008 will look very different from those in 1998. Indeed, if we project present trends into the future and believe what futurists tell us about emerging new careers, the 21st century will offer unprecedented job and career opportunities.

But such changes and opportunities have costs. The change in jobs and occupations will be so rapid that skills learned today may become obsolete in another five to ten years. Therefore, knowing what the jobs are becomes a prerequisite to knowing how to prepare for them, find them, and change them in the future.

Beware of Changing Occupational Profiles

A few words of caution are in order on how you should and should not use the information in this chapter. If you wish to identify a growing career field to plan a career, do so only after you identify your interests, skills, and abilities—the subjects of Chapters 7, 8, and 9. You need to determine if you have the proper skills or the aptitude and interests to acquire the necessary skills. The next step is to acquire the training before conducting a job search. Only then should you seriously consider pursuing what appears to be a growing field.

> If you wish to identify a growing career field to plan a career, do so only after you identify your interests, skills, and abilities.

At the same time, you should be aware that the statistics and projections on growing industrial and occupational fields may be inaccurate. First, they are based on traditional models and economic studies conducted by the U.S. Department of Labor, Bureau of Labor Statistics. Unlike fortune tellers and soothsayers who communicate in another world and many futurists who engage in "informed flights of fancy" and "brainstorming," the Bureau conducts "empirical studies" which assume a steady rate of economic growth—no major ups or downs. Such occupational projections are nothing more than "best guesses" based upon a traditional model which assumes continual, linear growth. This planning model does not deal well with the reality of cyclical changes, as evidenced by its failures during the turbulent 1980s and 1990s when boom and bust cycles, coupled with the emergence of unique events and crises, invalidated many of the Bureau's employment and occupational forecasts. For example, the Department of Labor projected a high unemployment rate of 7.6 percent for 1982; but in 1982 unemployment stood at 10.8 percent. In addition, the deepening recession and the government program cuts brought on by a series of international crises, domestic economic failures, and ideological changes were unanticipated developments which resulted in the actual decline in public employment for the first time since World War II. Thus, in 1982 there were 316,000 fewer public employees than in the year before!

The 1990s witnessed similar unexpected patterns of economic growth and decline. Federal government cutbacks, low inflation, and unprecedented growth of businesses and the stock market helped create an expected economic boom that saw federal government employment decline by nearly 300,000 and overall unemployment drop to 4.7 percent in 1998—the lowest in more than two decades. In an economy where full employment is considered to be at a 6 percent unemployment rate, the economy of the second half of the 1990s experienced major labor shortages especially in high tech industries and services. The slow growth predicted for the 1990s was anything but slow after 1995. The decade ahead may well provide us with more unique economic scenarios which produce similar unpredictable outcomes, from major recessions to economic booms.

Second, during a period of turbulent change, occupational profiles may become quickly outdated. Training requirements change, and thus individuals encounter greater uncertainty in career choices. For example, based on trend analyses, many people believe that promising careers lie ahead for computer programmers. This may be true if thousands of newly trained individuals do not glut the job market with computer programming skills. Moreover, it may be true if computer technology remains stagnant and the coming generation of self-programmed computers does not make computer programmers obsolete.

A similar situation arises for students pursuing the much glamorized MBA and law degrees. As more MBA's graduate and glut the job market with questionable skills, the glitter surrounding this degree has diminished, and the MBA may fast become an obsolete degree as employers turn to degree fields that emphasize greater communication and analytical skills. While the demand for lawyers increased substantially during the past decade and a large number of students continue to enroll in law schools, competition for legal positions has been keen during the past few years as more and more law graduates flooded a shrinking job market. Opportunities for lawyers may not increase much in the decade ahead. The demand for lawyers may actually decline due to substantial restructuring of the legal profession as lawyers become more competitive, promote more efficient legal services, hire more paralegals, change fee and billing practices, introduce more technology to traditional legal tasks, and develop more do-it-yourself legal approaches; as the criminal justice system undergoes restructuring; and as Americans become less litigious due to the high costs of pursuing legal action. But don't bet on it!

Expect Job Growth in Most Occupations

The growth in jobs has been steady during the past three to four decades. From 1955 to 1980, for example, the number of jobs increased from 68.7 to 105.6 million. This represented an average annual increase of about 1.5 million new jobs. During the 1970s the number of jobs increased by over 2 million per year. And between the years 1983 and 1994 the number of jobs increased by 24.6 million, a strong growth rate of 24 percent over an 11-year period or over 2 million new jobs each year.

Job growth during the 1990s slowed but remained steady at about 1.5 million new jobs each year. The slow down reflected demographic changes in society. By the year 2004 the labor force should grow to 149 million workers—up 13 percent from 1994.

Highlighting these patterns of job growth are 16 forecasts, based on U.S. Department of Labor data and projections and other recent analyses, which represent the confluence of demographic, economic, and technological changes in society during the 1990s:

1. **Growth of the labor force slows during the 1990s.**

   The growth in the labor force will slow to 149 million by the year 2006—a 13 percent increase over the 1994 level. This represents half the rate of increase during the previous 15-year period; it reflects an overall slow population growth, with a near zero population birth rate of 0.7 percent per year.

2. Labor force will be racially and ethnically more diverse.

The racial and ethnic mix of the work force in the year 2006 will be even more diverse than in the year 1990 given the differential birth and immigration rates of various racial and ethnic groups. Blacks, Hispanics, Asians, and other minority groups will represent 27 percent of the work force—up from 22 percent in 1990. These groups also will account for 35 percent of labor force entrants between 1990 and 2006. Hispanics, Asians, and other minorities will increase at a faster rate than blacks and white non-Hispanics.

3. Fewer young people will enter the job market.

The number of 16 to 24 year-olds entering the job market declined between 1975 and 1990 by 1.4 million or 6 percent. Their numbers will increase by 2.8 million during 1990-2006, reflecting a change of 13 percent. These new entrants represent the children of the baby-boom generation who began entering the job market after 1992. The number of 22 to 24 year-olds entering the job market will continue to decline until 1998. The youth share of the labor force will fall to 16 percent by 2006. This represents a significant de-cline—down from 23 percent in 1972, 20 percent in 1987, and 17 percent in 1990. Businesses depending on this age group for students, recruits, customers, and part-time work-ers—especially colleges, the Armed Forces, eating and drinking establishments, and retail stores—must draw from a smaller pool of young people. Competition among young people for entry-level jobs will decline accordingly.

4. The work force will continue to gray as it becomes older.

As the baby-boom generation of the 1960s and 1970s becomes more middle-aged, the number of 25 to 54 year olds in the labor force will increase substantially by the year 2000—with 72 percent or nearly 3 of every 4 workers, being between the ages of 25 and 54. This represents a significant increase from 40 percent in 1988 and 36 percent in 1976.

Between 1990 and 2006 the number of older workers, aged 55 years and above, will grow twice as fast as the labor force as a whole.

5. Women will enter the labor force in growing numbers.

Women will represent over half of all entrants into the labor force during the 1990s. While accounting for 39 percent of the labor force in 1972 and 41 percent of the labor force in 1976, women in the year 2006 are projected to constitute 47 percent of the labor force. By the year 2006, 4 out of 5 women ages 25-54 will be in the labor force.

6. Education requirements for most new jobs will rise.

Most new jobs will require strong basic education skills, such as reading, writing, oral communication, and computation. Many of these jobs will include important high-tech components which will require previous specialized education and training as well as the demonstrated ability to learn and acquire nontraditional education and training to continuously re-tool skills.

7. The fastest growing occupations will be in executive, managerial, professional, and technical fields—all requiring the highest levels of education and skill.

Three-quarters of the fastest growing occupational groups will be executive, administrative, and managerial; professional specialty; and technicians and related support occupations—occupations that require the highest levels of education and skill. Few opportunities will be available for high school dropouts or those who cannot read or follow directions. A combination of greater emphasis on productivity in the work place, increased automation, technological advances, innovations, changes in consumer demands, and import substitutions will decrease the need for workers with little formal education and few skills—helpers, laborers, assemblers, and machine operators.

8. **Employment will increase for most occupations.**

As the population continues to grow and become more middle-aged and affluent, demands for more services will increase accordingly. Except in the cases of agriculture, mining, and traditional manufacturing, the 1990s have seen a steady to significant job growth in all occupations. Over 26 million jobs will be added to the U.S. economy between the years 1990 and 2006. However, new jobs will be unevenly distributed across major industrial and occupational groups due to the restructuring of the economy and the increased education and training requirements for most jobs.

9. **The greatest growth in jobs will take place in service industries and occupations.**

Over 90 percent of all new jobs in the 1990s will be in the service-producing industries with services such as legal, business (advertising, accounting, word processing, and computer support), and healthcare leading the way. The number of jobs in services is expected to rise by 35 percent between 1990 and 2006, from 38 to 50.5 million. Health and business will be the fastest growing service industries during this period. Social, legal, engineering, and management services industries will also exhibit strong growth.

10. **Retail trade will be the second fastest growing industrial sector in the 1990s.**

Employment in the retail trade is expected to increase by 26 percent, from 19.7 to 24.8 million during the 1990-2006 period.

11. **Federal government employment will decline but state and local government employment will increase at different rates for different levels of government as well as for governmental units in different regions of the country.**

Federal government employment will continue to decline, reflecting the overall strategy to contract-out government services, downsize federal agencies, eliminate programs, and decentralize federal functions to state and local governments. The decline will average nearly 1.0 percent each year over the next five years. Except during recessionary periods, state and local government employment will increase by 1 to 2 percent each year with local governments in the rapidly developing and relatively affluent cities and counties of the West and Southwest experiencing the largest employment growth rates. State and local government employment is likely to decline in many areas of the Northeast. Excluding public education and public hospitals, for the period 1990 to 2006 government employment is expected to increase by 14 percent, from 9.5 million to 10.8 million jobs.

12. **Employment growth in education at all levels will be incremental.**

Both public and private education is expected to add 2.3 million jobs to the 9.4 million employed in 1990. Employment in education will increase slightly at all levels due to projected population and enrollment increases. Between 1990 and 2006, the elementary school age population should rise by 3.8 million, secondary by 3.2 million, and postsecondary by 1.4 million. Job opportunities should increase for teachers, teacher aides, counselors, and administrative staff.

13. **Jobs in manufacturing will decline throughout the 1990s.**

Manufacturing jobs are expected to decline by 3 percent, from the 1990 level of 19.1 million. Most of the decline will affect production jobs; professional, technical, and managerial positions in manufacturing will increase. These declines will be due to productivity gains achieved through automation and improved management as well as the closing of less efficient plants.

14. **Employment in agriculture, forestry, fishing, and mining jobs will continue to decline.**

Employment in agriculture, forestry, and fishing is expected to decline by 6 percent, from 3.3 to 3.1 million, reflecting a decrease of nearly 410,000 self-employed workers. Wage and salary positions in agricultural, forestry, and fishing services will increase by 214,000. Strong growth will take place in agricultural services industries, especially landscape, horticultural, and farm management services. Much of the self-employment decline in agriculture will be due to the closing of lucrative export markets as the productivity of agriculture abroad improves and new hybrid crops are introduced from genetic engineering breakthroughs to solve many of the world's food problems. Employment in mining is expected to decline by 6 percent—from 712,000 to 669,000. These figures assume that domestic oil production will drop and oil imports will rise sharply.

15. **Glamorous new occupations, responding to new technological developments and consumer demands, will offer exciting new opportunities for job seekers who are well educated and skilled in the jobs of tomorrow.**

New occupations, created through a combination of technological innovations and new service demands, will provide excellent career opportunities for those who possess the necessary skills and drive to succeed in the decade ahead. New occupations with such names as bionic-electronic technician, holographic inspector, cryonics technician, and aquaculturist will enter our occupational vocabulary during the coming decade.

16. **The hottest career fields for the first five years of the 21st century will be in science, engineering, computer technology, and health services.**

Look for these jobs to be the highest demand and highest paying jobs in the coming decade: biological scientist, physician, mechanical engineer, chemical engineer, computer scientist, computer engineer, materials engineer, medical technologist. Demand also will be high for these less well paid jobs: special education teachers, personal and home care aides, home health aides, and physical therapists.

Examine Growing and Declining Occupations

The Department of Labor divides occupations into 16 broad groups based on the Standard Occupational Classification, the classification system used by all government agencies for collecting occupational information:

- Executive, administrative, and managerial occupations
- Engineers, scientists, and related occupations
- Social science, social service, and related occupations
- Teachers, librarians, and counselors
- Health-related occupations
- Writers, artists, and entertainers
- Technologists and technicians
- Marketing and sales occupations
- Administrative support occupations, including clerical
- Service occupations
- Agricultural and forestry occupations
- Mechanics and repairers
- Construction occupations
- Production occupations
- Transportation and material moving occupations
- Handlers, equipment cleaners, helpers, and laborers

Assuming a moderate rate of economic growth throughout the 1990s—not boom and bust cycles—the U.S. Department of Labor projects an average growth rate of 20 percent for all occupations. Technical and service occupations will grow the fastest:

Projected Employment Changes, 1990-2005

Occupational group	Total increase/decrease in new jobs	Percentage change
All occupations	38,851,000	+20
▪ Services	7,403,000	+29
▪ Administrative support	6,413,000	+13

■ Operators	5,449,000	+4
■ Marketing and sales	5,379,000	+24
■ Precision production	4,764,000	+13
■ Professional specialty	4,281,000	+32
■ Managerial	3,085,000	+27
■ Technicians	1,200,000	+37
■ Agriculture-related	863,000	+5

More than one-half of all job growth in the 1990-2005 period will be contributed by 30 fast growing occupations:

Fastest Growing Occupations Contributing More Than 50% to Job Growth, 1990-2005

Occupation	New jobs created
■ Sales workers, retail	887,000
■ Registered nurses	767,000
■ Cashiers	685,000
■ General office clerks	670,000
■ Truck drivers, light and heavy	617,000
■ General managers and top executives	598,000
■ Janitors and cleaners	555,000
■ Nursing aides, orderlies, and attendants	552,000
■ Food counter, fountain, and related workers	550,000
■ Waiters and waitresses	449,000
■ Teachers, secondary school	437,000
■ Receptionists and information clerks	422,000
■ Systems analysts and computer scientists	366,000
■ Food preparation workers	365,000
■ Childcare workers	353,000
■ Gardeners and groundskeepers	348,000
■ Accountants and auditors	340,000
■ Teachers, elementary school	313,000
■ Guards	298,000
■ Teacher aids and educational assistants	278,000
■ Licensed practical nurses	269,000
■ Clerical supervisors and managers	263,000
■ Home health aids	263,000
■ Maintenance repairers, general utility	251,000
■ Secretaries except legal and medical	248,000
■ Cooks, short order and fast food	246,000
■ Stock clerks, sales floor	209,000
■ Lawyers	206,000

The patterns of growth and decline in industries and occupations during the 1990s generally follow the larger changes in the economy we discussed earlier. The U.S. Department of Labor studies have identified the fastest growing and declining occupations for the years 1990-2005. Occupations, for example, contributing the largest job growth in terms of the actual number of new jobs generated will be in service industries requiring a wide range of skills. Nearly half of the 30 fastest growing occupations will be in the health services alone, and most of the jobs will require advanced education and training:

30 Fastest Growing Occupations, 1990-2005

Occupation	Percent growth
■ Home health aides	92
■ Paralegals	85
■ Systems analysts and computer scientists	79
■ Personal and home care aides	77
■ Physical therapists	76
■ Medical assistants	74
■ Operations research analysts	73
■ Human services workers	71
■ Radiological technologists and technicians	70
■ Medical secretaries	68
■ Physical and corrective therapy assistants and aides	64
■ Psychologists	64
■ Travel agents	62
■ Correction officers	61
■ Data processing equipment repairers	60
■ Flight attendants	59
■ Computer programmers	56
■ Occupational therapists	55
■ Surgical technologists	55
■ Medical records technicians	54
■ Management analysts	52
■ Respiratory therapists	52
■ Childcare workers	49
■ Marketing, advertising, and public relations managers	47
■ Legal secretaries	47
■ Receptionists and information clerks	47
■ Registered nurses	44
■ Nursing aides, orderlies, and attendants	43
■ Licensed practical nurses	42
■ Cooks, restaurant	42

On the other hand, nearly half of the 30 fastest declining occupations will be in declining industries affected by technological change:

30 Fastest Declining Occupations, 1990-2005

Occupation	Numerical decline
▪ Farmers	224,000
▪ Bookkeeping, accounting, and auditing clerks	133,000
▪ Childcare workers, private household	124,000
▪ Sewing machine operators, garment	116,000
▪ Electrical and electronic assemblers	105,000
▪ Typists and word processors	103,000
▪ Cleaners and servants, private household	101,000
▪ Farm workers	92,000
▪ Electrical and electronic equipment assembler	81,000
▪ Textile draw-out and winding machine operators	61,000
▪ Switchboard operators	57,000
▪ Machine forming operators	43,000
▪ Machine tool cutting operators	42,000
▪ Telephone and cable TV line installers and repairers	40,000
▪ Central office and PBX installers and repairers	34,000
▪ Central office operators	31,000
▪ Statistical clerks	31,000
▪ Packaging and filling machine operators	27,000
▪ Station installers and repairers, telephone	26,000
▪ Bank tellers	25,000
▪ Lathe turning machine tool setters	20,000
▪ Grinders and polishers, hand	19,000
▪ Electromechanical equipment assemblers	18,000
▪ Grinding machine setters	18,000
▪ Service station attendants	17,000
▪ Directory assistance operators	16,000
▪ Butchers and meatcutters	14,000
▪ Chemical equipment controllers	14,000
▪ Drilling and boring machine tool setters	13,000
▪ Meter readers, utilities	12,000

The Department of Labor's latest figures cover the period 1996-2006. Occupations with the largest projected job growth include the following:

Occupations With Largest Projected Job Growth, 1996-2006

Occupation	Employment Change		Best training source
	Number	Percent	
▪ Cashiers	530,000	17	Short-term on-the-job
▪ Systems analysts	520,000	103	Bachelor's degree
▪ General managers and top executives	467,000	15	Work experience plus bachelor's or higher degree

■ Registered nurses	411,000	21	Associate's degree
■ Salespersons, retail	408,000	10	Short-term on-the-job training
■ Truckdrivers	404,000	15	Short-term on-the-job training
■ Home health aides	378,000	76	Short-term on-the-job training
■ Teacher aides and educational assistants	370,000	38	Short-term on-the-job training
■ Nursing aides, orderlies and attendants	333,000	25	Short-term on-the-job training
■ Receptionists and information clerks	318,000	30	Short-term on-the-job training
■ Teachers, secondary	312,000	22	Bachelor's degree
■ Child care workers	299,000	36	Short-term on-the-job training
■ Clerical supervisors and managers	262,000	19	Work experience in a related occupation
■ Database administrators, computer support specialists, and all other computer scientists	249,000	118	Bachelor's degree
■ Marketing and sales worker supervisors	246,000	11	Work experience in related occupation
■ Maintenance repairers, general utility	246,000	18	Long-term on-the-job training
■ Food counter, fountain related workers	243,000	14	Short-term on-the-job training
■ Teachers, special education	241,000	59	Bachelor's degree
■ Computer engineers	235,000	109	Bachelor's degree
■ Food preparation workers	234,000	19	Short-term on-the-job training
■ Hand packers and packagers	222,000	23	Short-term on-the-job training
■ Guards	221,000	23	Short-term on-the-job trainig
■ General office clerks	215,000	7	Short-term on-the-job trainig
■ Waiters and waitresses	206,000	11	Short-term on-the-job training

▪ Social workers	188,000	32	Bachelor's degree
▪ Adjustment clerks	183,000	46	Short-term on-the-job training
▪ Cooks, short order and fast food	174,000	22	Short-term on-the-job training
▪ Personal and home care aides	171,000	85	Short-term on-the-job training
▪ Food service and lodging managers	168,000	28	Work experience in a related occupation
▪ Medical assistants	166,000	74	Moderate-term on-the-job training

The Department of Labor also projects that the fastest growing occupations will be the following areas for the 1996-2006 period:

Fastest Growing Occupations, 1996-2006

| Occupation | Employment Change | | Best training source |
	Number	Percent	
▪ Databased administrators, computer support specialists, and all other computer scientists	249,000	118	Bachelor's degree
▪ Computer engineers	235,000	109	Bachelor's degree
▪ Systems analysts	520,000	103	Bachelor's degree
▪ Personal and home care aides	171,000	85	Short-term on-the-job training
▪ Physical and corrective therapy assistants/aides	66,000	79	Moderate-term on-the-job training
▪ Home health aides	378,000	76	Short-term on-the-job training
▪ Medical assistants	166,000	74	Moderate-term on-the-job training
▪ Desktop publishing specialist	22,000	74	Long-term on-the-job training
▪ Physical therapists	81,000	71	Bachelor's degree
▪ Occupational therapy assistants and aides	11,000	69	Moderate-term on-the-job training

- Teachers, special education | 241,000 | 59 | Bachelor's degree
- Human services workers | 98,000 | 55 | Moderate-term on-the-job training
- Data processing equipment repairers | 42,000 | 52 | Postsecondary vocational training
- Medical records technicians | 44,000 | 51 | Associate's degree
- Speech-language pathologists and audiologists | 44,000 | 51 | Master's degree
- Dental hygienists | 64,000 | 48 | Associate's degree
- Amusement and recreation attendants | 138,000 | 48 | Short-term on-the-job training
- Physician assistants | 30,000 | 47 | Bachelor's degree
- Respiratory therapists | 37,000 | 40 | Associate's degree
- Adjustment clerks | 183,000 | 46 | Short-term on-the-job training
- Engineering, science, and computer systems managers | 155,000 | 45 | Work experience plus bachelor's and/or higher degree
- Emergency medical technicians | 67,000 | 45 | Postsecondary vocational training
- Manicurists | 19,000 | 45 | Postsecondary vocational training
- Bill & account collectors | 112,000 | 42 | Short-term on-the-job training
- Residential counselors | 74,000 | 41 | Bachelor's degree
- Instructors and coaches sports and physical training | 123,000 | 41 | Moderate-term on-the-job training
- Dental assistants | 77,000 | 38 | Moderate-term on-the-job training
- Securities and financial services sales workers | 100,000 | 38 | Bachelor's degree

Determine "The Best" Jobs For You

The fastest growing occupational fields are not necessarily the best ones to enter. The best job and career for you will depend on your particular mix of skills, interests, and work and lifestyle values. Money, for example, is only one of many determiners of whether or not a job and career is particularly desirable. A job may pay a great deal of money, but it also may be very stressful and insecure, or it is found in an undesirable location. "The best" job for you will be one you find very rewarding in terms of your own criteria and priorities.

Periodically some observers of the labor market attempt to identify what are the best, the worst, the hottest, the most lucrative, or the most promising jobs and careers of the decade. One of the most ambitious attempts to assemble a list of "the best" jobs in America is presented in *The Jobs Rated Almanac*. Similar in methodology to *The Places Rated Almanac* for identifying the best places to live in America, the latest edition (1995) of this book evaluates and ranks 250 jobs in terms of six primary "job quality" criteria: income, stress, physical demands, environment, outlook, and security. According to their analyses, the 20 highest ranking jobs by accumulated score of these criteria are:

"The Best" Jobs in America

Job title	Overall rank	Overall score
■ Actuary	1	118
■ Software engineer	2	124
■ Computer systems analyst	3	131
■ Accountant	4	218
■ Paralegal assistant	5	222
■ Mathematician	6	223
■ Medical secretary	7	230
■ Computer Programmer	8	263
■ Parole officer	9	279
■ Medical Records Technician	10	294
■ Dietician	11	310
■ Medical Technologist	12	335
■ Statistician	13	336
■ Audiologist	14	342
■ Hospital administrator	15	349
■ Dental Hygienist	16	350

■ Medical Laboratory Technician	17	365
■ Urban/Regional Planner	18	367
■ Biologist	19	370
■ Sociologist	20	374

For the relative rankings of the remaining 230 jobs as well as the ratings of each job on individual criterion, consult the latest edition of *The Jobs Rated Almanac*, which should be available in your local library or bookstore. It can also be ordered from Impact Publications—see the order form at the end of this book.

100 "Best" Careers For the 21st Century

Several other observers of career trends have identified what they consider to be the 50 or 100 best careers for the 21st century. However, their definition of "the best" varies considerably, from "the fastest growing" to "the best paying" jobs. Few of these lists identify "the best" in terms of job satisfaction, security, or lifestyle considerations. In fact, many of the so-called best jobs defined as "the fastest growing" jobs are actually dead-end jobs that pay very little, such as home health aides and word processors. Consequently, you need to be very careful in interpreting such lists. "The best" means different things to different people.

Shelly Field in *100 Best Careers For the 21st Century* (New York: Arco/Macmillan, 1996) identifies the following careers as "the best":

MEDICAL TECHNOLOGY AND HEALTH CARE CAREERS

- Alcohol and Drug Abuse Counselor
- Audiologist
- Cardiology Technologist
- Chiropractor
- Clinical Laboratory Technologist
- Dance Therapist
- Dental Assistant
- Dental Hygienist
- Dietitian
- Dispensing Optician
- EEG Technologist/Technician
- Emergency Medical Technician
- Health Services Administrator
- Home Health Aide
- Licensed Practical Nurse (L.P.N.)

- Medical Records Technician
- Music Therapist
- Nurse's Aide
- Occupational Therapist
- Pharmacist
- Physical Therapist
- Physical Therapy Assistant
- Physician
- Physician Assistant
- Podiatrist
- Radiologic Technologist
- Registered Nurse (R.N.)
- Respiratory Therapist
- Surgical Technologist
- Veterinarian
- Veterinary Technician

GERIATRICS CAREERS

- Geriatric Assessment Coordinator
- Geriatric Care Manager
- Geriatric Social Worker
- Nursing Home Activities Director
- Recreational Therapist
- Retirement Planner

COMPUTER CAREERS

- CAD Specialist
- Computer Programmer
- Computer Salesperson—Retail
- Computer Service Technician
- Computer Trainer
- Systems Analyst
- Technical Documentation Specialist
- Word Processor Operator

CONSERVATION AND ENVIRONMENTAL CAREERS

- Environmental Engineer
- Environmental Technician (water and wastewater)
- Environmentalist
- Hazardous Waste Management Technician

ADVERTISING, COMMUNICATIONS, AND PUBLIC RELATIONS CAREERS

- Copywriter
- Graphic Artist

- Marketing Manager
- Print Advertising
- Public Relations Counselor
- Radio/Television Advertising Salesperson
- Reporter (print)
- Salesperson

SALES AND SERVICE CAREERS

- Accountant
- Actuary
- Child-Care Worker
- Correction Officer
- Hairstylist
- Insurance Sales Agent
- Lawyer
- Paralegal
- Personal Shopper
- Private Investigator
- Property Manager
- Real Estate Agent
- Salesperson
- Secretary

HOSPITALITY AND TRAVEL

- Flight Attendant
- Hotel/Motel Manager
- Pilot
- Restaurant Manager
- Travel Agent

SCIENCE AND ENGINEERING CAREERS

- Biochemist
- Civil Engineer
- Mechanical Engineer
- Meteorologist

FITNESS AND NUTRITION CAREERS

- Aerobics Exercise Instructor
- Personal Trainer
- Sports and Fitness Nutritionist

EDUCATION CAREERS

- Adult Education Teacher
- School Counselor
- Teacher (elementary and secondary school)

HOME-BASED BUSINESS CAREERS

- Adult Day Care Service
- Bed-and-Breakfast Inn Owner
- Bookkeeping and Accounting Service
- Catering Service
- Child-Care Service
- Cleaning Service
- Desktop Publishing Business
- Event Planning Service
- Gift Basket Service
- Home Instruction Service
- Image Consulting Service
- Information Broker Service
- Pet-Sitting Service
- Publicity Consulting Service
- Word Processing Service

Bradley G. Richardson in *JobSmarts 50 Top Careers* (New York: HarperPerennial, 1997) identifies a rather odd and confusing mix of 50 career fields, occupations, jobs, and/or employers that he considers to be "the top" based on conversations with lots of people who are interested in various career fields. "The best" in this case should be defined as ones that many people seem to be interested in knowing more about. In other words, these are "popular" career fields that may or may not do well in the future in terms of growth, income, security, and lifestyle:

- Accounting
- Administration
- Advertising
- Aerospace
- Airline Careers (commercial airline pilot and flight attendant)
- Architecture
- Child Care and Development
- Consulting
- Cops
- Education
- Engineering
- Entrepreneurship
- The Family Business
- Federal Bureau of Investigation (FBI)
- Film Industry
- Finance and Banking
- Firefighter
- Food Service
- Freelancing

- Government and Politics
- Graphic and Commercial Arts
- Healthcare
- High Tech: Computer and Software Technology
- Hospitality: Hotel and Lodging
- Human Resources
- Independent Filmmaking
- Insurance
- Journalism
- Law
- Marketing
- Odd Jobs: Career Off the Beaten Path
- Performing Arts
- Photojournalism
- Professional Speaking
- Professional Student: Pursuit of a Graduate Degree
- Public Relations and Communications
- Publishing
- Radio
- Real Estate
- Retail and Merchandising
- Retail Manufacturer's Representative
- Sales
- Television
- Temporary and Contract Careers
- Travel
- Web Site and Internet Developers
- Working Abroad: International Careers
- Writer/Author

Martin Yate in *CareerSmarts: Jobs With a Future* (New York: Ballantine, 1997) examines over 175 professional jobs that have a bright future because they are associated with healthy industries that should be experiencing steady growth in the years ahead. These, in turn, are linked to the author's creative classification system for identifying professional competencies and workplace realities; they may or may not be relevant to many organizations. His "best jobs" fall into these broad categories:

HEALTH CARE

- Administration
- Nursing
- Physical Health
- Dentistry
- Mental Health

THE TECHNOLOGIES

- Biotechnology and Environmental Technology
- Engineering
- Information Technology

BUSINESS AND PROFESSIONAL SERVICES

- Financial Services (Banking, Securities, Accounting, Insurance)
- Human Resources
- Law
- Media/Communications/Public Relations
- Sales and Marketing
- Food Services

PUBLIC SERVICE

- Social Services
- Education
- State and Local Government

You'll not have to look far for other lists of "the best" jobs for the future. The U.S. Department of Labor periodically revises its job growth projections. Several major magazines, such as *Working Woman* and *U.S. News & World Report*, publish annual surveys of "the best" jobs for the year and decade ahead. Newspapers, newsletters, and Internet sites publish similar lists.

Similarities and Differences

What is common and different about these predictions and projections? First, most are based upon data and analyses provided by the U.S. Department of Labor. Accordingly, they reflect the economic assumptions of the U.S. Department of Labor's planning model—steady-state economic growth. They do not, nor are they able to, incorporate what has become a pattern for most predictions during the past two decades—uncertainty attendant with recessionary cycles and unique events. As such, they should be examined with some degree of caution since many of the predictions are likely to be inaccurate due to the uncertain nature of future economic developments and the continuing restructuring of the economy.

Second, most writers identify a similar set of jobs and careers for the coming decade, no doubt based upon the U.S. Department of Labor's labor market data and economic projections. Indeed, nearly 80 percent of the so-called "best" jobs for the coming decade are repeated on others' lists of "the best" jobs. This remarkable degree of consensus and redundancy argues for serious examination of these similar lists.

Third, most differences lie in categorizing the major career areas— seven versus nine or ten different areas—which identify "the best" jobs. In the end, the career categories are very similar, as are the jobs identified.

Finally, several questionable jobs and careers appear on some of these lists. They question the credibility of the writers' research. Indeed, it is difficult to believe that jobs such as a home health aide, word processor operator, and personal shopper are good jobs since they are either low paying jobs that lead to little or no career advancement or fast declining occupations. Jobs such as the President of the U.S., NBA basketball player, and an NCAA basketball coach are so limited in number as to be useless information for most individuals who have little or no chance of ever attaining such positions.

Look For Exciting New Occupations in the 21st Century

In the early 1980s the auto and related industries—steel, rubber, glass, aluminum, railroads and auto dealers—accounted for one-fifth of all employment in the United States. Today that percentage continues to decline as service occupations further dominate America's occupational structure.

New occupations for the decade ahead will center around information, energy, high-tech, healthcare, and financial industries. They promise to create a new occupational structure and vocabulary relating to computers, robotics, biotechnology, lasers, and fiber optics. And as these fields begin to apply new technologies to developing new innovations, they in turn will generate other new occupations in the 21st century. While most new occupations are not major growth fields—because they do not initially generate a large number of new jobs—they will present individuals with fascinating new opportunities to become leaders in pioneering new fields and industries.

Futurists identify several emerging occupations for the coming decades. Most tend to brainstorm lists of occupational titles they feel will emerge in the next decade based on present trends. Others identify additional occupations which may be created from new, unforeseen technological breakthroughs. Feingold and Miller (*Emerging Careers*), for example, see 30 new careers emerging:

Emerging Careers For the 21st Century

- artificial intelligence technician
- aquaculturist
- automotive fuel cell battery technician
- benefits analyst
- bionic electron technician
- computational linguist
- computer microprocessor
- cryonics technician
- dialysis technologist
- electronic mail technician
- fiber optic technician
- fusion engineer
- hazardous waste technician
- horticulture therapy
- image consultant
- information broker
- information center manager
- job developer
- leisure consultant
- materials utilization specialist
- medical diagnostic imaging technician
- myotherapist
- relocation counselor
- retirement counselor
- robot technician
- shyness consultant
- software club director
- space mechanic
- underwater archaeologist
- water quality specialist

Most futurists agree that such new occupations will have two dominant characteristics during the coming decade:

- **They will generate fewer new jobs** in comparison to the overall growth of jobs in hundreds of more traditional service fields, such as sales workers, office clerks, truck drivers, and janitors.

- **They require a high level of education and skills** for entry into the fields as well as continuing training and retraining as each field transforms itself into additional growth fields.

If you plan to pursue any of these occupations, expect to first acquire highly specialized skills which may require years of higher education and training.

Consider the Implications of Future Trends For You

Most growth industries and occupations require skills training and experience. Moving into one of these fields will require knowledge of job qualifications, the nature of the work, and sources of employment.

Fortunately, the U.S. Department of Labor publishes several useful sources of information available in most libraries to help you. These include the *Dictionary of Occupational Titles*, which identifies over 13,000 job titles. The *Occupational Outlook Handbook* provides an overview of current labor market conditions and projections as well as discusses nearly 250 occupations that account for 107 million jobs, or 87 percent of the nation's total jobs, according to several useful informational categories: nature of work; working conditions; employment; training, other qualifications, and achievement; job outlook; earnings; related occupations; and sources of additional information.

At the same time, the U.S. Department of Labor is overhauling its traditional job classification system which is based on an analysis of the 1960s, 1970s, and 1980s U.S. job market. This system generates over 13,000 job titles as outlined in the *Dictionary of Occupational Titles*. Known as the O*NET project (The Occupational Information Network), the new system will more accurately reflect the structure of today's new job market; it condenses the 13,000+ job titles into approximately 1,200 job titles. The new system is being gradually introduced into career education and it will should soon replace the job classification system that has defined most jobs in the U.S. during the past four decades.

Anyone seeking to enter the job market or change careers should initially consult the U.S. Department of Labor publications as well as access information on the new O*NET project (see the new O*NET *Dictionary of Occupational Titles* available through Impact Publications at the end of this book) for information on trends and occupations.

However, remember that labor market statistics are for industries and occupations *as a whole.* They tell you little about the shift in employment emphasis *within the industry,* and nothing about the outlook of particular jobs for you, *the individual.* For example, employment in agriculture was projected to decline by 14 percent between 1985 and 2000, but the decline consisted of an important shift in employment emphasis within the industry: there would be 500,000 fewer self-employed workers but 150,000 more wage and salary earners in the service end of agriculture. The employment statistics also assume a steady-state of economic growth with consumers having more and more disposable income to stimulate a wide variety of service and trade industries.

Therefore, be careful in how you interpret and use this information in making your own job and career decisions. If, for example, you want to become a college teacher, and the data tells you there will be a 10 percent decline in this occupation during the next 10 years, this does not mean you could not find employment, as well as advance, in this field. It merely means that, on the whole, competition may be keen for these jobs, and that future advancement and mobility in this occupation may not be very good—on the whole. At the same time, there may be numerous job opportunities available in a declining occupational field as many individuals abandon the field for more attractive occupations. In fact, you may do much better in this declining occupation than in a growing field depending on your interests, motivations, abilities, job search savvy, and level of competition. And if the decade ahead experiences more boom and bust cycles, expect most of these U.S. Department of Labor statistics and projections to be invalid for the economic realities of this decade.

Use this industrial and occupational data to expand your awareness of various job and career options. By no means should you make critical education, training, and occupational choices based upon this information alone. Such choices require additional types of information—subjects of the next nine chapters—on you, the individual. If identified and used properly, this information will help clarify exactly which jobs are best for you.

5

Best Paying Jobs and Salary Ranges

T he best jobs for the 21st century are not necessarily the best paying jobs. Some, such as animal caretakers, are relatively low paying jobs that provide a great deal of personal satisfaction. Other occupations offer relatively low starting salaries which may substantially increase with experience. And still others may start at a relatively high salary level but they do not provide significant increases in compensation with experience.

Variable Compensation

If one of your criterion for identifying a "best job" is compensation, you need to carefully examine salary ranges for different occupations. They can vary greatly from one occupational field to another. In some occupations the salary spread from top to bottom is great, indicating a steady pattern of advancement or a system of compensation based upon sales performance. In other occupational fields, compensation levels may quickly plateau after just a few years on the job. In general, occupations requiring high levels of education and technical expertise pay the best. Jobs requiring less education but offering excellent compensation usually involve sales activities tied to commissions and bonuses or are found in the related field of finance (i.e., working with other people's money).

Salary Ranges For 229 Occupations

The following list should give you a rough estimate of salary ranges for 229 major occupations for 1997. We emphasize "rough" because the data is synthesized from several surveys and adjusted for inflation. The ranges include low entry-level and high experience levels. If, for example, you are seeking an entry-level position in one of the following occupational areas, chances are you will find a job that offers a starting salary 10-20 percent higher than our low entry-level range. Expect certain occupations to represent narrow salary ranges because they are primarily education or government positions, such as Mathematicians, Sociologists, Teacher Aides, Librarians, Meteorologists, Foresters, Air Traffic Controllers, and Urban Planners. On the other hand, several occupations represent very wide salary ranges, especially those of Lawyers, Financial Managers, Physicians, and Actors.

> **Occupations requiring high levels of education and technical expertise tend to pay the best. Those involving sales can also pay well.**

■ Accountants	$28,000 - 88,000+
■ Actors, Directors, and Producers	$6,000 - 2+ million
■ Actuaries	$35,000 - 130,000+
■ Adjusters, Investigators, Collectors	$18,000 - 70,000
■ Administrative Services Managers	$31,000 - 56,000+
■ Adult Education Teachers	$14,000 - 60,000
■ Agricultural Scientists	$24,000 - 60,000
■ Aircraft Mechanics and Engineer Specialists	$25,000 - 55,000
■ Aircraft Pilots	$30,000 - 200,000+
■ Air Traffic Controllers	$24,000 - 60,000
■ Animal Caretakers, Except Farm	$10,000 - 26,000
■ Apparel Workers	$14,000 - 28,000
■ Architects	$20,000 - 100,000+
■ Archivists and Curators	$20,000 - 60,000
■ Armed Forces Occupations	$12,000 - 100,000+
■ Automotive Mechanics	$24,000 - 48,000
■ Bank Tellers	$13,000 - 27,000
■ Barbers and Cosmetologists	$15,000 - 30,000

- Billing Clerks $14,000 - 25,000
- Bindery Workers $14,000 - 40,000
- Biological Scientists $15,000 - 60,000+
- Blue-Collar Work Supervisors $20,000 - 54,000
- Boilermakers $15,000 - 42,000
- Bookkeeping, Accounting, and
  Auditing Clerks $14,000 - 26,000
- Bricklayers and Stonemasons $16,000 - 42,000
- Broadcast Technicians $17,000 - 80,000
- Budget Analysts $25,000 - 60,000
- Busdrivers $14,000 - 38,000
- Butchers and Meat, Poultry, and Fish Cutters $15,000 - 38,000
- Carpenters $15,000 - 47,000
- Carpet Installers $18,000 - 43,000
- Cashiers $12,500 - 24,000
- Chefs, Cooks, Other Kitchen Workers $13,000 - 52,000
- Chemists $30,000 - 90,000
- Chiropractors $30,000 - 200,000+
- Clerical Supervisors and Managers $18,000 - 50,000
- Clinical Laboratory Technologists
  and Technicians $28,000 - 60,000
- College and University Faculty $32,000 - 80,000+
- Commercial and Industrial Electronics
  Equipment Repairers $21,000 - 45,000
- Communications Equipment Mechanics $25,000 - 48,000
- Computer and Office Machine Repairers $22,000 - 45,000
- Computer and Peripheral Equipment
  Operators $18,000 - 48,000
- Computer Programmers $30,000 - 70,000
- Computer Systems Analysts $29,000 - 75,000
- Concrete Masons and Terrazzo
  Workers $20,000 - 47,000
- Construction and Building Inspectors $23,000 - 50,000
- Construction Contractors and Managers $32,000 - 100,000+
- Correction Officers $20,000 - 50,000
- Cost Estimators $20,000 - 80,000
- Counselors $22,000 - 60,000
- Credit Clerks and Authorizers $16,000 - 27,000
- Counter and Rental Clerks $13,000 - 25,000

- Dancers and Choreographers　　　　$12,000 - 40,000
- Dental Assistants　　　　$18,000 - 27,000
- Dental Hygienists　　　　$33,000 - 60,000
- Dental Laboratory Technicians　　　　$18,000 - 43,000
- Dentists　　　　$95,000 - 200,000+
- Designers　　　　$17,000 - 100,000
- Dietitians and Nutritionists　　　　$31,000 - 45,000
- Diesel Mechanics　　　　$25,000 - 50,000
- Dispensing Opticians　　　　$23,000 - 45,000
- Drafters　　　　$20,000 - 48,000
- Drywall Workers and Lathers　　　　$21,000 - 48,000
- Education Administrators　　　　$36,000 - 200,000
- EEG Technologists　　　　$24,000 - 38,000
- EKG Technicians　　　　$21,500 - 34,000
- Electric Power Generating Plant Operators
  and Power Distributors and Dispatchers　　　　$23,000 - 64,000
- Electricians　　　　$20,000 - 55,000
- Electronic Equipment Repairers　　　　$21,000 - 48,000
- Electronic Home Entertainment
  Equipment Repairers　　　　$23,000 - 45,000
- Electronic Installers and Repairers　　　　$24,000 - 55,000
- Elevator Installers and Repairers　　　　$24,000 - 55,000
- Emergency Medical Technicians　　　　$23,000 - 45,000
- Employment Interviewers　　　　$21,000 - 30,000
- Engineering, Science, and
  Data Processing Managers　　　　$47,000 - 120,000+
- Engineering Technicians　　　　$20,000 - 46,000
- Engineers　　　　$33,000 - 100,000+
- Environments and Marketing
  Research Analysts　　　　$23,000 - 90,000
- Farm Equipment Mechanics　　　　$19,000 - 38,000
- Farm Operators and Managers　　　　$15,000 - 42,000
- File Clerks　　　　$13,000 - 24,000
- Financial Managers　　　　$40,000 - 75,000
- Firefighting Occupations　　　　$22,000 - 40,000
- Fishers, Hunters, and Trappers　　　　$13,000 - 100,000
- Flight Attendants　　　　$16,000 - 40,000
- Food and Beverage Service Workers　　　　$13,000 - 26,000
- Foresters and Conservation Scientists　　　　$21,000 - 63,000

- Gardeners and Groundskeepers $16,000 - 42,000
- General Maintenance Mechanics $17,000 - 35,000
- General Managers and Top Executives $60,000 - 2+ million
- General Office Clerks $14,000 - 35,000
- Geologists and Geophysicists $29,000 - 90,000
- Glaziers $23,000 - 55,000
- Government Executive and Legislators $2,500 - 200,000
- Guards $13,000 - 25,000
- Handlers, Equipment Cleaners,
  Helpers, and Laborers $13,000 - 37,000
- Health Services Managers $42,000 - 250,000+
- Heating, Air Conditioning, and
  Refrigeration Technicians $18,000 - 45,000
- Home Appliances and Power Tool Repairers $17,000 - 42,000
- Homemaker and Home Health Aides $13,000 - 25,000
- Hotel and Motel Desk Clerks $13,000 - 20,000
- Hotel Managers and Assistants $23,000 - 95,000
- Human Services Workers $15,000 - 32,000
- Industrial Machinery Repairers $18,000 - 45,000
- Industrial Production Managers $58,000 - 95,000
- Information Clerks $14,000 - 25,000
- Inspectors and Compliance Officers,
  Except Construction $23,000 - 58,000
- Inspectors, Testers, and Graders $15,000 - 37,000
- Insulation Workers $20,000 - 49,000
- Insurance Agents and Brokers $18,500 - 75,000
- Interviewing and New Accounts
  Clerks $15,000 - 23,000
- Janitors and Cleaners $13,000 - 28,000
- Jewelers $18,000 - 53,000
- Kindergarten and Elementary
  School Teachers $24,000 - 48,000
- Landscape Architects $21,000 - 51,000
- Lawyers and Judges $38,000 - 200,000+
- Librarians $23,000 - 57,000
- Library Assistants and Bookmobile Drivers $14,000 - 25,000
- Library Technicians $17,000 - 32,000
- Licensed Practical Nurses $19,000 - 33,000
- Line Installers and Cable Splicers $19,000 - 45,000

- Machinists $16,000 - 45,000
- Mail Clerks and Messengers $14,000 - 30,000
- Management Analysts and Consultants $25,000 - 200,000+
- Manufacturers' and Wholesale Sales Reps $20,000 - 75,000
- Marketing, Advertising, and Public
  Relations Managers $23,000 - 95,000
- Material Moving Equipment Operators $15,000 - 48,000
- Material Recording, Scheduling,
  Dispatching, and Distributing Operations $14,000 - 39,000
- Mathematicians $31,000 - 64,000
- Medical Assistants $18,000 - 30,000
- Medical Record Technicians $19,000 - 31,000
- Metalworking and Plastics-Working
  Machine Operators $15,000 - 39,000
- Meteorologists $20,000 - 63,000
- Millwrights $18,000 - 47,000
- Mobile Heavy Equipment Mechanics $18,000 - 47,000
- Motorcycle, Boat, and Small-
  Engine Mechanics $16,000 - 43,000
- Musical Instrument Repairers & Tuners $18,000 - 47,000
- Musicians $13,000 - 44,000
- Nuclear Medicine Technologists $26,000 - 43,000
- Numerical-Control Machine-Tool
  Operators $17,000 - 42,000
- Nursing Aides and Psychiatric Aides $13,000 - 27,000
- Occupational Therapists $29,000 - 52,000
- Operations Research Analysts $34,000 - 100,000+
- Ophthalmic Laboratory Technicians $15,000 - 22,000
- Optometrists $53,000 - 100,000+
- Order Clerks $20,000 - 32,000
- Painters and Paperhangers $18,000 - 44,000
- Painting & Coating Machine Operators $15,000 - 43,000
- Paralegals $23,000 - 41,000
- Payroll and Timekeeping Clerks $19,000 - 30,000
- Personnel, Training, and Labor
  Relations Specialists and Managers $23,000 - 100,000+
- Pharmacists $32,000 - 70,000
- Photographers and Camera Operators $24,000 - 53,000
- Photographic Process Workers $15,000 - 37,000

- Physical Therapists $31,000 - 48,000
- Physicians $90,000 - 300,000+
- Physicists and Astronomers $33,000 - 83,000
- Plasterers $20,000 - 49,000
- Plumbers and Pipefitters $18,000 - 47,000
- Podiatrists $73,000 - 150,000+
- Police, Detectives, Special Agents $25,000 - 100,000+
- Postal Clerks and Mail Carriers $28,000 - 40,000
- Precision Assemblers $14,000 - 37,000
- Prepress Workers $18,000 - 58,000
- Preschool Workers $12,000 - 22,000
- Printing Press Operators $16,000 - 47,000
- Private Household Workers $11,000 - 24,000
- Property and Real Estate Managers $14,000 - 82,000
- Protestant Ministers $25,000 - 63,000
- Psychologists $22,000 - 93,000
- Public Relations Specialists $17,000 - 55,000
- Purchasing Agents and Managers $19,500 - 63,000
- Rabbis $32,000 - 100,000
- Radio and Television Announcers
  and Newscasters $24,000 - 200,000+
- Radiologic Technologists $28,000 - 48,000
- Rail Transportation Workers $28,000 - 67,000
- Real Estate Agents, Brokers,
  and Appraisers $13,000 - 100,000+
- Receptionists $14,000 - 21,000
- Recreation Workers $12,000 - 100,000
- Recreational Therapists $17,000 - 48,000
- Registered Nurses $27,000 - 68,000
- Reporters and Correspondents $18,000 - 82,000
- Reservation and Transportation
  Agents and Travel Clerks $17,000 - 26,000
- Respiratory Therapists $25,000 - 47,000
- Restaurant and Food Service Managers $20,000 - 52,000
- Retail Sales Workers $13,000 - 37,000
- Roman Catholic Priests $11,000 - 23,000
- Roofers $18,000 - 44,000
- Roustabouts $22,000 - 48,000
- Science Technicians $18,000 - 49,000

- Secondary School Teachers $27,000 - 52,000
- Secretaries $20,000 - 42,000
- Securities and Financial Services Sales Reps $23,000 - 1+ million
- Services Sales Representatives $21,000 - 250,000+
- Sheet-Metal Workers $32,000 - 82,000
- Shoe and Leather Workers
  and Repairers $14,000 - 40,000
- Speech-Language Pathologists
  and Audiologists $26,000 - 52,000
- Social Workers $26,000 - 42,000
- Sociologists $21,000 - 93,000
- Stationary Engineers $18,000 - 62,000
- Statisticians $37,000 - 63,000
- Stenographers and Court Reporters $17,000 - 30,000
- Structural and Reinforcing Ironworkers $23,000 - 53,000
- Surgical Technologists $21,000 - 37,000
- Surveyors $18,000 - 50,000
- Teacher Aids $15,000 - 25,000
- Telephone Installers and Repairers $25,000 - 47,000
- Telephone, Telegraph, and Teletype
  Operators $14,000 - 34,000
- Textile Machinery Operators $15,000 - 37,000
- Tilesetters $17,000 - 52,000
- Timber Cutting and Logging Workers $16,000 - 32,000
- Tool and Die Makers $20,000 - 52,000
- Tool Programmers, Numerical Control $27,000 - 45,000
- Travel Agents $12,000 - 27,000
- Truckdrivers $17,000 - 50,000
- Typists, Word Processors, and Data
  Entry Keyers $16,000 - 27,000
- Underwriters $28,000 - 62,000
- Upholsterers $14,000 - 32,000
- Urban and Regional Planners $22,000 - 75,000
- Vending Machine Servicers and Repairers $18,000 - 44,000
- Veterinarians $33,000 - 100,000+
- Visual Artists $15,000 - 47,000
- Water and Wastewater Treatment
  Plant Operators $17,000 - 47,000
- Water Transportation Occupations $16,000 - 72,000

- Webmasters $50,000 - 100,000+
- Welders, Cutters, and Welding
  Machine Operators $15,000 - 47,000
- Wholesale and Retail Buyers and
  Merchandise Managers $18,000 - 52,000
- Woodworkers $15,000 - 43,000
- Writers and Editors $22,000 - 77,000

Pursuing a $100,000+ Job

If you are interested in joining the less than 5 percent of the population who makes in excess of $100,000 a year, you need to select an occupational field where salary ranges exceed the $100,000 level. To get you started on this journey and to familiarize yourself with the types of skills, experience, and qualifications required of such individuals, we recommend five books that focus on this level of compensation:

➤ *100 Winning Resumes For $100,000+ Jobs*, Wendy S. Enelow (Impact Publications, 1997)

➤ *201 Winning Cover Letters For $100,000+ Jobs*, Wendy S. Enelow (Impact Publications, 1998)

➤ *1500+ KeyWords For $100,000+ Jobs*, Wendy S. Enelow (Impact Publications, 1998)

➤ *The New Rites of Passage at $100,000+*, John Lucht (Viceroy, 1995)

➤ *The $100,000 Club*, D. A. Benton (Warner, 1998)

In contrast to most job search books that tend to be geared toward entry-level job seekers or those with only a few years of experience, these five books will give you an inside view as to what it really takes to join the $100,000+ circle. You may want to examine Wendy Enelow's three resume and cover letter books, which are organized by upscale occupations, to get a good snapshot of what it's really like working at the top of many occupations and organizations.

6

The Best Places to Live and Work

Knowing what are the best jobs tells you nothing about where they are located. Unless you are totally obsessed with your career, we assume you also have a personal life and thus would like to reach a satisfying balance between your work and the rest of your life. Moreover, we assume you wish to make important lifestyle choices related to your career.

So where do you really want to live and work during the next ten years? Are the best jobs also found in the best communities?

Relocation is an important job concern for millions of Americans. Indeed, most people change residences as frequently as they change jobs. One in every five families moves residences each year; the average person changes addresses eleven times during their life. Each year approximately 7 million Americans move to another state. In many cases relocation also means changing jobs and lifestyles.

People relocate for many reasons. Some are forced to move because of a company policy that routinely moves personnel from one branch office to another or from headquarters to field offices, and vice versa. Others choose to relocate when their company closes in one community, consolidates its operations in another community, or opens a new office elsewhere. And still others choose to seek employment in communities that offer better job opportunities or more attractive lifestyles. For them, relocation becomes another strategy in their arsenal of job search techniques.

Whether you are forced to relocate due to company policies or you seek new opportunities in other communities, chances are you will consider relocating sometime during the coming decade. When you are faced with a relocation decision, you need to be prepared to deal with many new job, community, and lifestyle issues.

Relocate For New Opportunities

Where will you be working and living next year, five years, or ten years from today? If you had the freedom to pick up and move today, where would you love to live? Choosing where you want to live can be just as important as choosing what you want to do. Such a choice involves making career and lifestyle changes.

When you conduct a job search, you do so by targeting specific employers in particular communities. In most cases, individuals will conduct their job search in the same community in which they live. For other people, moving to another community is desirable for career and lifestyle purposes. And for others, unemployment may be preferred to leaving their present community.

Whatever your choices, you should weigh the relative costs and benefits of relocating to a new community where job opportunities for someone with your skills may be plentiful. If you live in a declining community or one experiencing little economic growth, job and career opportunities for you may be very limited. You should consider whether it would be better for you to examine job opportunities in other communities which may offer greater long-term career advancement as well as more opportunities for careering and re-careering in the future.

In recent years economic development has shifted toward the West, Southwest, and Southeast as well as to selected metropolitan areas in the East and South. Even the Midwest has experienced an economic turnaround. Millions of job seekers will continue to migrate to these areas in the decade ahead in response to growing job opportunities. Perhaps you, too, will look toward these areas as you make important job and career decisions in the years ahead.

Nowhere do we recommend that you pull up stakes and take to the road in search of new opportunities. Many people did so in the 1980s as they headed for the reputed promised lands of Houston and Denver. As the booming economies in these communities went bust by the mid-1980s, many of these people experienced a new round of unemployment. The situation is likely to be repeated in today's reputed promised lands for the decade ahead—Seattle, Denver, Las Vegas, Cincinnati, St. Louis, Philadelphia, Boston, and Atlanta.

Don't ever take to the road until you have done your homework by researching communities, organizations, and individuals as well as created the necessary *bridges* for contacting employers in a new community. Most important, be sure you have the appropriate work-content and networking skills for finding employment available in specific communities.

Target Communities

Many people are attached to their communities. Friends, relatives, churches, schools, businesses, and neighborhoods provide an important sense of identity which is difficult to leave for a community of strangers. Military and diplomatic personnel—the truly transient groups in society—may be the only ones accustomed to moving to new communities every few years.

The increased mobility of society is partly due to the nature of the job market. Many people voluntarily move to where job opportunities are most plentiful. Thus, Atlanta becomes a boom city with hundreds of additional cars entering the already congested freeways each week. The corporate structure of large businesses, with branches geographically spread throughout the national production and distribution system, requires the movement of key personnel from one location to another—much like military and diplomatic personnel.

When you begin your job search, you face two alternative community approaches. You can concentrate on a particular job, regardless of its geographic setting, or you can focus on one or two communities. The first approach, which we term *follow-the-job*, is widely used by migrant farm workers, cowboys, bank robbers, mercenaries, oil riggers, construction workers, newspaper reporters, college and university professors, and city managers. These people move to where the jobs are in their particular profession. Not surprising, many of these job seekers end up in boring communities which may limit their lifestyle options.

If you *follow-the-job*, you will need to link into a geographically mobile communication system for identifying job opportunities. This often means subscribing to specialized trade publications, maintaining contacts with fellow professionals in other communities, joining a nationwide electronic resume and networking bank, or creatively advertising yourself to prospective employers through newspaper ads or letter blitzes.

On the other hand, you may want to *target a community*. This may mean remaining in your present community or locating a community you find especially attractive because of job opportunities, climate, recreation, or social and cultural environments. Regardless of rumored job opportunities, many people, for instance, would not move to North Dakota— the state with the lowest unemployment rate in the country (2.5%)—or to the "deep South" where the local economies, cultures, and public services may be less supportive of desired lifestyles best found in other parts of the country. The same is true for Southerners who are not particularly interested in moving to what are reputed to be cold, dreary, and crime ridden northern cities. At the same time, Seattle, Madison (WI), Gainesville (FL), Philadelphia, Raleigh-Durham, Minneapolis, Austin, Boston, Baltimore, Cincinnati, Nashville, Denver, Ft. Lauder-dale, Las Vegas, St. Louis, and Washington, DC are reputed to be the new promised lands for many people. Seeming oases of prosperity and centers for attractive urban lifestyles, these cities are on the community target list of many job seekers.

We recommend using this second approach of targeting specific communities. The follow-the-job approach is okay if you are young, adventuresome, or desperate; you find yourself in a geographically mobile profession; your career takes precedence over all other aspects of your life; or you have a bad case of wanderlust and thus let others arrange your travel and housing plans. By targeting a community, your job search will be more manageable. Furthermore, moving to another community can be a liberating experience which will have a positive effect on both your professional and personal lives.

Why not find a great job in a community you really love? Fortunately you live in a very large country consisting of numerous communities that offer a terrific range of career and lifestyle opportunities. Let's identify some communities that might be a good "fit" for you as well as eliminate many which you may wish to avoid.

Know the Growing States and Communities

Frictional unemployment—the geographic separation of underemployed and unemployed individuals from high labor demand regions and communities—should present new options for you. Numerous job opportunities may be available if you are willing to relocate.

Unemployment in the 1980s was most pronounced in the states of West Virginia, Michigan, Alabama, Mississippi, and Louisiana. South Dakota, Nebraska, Connecticut, Massachusetts, and Arizona had the lowest unemployment rates. These patterns of unemployment shifted significantly in the 1990s in response to a restructured and revitalized economy. In February 1997, for example, unemployment nationwide stood at 5.4 percent. It was differentially distributed by state and metropolitan areas as follows:

Unemployment by States

	Number Unemployed	Percentage
Alabama	104,300	5.0
Alaska	22,500	7.2
Arizona	119,800	5.6
Arkansas	69,000	5.5
California	1,069,200	6.9
Colorado	78,900	3.8
Connecticut	87,600	5.0
Delaware	19,900	5.2
District of Columbia	22,400	8.4
Florida	359,100	5.1
Georgia	162,900	4.3
Hawaii	32,500	5.5
Idaho	30,400	4.8
Illinois	314,000	4.8
Indiana	119,800	3.9
Iowa	52,800	3.3
Kansas	55,700	4.1
Kentucky	90,300	4.4
Louisiana	146,400	7.2
Maine	33,500	5.0
Maryland	129,400	4.6
Massachusetts	126,700	4.1

Michigan	234,500	4.8
Minnesota	94,200	3.6
Mississippi	73,300	5.8
Missouri	117,300	4.1
Montana	22,300	4.9
Nebraska	24,900	2.7
Nevada	44,100	5.2
New Hampshire	27,700	4.4
New Jersey	252,300	6.1
New Mexico	57,300	7.0
New York	505,300	5.9
North Carolina	158,200	4.2
North Dakota	8,700	2.5
Ohio	270,000	4.7
Oklahoma	64,200	4.0
Oregon	90,400	5.2
Pennsylvania	293,800	5.0
Rhode Island	21,400	4.3
South Carolina	113,400	6.1
South Dakota	11,000	2.8
Tennessee	135,700	4.9
Texas	510,400	5.2
Utah	31,900	3.1
Vermont	14,800	4.5
Virginia	147,100	4.2
Washington	167,000	5.8
West Virginia	59,500	7.4
Wisconsin	90,400	3.1
Wyoming	12,100	4.7
Puerto Rico	166,000	12.8

Throughout the coming decade we expect Colorado, Georgia, Idaho, Illinois, Indiana, Iowa, Kansas, Kentucky, Massachusetts, Michigan, Minnesota, Montana, Nebraska, New Hampshire, North Carolina, North Dakota, Oklahoma, Rhode Island, South Dakota, Tennessee, Utah, Vermont, Virginia, and Wisconsin to have above average employment rates. Numerous communities within these states, especially in the 250,000 to 500,000 population range, will offer some of the best job opportunities.

We foresee major population and economic growth in and around several large cities: Seattle, Portland, Las Vegas, Salt Lake City-Ogden, Denver, Minneapolis-St. Paul, Rochester (MN), Milwaukee, Nashville,

Dallas-Ft. Worth, Houston, Austin, San Antonio, Albuquerque, Phoenix, Gainesville (FL), Fort Lauderdale, Atlanta, Tampa-St. Petersburg, Raleigh-Durham, Pittsburgh, Philadelphia, Washington-Baltimore, Madison (WI), Boston, Indianapolis, Louisville, and Cleveland. We do not expect Southern California—especially the Los Angeles-San Diego corridor—to be a major growth region for population and jobs. While the California economy is slowly rebounding after a difficult recession—largely driven by its exports to Pacific Rim economies and Mexico—we do not expect California to transform itself into a new job mecca. Its recovery and future growth has been further complicated by the economic melt down in several East and Southeast Asia. economies during 1997 and 1998.

Even though the overall growth predictions point to the Northwest, Far West, and Southwest, these trends should not deter you from considering older cities in the Northeast and North Central regions. After all, nearly 2 million new jobs are created nationwide each year. New jobs will continue to develop in cities such as Chicago, Philadelphia, and New York; these are still the best places to pursue careers in the fields of banking, publishing, and advertising. Boston is again becoming an attractive employment center. Several communities in the Midwest—especially those with strong educational infrastructures—have rebounded as they transformed their local economies in the direction of new high-tech and service industries. Rochester (MN), Minneapolis-St. Paul, Madison, Chicago, Detroit, St. Louis, Kansas City, Indianapolis, Columbus, Cleveland, and Cincinnati in the Midwest and Philadelphia, Pittsburgh, Baltimore, Washington DC, Raleigh-Durham-Chapel Hill, and Atlanta in the central to southern Atlantic coast area will remain some of the best cities for jobs and lifestyles in the decade ahead.

Consider the Best Places to Work

If you contemplate relocating to a new community, you should consider communities that are experiencing low unemployment coupled with steady job growth as well as attractive lifestyles. A *Fortune Magazine* survey (November 11, 1996) identified fifteen cities as the best places to balance work and family life. These are places where you can have a good job as well as enjoy a fine lifestyle:

1. Seattle
2. Denver
3. Philadelphia
4. Minneapolis
5. Raleigh-Durham
6. St. Louis
7. Cincinnati
8. Washington, DC
9. Pittsburgh
10. Dallas-Fort Worth
11. Atlanta
12. Baltimore
13. Boston
14. Milwaukee
15. Nashville

If you are planning to go international, you might want to include these great international cities in your job search plans:

1. Toronto
2. London
3. Singapore
4. Paris
5. Hong Kong

Located outside the Sunbelt, most of the American cities are likely to experience solid growth in the decade ahead. The cities of Raleigh-Durham and Minneapolis are already star performers because of their extensive medical facilities and high-tech infrastructure as well as their attractive lifestyles. These two cities will probably continue to be great growth communities during the coming decade. They will generate a disproportionate number of high paying jobs due to the high quality nature of their jobs and workforces. They may well provide models of a new economy and workforce for the 21st century.

Find the Best Place to Live

Community growth and decline trends should be considered as part of your job and career options. If you live in a declining community with few opportunities for your skills and interests, seriously consider relocating to a growth community. Depressed communities simply do not generate enough jobs for their populations. Many communities with populations of 100,000 to 500,000 offer a nice variety of job and lifestyle options.

Except for a few people, one's work should not become one's life. After all, there are more important things in life than one's work. Different communities offer many life choices in addition to jobs. Economic development and job generation are only two of many important community choice concerns. Using ten indicators of "living," the 1997 edition of *Places Rated Almanac* identifies what it considers to be the 50 best communities in North America (USA and Canada) in terms of their mix of cost of living, jobs, housing, transportation, education, health care, crime, the arts, recreation, and climate:

North America's Top 50 Metro Areas

1. Orange County, CA
2. Seattle-Bellevue-Everett, WA
3. Houston, TX
4. Washington, DC-MD-VA-WV
5. Phoenix, AZ
6. Minneapolis-St. Paul, MN-WI
7. Atlanta, GA
8. Tampa-St. Petersburg, FL
9. San Diego, CA
10. Philadelphia, PA-NJ
11. San Jose, CA
12. Long Island, NY
13. Riverside-San Bernardino, CA
14. Pittsburgh, PA
15. Toronto, OH
16. Portland-Vancouver, OR-WA
17. Oakland, CA
18. Denver, CO
19. Cincinnati, OH-KY-IN
20. San Francisco, CA
21. Detroit, MI
22. Dallas, TX
23. Chicago, IL
24. Miami, FL
25. Cleveland-Lorain-Elyria, OH
26. Salt Lake City-Ogden, UT
27. San Antonio, TX
28. Milwaukee-Waukesha, WI
29. Orlando, FL
30. Vancouver, BC
31. Montreal, PQ
32. Raleigh-Durham-Chapel Hill, NC
33. Fort Lauderdale, FL
34. Los Angeles-Long Beach, CA
35. New Orleans, LA
36. Indianapolis, IN
37. Nashville, TN
38. Sacramento, CA
39. Kansas City, MO-KS
40. Rochester, NY
41. Richmond-Petersburg, VA
42. Norfolk-Virginia Beach, VA-NC
43. Syracuse, NY
44. Ventura, CA
45. Austin-San Marcos, TX
46. Oklahoma City, OK
47. Middlesex-Somerset, NJ
48. Montreal, PQ
49. Boston, MA
50. Omaha, NE-IA

These 1997 rankings have already changed in other surveys; they will undoubtedly change in the coming decade. It is best to consult the latest edition of *Places Rated Almanac* to see how particular communities rank.

Money Magazine's most recent annual survey (July 1997) of the best places to live came up with a different set of conclusions on the lifestyle side of the relocation equation. They found that when considering a community move, respondents most valued safety, clean water, clean air, the availability of doctors and hospitals, housing appreciation, good schools, low property taxes, low income taxes, strong state government, and recession resistance. "Future job growth" ranked 14th and "recent job growth" ranked 16th amongst their concerns. Based on such values, *Money Magazine* identified these 50 cities as the best places to live:

America's Top 50 Cities to Live In, 1997

1. Nashua (NH)
2. Rochester (MN)
3. Monmouth/Ocean counties (NJ)
4. Punta Gorda (FL)
5. Portsmouth (NH)
6. Manchester (NH)
7. Madison (WI)
8. San Jose (CA)
9. Jacksonville (FL)
10. Fort Walton Beach (FL)
11. Seattle (WA)
12. Gainesville (FL)
13. San Francisco (CA)
14. Lakeland (FL)
15. Fort Lauderdale (FL)
16. Raleigh/Durham/Chapel Hill (NC)
17. West Palm Beach (FL)
18. Orlando (FL)
19. Boulder (CO)
20. Long Island (NY)
21. Sarasota/Bradenton (FL)
22. Los Angeles/Long Beach (CA)
23. Boston (MA)
24. Oakland (CA)
25. Lafayette (IN)
26. Sheboygan (WI)
27. Orange County (CA)
28. San Diego (CA)
29. Central New Jersey
30. Naples (FL)
31. Tampa/St. Petersburg (FL)
32. Daytona Beach (FL)
33. Pensacola (FL)
34. Stamford/Norwalk (CT)
35. Fort Myers/Cape Coral (FL)
36. Phoenix (AZ)
37. Portland (OR)
38. Fort Collins (CO)
39. Tucson (AZ)
40. Dallas (TX)
41. Provo/Orem (UT)
42. Tacoma (WA)
43. Columbia (MO)
44. Austin (TX)
45. Tallahassee (FL)
46. Denver (CO)
47. Ocala (FL)
48. Fayetteville (AR)
49. Olympia (WA)
50. Houston (TX)

Most of their communities had populations ranging from 250,000 to 500,000. In fact, large cities did not do well in their survey. For example, ten of the cities appearing on *Fortune's* top 15 list ranked much lower on the *Money's* list: Nashville (116th), Minneapolis (118th), Baltimore (156th), Atlanta (159th), Washington (162nd), Pittsburgh (164th), Milwaukee (175th), Philadelphia (187th), Cincinnati (194th), and St. Louis (268th). The relative importance of jobs in comparison to other relocation concerns is exemplified by McAllen, Texas which ranked as *Money's* 104th best place to live. In October 1996 this city had one of the highest unemployment rates in the country—16.1%!

Seek Out the Best Employers

You might also want to consider some of America's best employers when identifying your ideal community. According to Robert Levering and

Milton Moskowitz in their latest edition of *The 100 Best Companies to Work For in America,* these are the best companies to work for:

100 Best Companies in America

Company	Headquarters
Acipco	Birmingham, AL
Advanced Micro Devices	Sunnyvale, CA
Alagasco	Birmingham, AL
Anheuser-Busch	St. Louis, MO
Apogee Enterprise	Minneapolis, MN
Armstrong	Lancaster, PA
Avis	Garden City, NY
Baptist Hospital of Miami	Miami, FL
BE&K	Birmingham, AL
Ben & Jerry's Homemade	Waterbury, VT
Beth Israel Hospital Boston	Boston, MA
Leo Burnett	Chicago, IL
Chaparral Steel	Midlothian, TX
Compaq Computer	Houston, TX
Cooper Tire	Findlay, OH
Corning	Corning, NY
Cray Research	Eagan, MN
Cummins Engine	Columbus, TN
Dayton Hudson	Minneapolis, MN
John Deere	Moline, IL
Delta Air Lines	Atlanta, GA
Donnelly	Holland, MI
Du Pont	Wilmington, DE
A. G. Edwards	St. Louis, MO
Erie Insurance	Erie, PA
Federal Express	Memphis, TN
Fel-Pro	Skokie, IL
First Federal Bank of California	Santa Monica, CA
H. B. Fuller	St. Paul, MN
General Mills	Minneapolis, MN
Goldman Sachs	New York, NY
W. L. Gore & Associates	Newark, DE
Great Plains Software	Fargo, ND
Hallmark Cards	Kansas City, MO
Haworth	Holland, MI
Hershey Foods	Hershey, PA
Hewitt Associates	Lincolnshire, IL
Hewlett-Packard	Palo Alto, CA

Honda of America Manufacturing	Marysville, OH
IBM	Armonk, NY
Inland Steel	Chicago, IL
Intel	Santa Clara, CA
Johnson & Johnson	New Brunswick, NJ
SC Johnson Wax	Racine, WI
Kellogg	Battle Creek, MI
Knight-Ridder	Miami, FL
Lands' End	Dodgeville, WI
Lincoln Electric	Cleveland, OH
Los Angeles Dodgers	Los Angeles, CA
Lotus Development	Cambridge, MA
Lowe's	North Wilkesboro, NC
Lyondell Petrochemical	Houston, TX
Marquette Electronics	Milwaukee, WI
Mary Kay Cosmetics	Dallas, TX
McCormick	Hunt Valley, MD
Merck	Whitehouse Station, NJ
Methodist Hospital	Houston, TX
Microsoft	Redmond, CA
Herman Miller	Zeeland, MI
3M	St. Paul, MN
Moog	East Aurora, NY
J. P. Morgan	New York, NY
Morrison & Foerster	San Francisco, CA
Motorola	Schaumburg, IL
Nissan Motor Manufacturing	Smyrna, TN
Nordstrom	Seattle, WA
Northwestern Mutual Life	Milwaukee, WI
Odetics	Anaheim, CA
Patagonia	Ventura, CA
J. C. Penney	Plano, TX
Physio-Control	Redmond, WA
Pitney Bowes	Stamford, CT
Polaroid	Cambridge, MA
Preston Trucking	Preston, MD
Procter & Gamble	Cincinnati, OH
Publix Super Markets	Lakeland, FL
Quad/Graphics	Pewaukee, WI
Reader's Digest	Pleasantville, NY
Recreational Equipment, Inc.	Seattle, WA
Rosenbluth International	Philadelphia, PA
SAS Institute	Cary, NC
J. M. Smucker	Orrville, OH
Southwest Airlines	Dallas, TX
Springfield ReManufacturing	Springfield, MO
Springs	Fort Mill, SC

Steelcase	Grand Rapids, MI
Syntex	Palo Alto, CA
Tandem	Cupertino, CA
TDIndustries	Dallas, TX
Tennant	Minneapolis, MN
UNUM	Portland, ME
USAA	San Antonio, TX
U S WEST	Eaglewood, CO
Valassis Communications	Livonia, MI
Viking Freight System	San Jose, CA
Wal-Mart	Bentonville, AR
Wegmans	Rochester, NY
Weyerhaeuser	Tacoma, WA
Worthington Industries	Columbus, OH
Xerox	Stamford, CT

While the headquarters will be the main employment centers for most of these companies, please keep in mind that many of these companies—such as Federal Express, Delta Air Lines, Avis, IBM, Lowe's, J.C. Penney, Wal-Mart, and Nordstrom—have offices, plants, and stores in other locations throughout the United States as well as abroad. If you are interested in working for one of these companies, contact the headquarters for information on their other locations as well as refer to *The 100 Best Companies to Work For in America* for more detailed information on these companies.

A. David Silver, author of *Quantum Companies*, identifies 100 of the most exciting, cutting-edge companies that appear destined to grow and redefine business in the 21st century. A disproportionate number of these companies are located in California and Massachusetts as well as represent the hot computer and health care fields. Indeed, 37 percent of these firms specialize in computers, electronics, and communications; 27 percent represent the closely related medical and pharmaceutical industries; and 30 percent of the companies are based in California.

Acxiom Corporation	Cambridge Technology Partners
American Medical Response	Catalina Marketing Corp.
Asante Technologies	C-Cube Microsystems
Ascend Communications	Cerner Corporation
Atmel Corporation	Chipcom Corporation
Bay Networks	Cirrus Logic
Better Education	Computer Network Technology
The Body Shop International PLC	Corel Corporation
Cambridge Neuroscience	

Corrections Corporation of
  America
Davidson & Associates
Decision Quest
Digital Link Corp.
Dionex Corporation
DNX Corporation
Ecoscience Corp.
Education Alternatives
Ensys Environmental Products
Envirotest Systems Corp.
Fore Systems
Frontier Insurance Group
GTI Corporation
Harmony Brook
Hauser Chemical Research
Health Management Associates
Healthdyne Technologies
Heart Technology
Hemosol
Homecare Management
Information America
Informix Corporation
Integrated Health Services
International High Tech
  Marketing
Invision Systems Corporation
Just for Feet
Landstar Systems
Life Resuscitation Technologies
Medicenter
Medicus Systems Corp
Medrad
Megahertz Holding Corp.
Mitek Surgical Products
Molten Metal Technology
Mothers Work
National Health Corp.
NetFrame Systems
Neurogen Corp.
Newbridge Networks Corp.
Nextel Communications

On Assignment
Orbital Sciences Corp.
Orthogene
Parametric Technology Corp.
Phenix Biocomposites
Pleasant Company
Progressive Corp.
Qualcomm
Quantum Health Resources
Quorum Health Group
Res-Care
Research Management Conslts.
Roper Industries
Ryka
Sentinel Systems
Shaman Pharmaceuticals
SRX
Stores Automated Systems
Sunrise Medical
Swift Transportation Co.
Sybase
Synaptic Pharmaceutical
Synopsys
Systemix
Tecnol Medical Products
Tetra Tech
Thermo Electron Corp.
3Com Corp.
Three-Five Systems
Transmedia Network
Tresp Associates
Vivra
Vivus
Wall Data
Whole Foods Market
Wholesome & Hearty Foods
Work/Family Directions
Workstation Technologies
Xilinx
Xircome
Zebra Technologies Corp.
Zia Metallurgical Processes

Look For Solid Metro Areas

Five metropolitan areas exhibiting strong performance in several sectors—cost of living, jobs, housing, transportation, education, health care, crime, the arts, recreation, and climate—should prove to be very attractive areas in the long-term according to *Places Rated Almanac*:

Super-Solid Metro Areas

Metro Area (Overall Rank)	Highest Rank	Lowest Rank
Boise City, ID	Crime	Health Care
Indianapolis	Jobs	Crime
Lexington, KY	Health Care	Crime
Louisville, KY-IN	Climate	Recreation
Salt Lake City-Ogden, UT	Transportation	Housing

However, keep in mind that while many of these communities are *statistically* good places to live, they may or may not be the best places for *you* to find a job and re-career. Be sure to thoroughly investigate communities before deciding to target your job search on any one community.

Select a Location Properly

You and your family should take into consideration several factors and questions when deciding on which communities to target your job search:

- What's most important to me/us in making a move—environment, health care, safety, education, employment, economy, taxes, culture, recreation, climate?

- Where would I/we ideally like to live for the next 5, 10, or 20 years?

- What is the relative cost of living?

- How attractive are the educational, social, recreational, and cultural opportunities?

- What are the economic and psychological costs of making a move?

- What job and career opportunities are there for me/us?

- How can I/we best conduct a job search in another community?

Many people answer these questions by remaining in their community or by targeting economically growing communities or ones offering excellent lifestyle options. The exodus from the declining industrial cities in the Northeast and North Central regions to the Sunbelt began in the 1960s, expanded in the 1970s, continued into the 1980s with the inclusion of the energy-rich Rocky Mountain states, and further expanded in the 1990s with high tech industries in the West. Several metropolitan areas in all regions, but especially in the West, will have abundant job opportunities for skilled workers in the decade ahead. Many of these communities also offer attractive lifestyles. Targeting a job search in metropolitan Seattle, San Francisco, Las Vegas, Denver, Phoenix, Dallas, St. Louis, Minneapolis, Atlanta, Raleigh-Durham, Nashville, and Boston may be a wise move. While these areas may experience numerous urban problems over the next decade, their problems are ones of growth— traffic congestion, pollution, city planning, crime, and housing shortages—not ones of decline. We believe it is better to experience the problems of growth than of decline, especially since growing economies are more likely to respond to their problems. In a situation of decline, your livelihood becomes threatened. In a situation of growth, your major problem may be fighting the traffic congestion in order to get to a job which offers a promising career.

New frontiers for renewed job and career prosperity abound throughout America if you are willing to pack your bags and move. But most such frontiers require highly skilled individuals, and there can be major financial costs in making such a move, especially if you are a homeowner. If you lack the necessary skills for industries in other communities, consider getting retrained before making a move. Unfortunately, many people making moves today do not have the necessary skills to succeed in many of today's growing communities.

Making a community move on your own involves taking risks. Many people, for example, are locked into financial obligations, such as a mortgaged house which doesn't sell well in what may be a depressed housing market. If you find yourself locked in financially, you may want to consider taking an immediate financial loss in anticipation of renewed prosperity in a community which is experiencing promising growth and prosperity. You may recoup your immediate losses within a year or two. However, you will have to pass through a transition period which can be difficult if you don't approach it in a positive, up-beat manner. The old saying, *"There is no gain without pain"* is appropriate in many situations involving community moves.

Consider Your Financial Costs

The financial costs of relocating will vary depending on your situation. They can be major, especially if you move to a community with high housing costs. Studies conducted by Runzheimer International, for example, found the average costs of relocating in 1995 to be $34,700 for homeowners and $8,938 for non-homeowners. The major costs include:

1. Search for housing—travel, child care, and associated expenses.
2. Closing costs on both the old and new homes.
3. Increases in mortgage payments or apartment rent.
4. Temporary living expenses.
5. Cost of a bridge, equity, or swing loan.
6. Costs of maintaining two residences during the relocation period—very high if the old home does not sell immediately.
7. Shipment of household goods.
8. Final moving expenses.
9. Possible increase in cost of living—property and sales taxes, food, utilities.
10. Travel and job search costs for working spouse.
11. Expenses for marketing a home or subletting an apartment.
12. Miscellaneous costs—deposits, decorating costs, fees, dues.

Housing can be a major cost if you move to a community with expensive housing. The National Association of Realtors reported the median home price for the top 25 metropolitan areas in November 1996 to be as follows:

Median Home Prices For the Top 25
Metropolitan Areas, 1996

1.	Honolulu, HI	$335,000
2.	San Francisco Bay Area, CA	$269,900
3.	Orange County, CA	$216,800
4.	Newark, NJ	$197,300
5.	Bergen/Passaic, NJ	$195,800
6.	Boston, MA	$195,300
7.	San Diego, CA	$173,600
8.	New York/Northern New Jersey-Long Island, NY-NJ-CT	$174,500
9.	Middlesex/Somerset/Hunterdon, NJ	$174,000
10.	Los Angeles Area, CA	$172,400
11.	Washington, DC/MD/VA	$164,100
12.	Seattle, WA	$163,800
13.	Nassau/Suffolk, NY	$161,800
14.	Chicago, IL	$153,400
15.	Monmouth/Ocean, NJ	$144,200
16.	Lake County, IL	$142,500
17.	Hartford, CT	$142,500
18.	Providence, RI	$139,400
19.	Reno, NV	$139,000
20.	Aurora/Elgin, IL	$138,400
21.	New Haven/Meriden, CT	$136,800
22.	Trenton, NJ	$136,500
23.	Raleigh/Durham, NC	$132,700
24.	Denver, CO	$132,300
25.	Colorado Springs, CO	$132,100

On the other hand, once you buy into these communities, your housing investment might appreciate. In the long-term, you will probably realize a return on your investment. The basic problem is initially buying into the higher priced housing, and especially if comparable housing was much less expensive in your last community.

When considering a community move, you should be aware of the relative cost of living in various communities. According to the U.S. Bureau of the Census, the following metropolitan areas exhibited the highest and lowest costs of living in 1995:

Highest Costs of Living, 1995

1. New York, NY
2. Honolulu, HI
3. San Francisco, CA
4. Marin County, CA
5. San Mateo County, CA
6. West Chester, NY
7. Boston, MA
8. Philadelphia, PA
9. Washington, DC
10. Anchorage, AK

Lowest Costs of Living, 1995

1. Ft. Smith, AR
2. Little Rock-North Little Rock, AR
3. Joplin, MO
4. Lincoln, NE
5. Johnson City-Kingsport-Bristol, TN
6. South Bend, IN
7. Tulsa, OK
8. Texarkana, TX
9. Bryan-College Station, TX
10. Clarksville-Hopkinsville, TN

Unfortunately, communities with the lowest cost of living also tend to have low rewards of living. Offering few job opportunities, many of these communities offer a disproportionate number of low paying jobs—the reason they have a low cost of living. Not surprising, communities with the highest cost of living tend to offer more job opportunities which also pay the highest wages. Our advice to people with marketable skills: consider heading for communities with a higher cost of living. You'll probably find better job opportunities and face quality lifestyle options in these places.

Do you hate commuting to a job? If you've ever driven to work in Los Angeles, Washington, DC, Chicago, or New York City, you know why many people hate commuting. They can easily spend two to three hours a day in the traffic trying to get to and from work. In 1997 Washington, DC, for example, ranked No. 1 in the country for per capita cost of wasted fuel and time: $820 a year per person. Therefore, you should consider the costs of commuting to and from work in different communities.

Conduct a Long-Distance Community Search

How do you target your job search on a particular community? If you decide to remain in your present community, your job search is relatively manageable on a day-to-day basis. If you target another community, you will need to conduct a long-distance job search which requires more extensive use of the mail and telephone as well as carefully planned visits to the community. In fact, you will probably use your job search time more efficiently with a long-distance campaign. In both situations, you need to conduct community research prior to initiating the major communication steps in your job search.

Most of your community research can be conducted in the library or on the Internet. You need names, addresses, and phone numbers of potential employers. Use major directories such as the *Dun & Bradstreet's Middle Market Directory* and *Who's Who in Commerce and Industry* to get this information. The *Business Phone Book USA 1998* is an especially useful directory for anyone contemplating a long-distance job search.

Three publishers—Adams Media, Surrey Books, and NET Research—publish job bank books which identify hundreds of employers and job search services in the following cities and states: Atlanta, Boston, the Carolinas, Chicago, Dallas/Fort Worth, Denver, Detroit, Florida, Houston, Los Angeles, Minneapolis, New York City, Ohio, Philadelphia, Phoenix, Portland, San Diego, San Francisco, Seattle, St. Louis, Tennessee, and Washington, DC. Each book includes annotated descriptions of employers along with addresses and telephone numbers.

Numerous online resources are available for accessing information on communities, businesses, and relocation. Again, we refer you to the World Wide Web and recommend using a powerful search engine like Yahoo, Excite, or InfoSeek to glean information about almost any community worldwide. Most libraries now have access to a variety of online resources relevant to job seekers and those interested in relocating. If you use the Internet, you can access information on numerous communities and employers throughout the country.

Homequity provides relocation counseling services. If you call their toll-free number (800/243-1033), you can receive free information on housing and schools in any community as well as spouse career counseling. You can also write to them for information: Homequity Destination Services, 40 Apple Ridge Road, Danbury, CT 06810.

United Van Lines' Relocation Services (800/325-3870) maintains a database on over 7,000 cities in the U.S. and abroad. They will send you detailed relocation information on two cities upon request for free. Many banks will supply you with relocation information.

Part of your research may involve narrowing the number of communities you are considering. If you identify 10 alternative communities, outline the criteria by which to evaluate the 10 communities. For example, you may be particularly interested in moving to a community which has a good climate, excellent cultural facilities, unique recreational opportunities, and a sound educational infrastructure in addition to numerous job and career opportunities in your area of interest and skill. Select three communities and initiate a writing campaign for more information. If at all possible, schedule a trip to the cities to get an on-site view or feel for the relative environments. Further try to narrow your choices by rank-ordering your preferences among the three communities. Concentrate most of your job search efforts on your top priority community.

Your next step is to develop a strategy for penetrating both the advertised and hidden job markets. If you are conducting a job search outside your present community, the advertised job market will be most accessible to you. However, you need to link into the hidden job market, where most of the good jobs are located. While doing this from a distance is somewhat difficult, nonetheless it can be managed.

Penetrate the Local Job Market

The advertised job market is always the easiest to access. Buy a newspaper and read the classified ads. Contact an employment firm and they will eagerly assist you. Walk into a personnel office and fill out an application.

Efforts to penetrate the advertised job market should be geared toward uncovering the hidden job market. For example, in reading the Sunday newspaper, watch for names of important people in the society or *"Living"* section. You may want to contact some of these people by writing an approach letter. The employment agencies may give some indication of the general employment situation in the community—both advertised and hidden job markets. The chamber of commerce might be able to give you some job leads other than those advertised. Perhaps you can develop local contacts through membership in an alumni network, professional association, or church.

If you are conducting a long-distance job search, we recommend networking for information, advice, and contacts. Preparation is the key to success. Do your research on potential employers, write letters, make phone calls, and schedule informational and referral interviews. The major difference in this situation is your timing. In addition, you need to give more information to your contacts. In your letter mention that you are planning to move to their community and would appreciate their advice on job opportunities for someone with your qualifications. Mention that you plan to visit the community on such and such a date and would appreciate an opportunity to discuss your job search plan at that time. In this case, enclose your resume with the letter and request a reply to your inquiry. Most people will reply and schedule an interview or refer you to someone else.

You should set aside one or two weeks—preferably more—to literally blitz the community with informational interviews. This requires doing a considerable amount of advance work. For example, use your present community to practice informational and referral interviewing. Contact employers in your area who are in similar positions. Many of them may give you referrals to friends and colleagues in your targeted community.

If you have limited contacts when conducting a long-distance job search, you will probably need to use the "cold turkey" approach more frequently. You should make most of your key contacts at least four weeks before you plan to visit your targeted community. Within two weeks of your visit, you should have scheduled most of your interviews.

Try to schedule at least three interviews each day. You will probably do more because each interview will yield one or two referrals to others. Five interviews a day are manageable if you don't need to spend a lot of time traveling from one site to another. Plan to keep the sites near each other for each day. Within a two week period, you should be able to conduct 40 to 60 interviews. Use the weekends to research the community further. Contact a realtor who will be happy to show you around the community and inform you of different housing alternatives, neighborhoods, schools, taxes, public services, shopping centers, and a wealth of other community information. You should reserve the last two days for following up on referrals. Scheduling interviews with referrals will have to be made by telephone because of the time factor.

After concluding your one to two week visit, follow up your interviews with thank you letters, telephone calls, and letters indicating continuing interest and requesting referrals.

If you receive an invitation to a formal job interview in another city, be sure to clarify the financial question of who pays for the interview. Normally if the employer has requested the interview, the company pays the expense to and from the out of town interview. However, if you have invited yourself to an interview by stating that you will be "in town," expect to pay your own expenses. If you are unclear about who initiated the interview, simply ask *"How should we handle the travel expenses?"* This question should clarify the matter so there's no misunderstanding.

Identify Opportunity Structures

Each community has its own set of social, economic, political, and job market structures. Your job is to understand and use the particular job market structure in your targeted community. The degree of structure differs for every community. However, one thing is relatively predictable: most communities lack a coherent structure for processing job information efficiently and effectively. But communities are made up of networks which enable individuals to network for job information, advice, and referrals. Each community consists of numerous individuals, groups, organizations, and institutions—many of which constitute mutually dependent networks—that are involved in pursuing their own interests in cooperation and competition with one another. The Yellow Pages of your telephone book best outline the major actors. Banks, mortgage companies, advertising firms, car dealers, schools, churches, small businesses, industries, hospitals, law firms, governments, and civic and voluntary groups do their "own thing" and have their own internal power structure. No one dominates except in small communities which also are company towns—paper mills, mining companies, universities, or steel mills. At the same time, the groups overlap with each other because of economic, political, and social needs. The bank, for example, needs to loan money to the businesses and churches. The businesses, in turn, need the educational institutions. And the educational institutions need the businesses to absorb their graduates. Therefore, individuals tend to cooperate in seeing that people playing the other games also succeed. Members of school boards, medical boards, and the boardrooms of banks and corporations will overlap and give the appearance of a "power structure" even though power is structured in the loosest sense of the term. The game players compete and cooperate with each other as well as coop one another. The structures they create are your opportunity structures for penetrating the hidden job market.

Examine the case of Washington, DC. The opportunity structures are relatively clear in this city. While government is the major institution, other institutions are well defined in relation to the government. Within government, both the political and administrative institutions function as alternative opportunity structures: congressional staffs, congressional committees, congressional subcommittees, congressional bureaucracy, executive staff, departments, independent executive agencies, and independent regulatory agencies. Outside, but clinging to, government are a variety of other groups and networks: interest groups, the media, professional associations, contractors, consultants, law firms, banks, and universities and colleges. As illustrated on page 131, these groups constitute an integrated network.

Washington is the ultimate networking community. For years Washington insiders have learned how to use networks to advance their careers. A frequent career pattern would be to work in an agency for three to four years. During that time, you would make important contacts on Capitol Hill with congressional staffs and committees as well as with private consultants, contractors, and interest groups. Your specialized knowledge on the inner workings of government is marketable to these other people. Therefore, you make a relatively easy job change from a federal agency to a congressional committee or to an interest group. Later you move to another group in the network. Perhaps you also work on a law degree so that in another five years you can get a job with a law firm. The key to making these moves is the personal contact—whom you know. Particular attention is given to keeping a current federal application or resume, just in case an opportunity happens to come by. Congressional staff members usually last no more than two years; they set their sights on consulting and contracting firms, agencies, or interest groups for their next job move.

Whatever community you decide to focus your job search on, expect it to have its particular networks. Do as much research as possible to identify the structure of the networks as well as the key people who can provide access to various elements in the opportunity structures. Washington is not unique in this respect; it is just better known, and Washingtonians talk about it more because of their frequent job moves.

Your Ideal Marriage

Whatever your job choices, keep in mind that where you work—the specific community or employer—can make a major difference in how much you enjoy your work. If you are open to relocating, we recommend taking a serious look at some of the best communities. Many of these places offer wonderful lifestyle options, numerous job alternatives, and a bright economic future.

We believe it's wise to put yourself into a quality environment for living and working in the 21st century. When considering the best jobs, do include the best places to live and work in the decade ahead. You may

Washington Networks

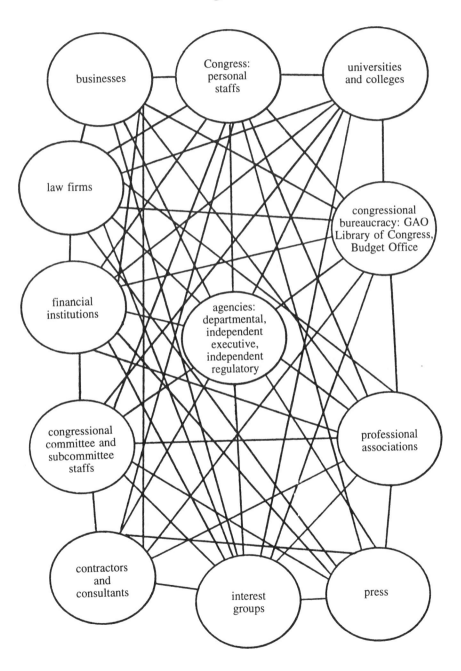

discover an ideal marriage of work and play in one of the many communities we have identified in this chapter.

Part II

The Best Jobs

7

Medical & Health Care Careers

S ome of the hottest careers for the 21st century will be in the fields of medicine and health care. Indeed, five of the ten fastest growing jobs in the decade ahead will be found in health care. Altogether, over 15 million people will work in the health care industry by the year 2006. While major restructuring of health care finance and services may negatively affect some jobs in these fields, especially nurses in hospitals and physicians in private practice, despite such restructuring, medicine and health care are hot career fields for the decade ahead. Entry into the medical field will most likely result in a rewarding long-term career.

Increased job opportunities are largely due to four major changes which translate into a boom for the health care industry:

- Increased public and private financing of health care services.

- New medical breakthroughs for the prevention and detection of diseases.

- An increasingly aging population requiring and demanding more health care services.

- The increasing acceptance of alternative medical approaches.

In general, jobs in the medical and health care industries pay better than in most other industries. The best paying jobs will be for those with high levels of education and specialized training, such as surgeons, radiologists, gynecologists, and anesthesiologists. These industries also will generate hundreds of thousands of lower paying entry-level support positions, especially for medical assistants, nursing aids, and home health aids, which require the least amounts of medical education and training.

We expect job opportunities in medicine and health care to continue to expand throughout the coming decade. New medical breakthroughs relating to genetic engineering and biochemistry will create new occupational specialties. However, don't expect this to be a constantly expanding and rosy occupational field. The organization and management of medical and health care services will continue to undergo major changes in the next decade. The field faces some difficult and challenging years ahead with hospitals and HMOs being at the center of a major upheaval in health care services. Key service delivery centers, such as hospitals and HMOs, are experiencing numerous difficulties relating to financing and the delivery of quality services. Indeed, the health care field is undergoing a fundamental revolution in how it finances, delivers, and gets paid for its services.

The revolution in medicine and health care will have a significant impact on traditional medical roles and medical providers, such as physicians, nurses, and hospitals. The major factors affecting the job outlook will be the financing of health care and the restructuring of health care roles. Changes in health care financing are the key to understanding the increased demand for health care services. As health care financing undergoes major changes, expect the demand for health care services to change accordingly. The current system of health care financing, as well as proposals to increase the scope of financing, could result in an even greater demand for medical and health care services in the decade ahead. Be prepared for new approaches to health care financing as well as new roles for nurses and medical aids in delivering health care services—changes which could significantly alter job opportunities within the health care field in the coming decade.

Twelve of the 24 jobs and careers appearing in this chapter are normally included on most lists of the "50 best jobs":

- Dental Hygienists
- Dietitians and Nutritionists
- Electroneurodiagnostic Technologists

- Emergency Medical Technicians
- Licensed Practical Nurses
- Medical Assistants
- Medical Record Technician
- Physical Therapists
- Physicians
- Radiologic Technologists
- Registered Nurses
- Respiratory Therapists
- Speech-Language Pathologists and Audiologists

We've identified these jobs with one or two stars. One star (★) means the job outlook for the field is excellent; two stars (★ ★) means the job outlook is outstanding.

CHIROPRACTORS

➤ **EMPLOYMENT OUTLOOK:** Demand for chiropractic services is expected to grow faster than average given the rapidly growing older population experiencing a disproportionate number of physiological problems; the increased emphasis on alternative medicine and heathier lifestyles; greater public awareness of the profession; and the financing of chiropractic services through health insurance. In 1998 there were approximately 45,000 chiropractors. Expect a 10 to 20% increase in chiropractors through the year 2006—from 45,000 to 54,000.

➤ **NATURE OF WORK:** If you are interested in alternative medicine, health lifestyles, and having an independent practice, this can be a very attractive and rewarding medical field. Once viewed as quacks by physicians, chiropractors have come of age as professionals practicing an important and respected alternative field of medical care. Emphasizing vitamins, nutrition, and exercise rather than drugs and surgery, chiropractic health care especially appeals to individuals whose muscular ailments have not been treated adequately by traditional medicine. Chiropractors diagnose, treat, and work to prevent physiological disorders and injuries. Using a holistic approach, they treat health problems associated with the body's muscular, nervous, and skeletal systems, especially the spine, by manipulating the muscular system, using X-rays, and prescribing nondrug therapy. Many chiropractors specialize in sports injuries, neurology, orthopedics, nutrition, internal disorders, or diagnostic imaging.

➤ **WORKING CONDITIONS:** Most chiropractors work in clean, comfortable office settings. Over 70 percent have their own practices whereas 25 percent work in group practices or partnerships. They average a 42-hour work week and receive over 100 patients each week.

➤ **EDUCATION, TRAINING, QUALIFICATIONS:** All states require chiropractors to meet educational standards and have a license. Most licensing boards require a 4-year chiropractic college education in addition to a 2-4 year undergraduate education.

➤ **EARNINGS:** Medium income for chiropractors in 1998 was approximately $87,000, after expenses, although the range of earnings varied greatly. The lowest 10 percent averaged $31,000 a year; the highest 10 percent averaged over $200,000 a year.

➤ **KEY CONTACTS:** Chiropractic education and career information is available through:

- **American Chiropractic Association:** 1701 Clarendon Blvd., Arlington, VA 22209. Email: Amerchiro@aol.com Web site: *http://www.amerchiro.org/aca*

- **Council on Chiropractic Education:** 7975 North Hayden Road, Suite A-210, Scottsdale, AZ 85258

- **Federation of Chiropractic Licensing Boards:** 901 54th Avenue, Suite 101, Greeley, CO 80634

- **International Chiropractors Association:** 1110 North Glebe Rd., Suite 1000, Arlington, VA 22201

- **World Chiropractic Alliance**, 2950 N. Dobson Rd., Suite 1, Chandler, AZ 85224-1802.

CLINICAL LABORATORY
TECHNOLOGISTS & TECHNICIANS

➤ **EMPLOYMENT OUTLOOK:** Expect steady job growth in response to overall demand for health care services. Employment is expected to increase from 280,000 in 1998 to 340,000 in 2006.

➤ **NATURE OF WORK:** Also known as medical technologists and technicians, individuals in these jobs play a key role in the detection, diagnosis, and treatment of diseases. They examine and analyze body fluids, tissues, and cells to determine bacteria, parasites, and other micro-organisms; match blood for transfusions; test for drug levels; prepare specimens; and conduct numerous medical tests using a variety of sophisticated laboratory equipment.

➤ **WORKING CONDITIONS:** Work settings and conditions vary, from large hospitals to small commercial laboratories. While half work in hospitals, the trend is to employ more and more medical technologists and technicians in independent laboratories. Hours also vary, from day, evening, night shift, and weekend and holiday work. Given proper precautions, clinical laboratory work is relatively safe.

➤ **EDUCATION, TRAINING, QUALIFICATIONS:** Most entry-level medical technology positions require a bachelor's degree in one of the life sciences or in medical technology. Course work usually includes chemistry, biological sciences, microbiology, mathematics, and computer technology. Medical laboratory technicians receive training in 2-year community college programs, hospitals, vocational and technical schools, or in the Armed Forces.

➤ **EARNINGS:** Median annual earnings of full time, salaried clinical laboratory technologists and technicians were $28,134 in 1998. Half earned between $19,636 and $33,864. The lowest 10 percent earned less than $15,664 and the top 10 percent earned more than $47,000. The median annual salary of medical technologists was $34,202. For medical laboratory technicians, the median was $26,583; for histology technicians, the median was $28,264; for cytotechnologists, the median was $41,414; and for phlebotomists, the median was $19,209.

➤ **KEY CONTACTS:** Career and certification information is available through:

- **American Association of Blood Banks:** 8101 Glenbrook Rd., Bethesda, MD 20814-2749

- **American Medical Technologists:** 710 Higgins Rd., Park Ridge, IL 60068

- **American Society of Clinical Pathologists:** Board of Registry, P.O. Box 12270, Chicago, IL 60612

- **American Society of Cytopathology:** 400 West 9th St., Suite 201, Wilmington, DE 19801

- **National Certification Agency for Medical Laboratory Personnel:** 7910 Woodmont Ave., Suite 1301, Bethesda, MD 20814

- **International Society for Clinical Laboratory Technology:** 818 Olive St., Suite 918, St. Louis, MO 63101

DENTAL ASSISTANTS

➤ **EMPLOYMENT OUTLOOK:** The employment outlook for dental assistants should be excellent in the decade ahead as more individuals use the services of dentists. Dentists currently employ nearly 210,000 dental assistants. This number should increase to 265,000 by 2006.

➤ **NATURE OF WORK:** Dental assistants perform a wide range of office, patient care, and laboratory tasks. Office duties include scheduling appointments, receiving patients, keeping records, sending bills, receiving payments, and ordering dental supplies. Patient care involves preparing patients for treatment, assisting dentists with instruments and materials, and keeping patients comfortable. Some dental assistants may perform the roles of dental hygienists, such as process dental X-ray film, remove sutures, and apply anesthetics. Laboratory duties includes making casts of teeth, make temporary crowns, and maintain cleanliness of appliances.

➤ **WORKING CONDITIONS:** Dental assistants work in well-lighted, clean environments where infectious diseases and dangers posed by radiographic equipment is minimized by proper safety procedures. Most work in private dental offices but some also work in dental schools, hospitals, and public health clinics. One out of three dental assistants work part time, averaging a 32- to 40-hour workweek.

➤ **EDUCATION, TRAINING, QUALIFICATIONS:** While many dental assistants attend dental assisting programs sponsored by community colleges, trade schools, and technical institutes, most dental assistants pick up their skills through on the job experience. Many dental assistants with chairside experience go back to school to become dental hygienists. Others go on to become office managers.

➤ **EARNINGS:** Mediam weekly earnings for dental assistants in 1998 were about $380. The lowest 10 percent earned less than $225; the top 10 percent earned more than $525. Full-time dental assistants can expect to earn between $18,000 and $27,000 a year.

➤ **KEY CONTACTS:** Information on careers for dental assistants is available through:

- **American Association of Dental Examiners:** 211 East Chicago Avenue, Suite 760, Chicago, IL 60611, Tel. 312/440-7464

- **American Association of Dental Schools:** 1625 Massachusetts Avenue, NW, Washington, DC 20036, Tel. 202/667-9433. Email: aads@aads.jhu.edu

- **American Dental Assistants Association:** 203 North LaSalle Street, Suite 1320, Chicago, IL 60601, Tel. 312/541-1320

- **American Dental Association:** 211 East Chicago Avenue, Chicago, IL 60611, Tel. 312/440-2500
  Web site: *http://www.ada.org/prac/careers/dc-menu.html*

- **Dental Assisting National Board:** 216 East Ontario Street, Chicago, IL 60611, Tel. 312/642-3368

- **National Association of Dental Assistants:** 900 South Washington Street, Suite G13, Falls Church, VA 22046, Tel. 703/237-8616

- **National Association of Health Career Schools:** 750 First St., NE, Suite 940, Washington, DC 20002, Fax 202-842-1565

★ DENTAL HYGIENISTS

➤ **EMPLOYMENT OUTLOOK:** Should have no trouble finding a job in this field as the population continues to grow and age and requires more dental services and as incomes rise. Through the year 2006 employment for dental hygienists is expected to grow at a faster rate than other occupations. An estimated 146,000 dental hygienists in 1998 is expected to increase by 15% to 167,000 by the year 2006.

➤ **NATURE OF WORK:** Dental hygienists provide preventive dental care and teach patients about good oral hygiene. Depending on State regulations, dental hygienists may provide any or all of these services: remove calculus, stain, and plaque; apply cavity preventive agents such as fluorides and pit and fissure sealants; take and develop dental X-rays; place temporary fillings and periodontal dressings; remove sutures; and smooth and polish metal restorations.

➤ **WORKING CONDITIONS:** This is a terrific career field for someone who prefers a flexible work schedule. Most dental hygienists work in dental offices where they may have a wide range of flexible work schedules—full-time, part-time, evening, and weekend. Many work two or three days a week in one office and two or three days in other offices.

➤ **EDUCATION, TRAINING, QUALIFICATIONS:** Each state licenses dental hygienists who are required to graduate from an accredited dental hygiene school as well as pass both a written and a clinical examination. Over 200 dental hygiene programs are accredited by the commission on Dental Accreditation; most grant an associate degree but some also offer both bachelor's and master's degrees. Many of these programs require applicants to have completed 1-2 years of undergraduate education with course work in biology, health, chemistry, physiology, pharmacology, and nutrition.

➤ **EARNINGS:** This is a relatively well paying field for individuals with 1-2 years of college education. The average weekly earnings for dental hygienists in 1998, who worked 32 hours a week or more, was $839. The average hourly earnings of all dental hygienists was $23.70.

➤ **KEY CONTACTS:** Information on careers in dental hygiene and educational requirements is available through:

- **American Association of Dental Examiners:** 211 E. Chicago Ave., Suite 760, Chicago, IL 60611, Tel. 312/440-7464

- **American Association of Dental Schools:** 1625 Massachusetts Avenue, NW, Washington, DC 20036, Tel. 202/667-9433. Email: aads@aads.jhu.edu

- **American Dental Association/American Association of Dental Schools:** SELECT, 211 E. Chicago Ave., Suite 1804, Chicago, IL 60611. Tel. 312/440-2500
  Web site: *http://www.ad.org/prac/careers/dc-menu.html*

- **American Dental Hygienists' Association:** Division of Professional Development, 444 N. Michigan Ave., Suite 3400, Chicago, IL 60611, Tel. 312/440-8929

- **National Dental Hygienists' Association:** 5506 Connecticut Avenue, NW, Suite 24-25, Washington, DC 20015, Tel. 202/244-7555

DENTISTS

➤ **EMPLOYMENT OUTLOOK:** After nearly a decade and a half of declining job opportunities for dentists—due to the glut of dental graduates in the 1970s—job prospects for dentists have improved considerably in recent years. However, despite increased demand for dental services in the decade ahead, employment prospects for dentists will grow slower than average. Dentists will cope with increased demand for services by working longer hours and hiring more dental hygienists and dental assistants. Dental jobs are expected to grow by 5% during the next decade, from 165,000 jobs in 1998 to 173,000 jobs in 2008. Job prospects should continue to improve, because of the sharp decline in dental school graduates since the early 1980's and the increased demand for a wide range of dental services amongst the elderly.

➤ **NATURE OF WORK:** Dentists perform a host of dental jobs, from drilling and filling cavities to diagnosing and treating problems of the teeth and tissues of the mouth. This includes examining X-rays, straightening teeth, repairing fractured teeth, performing corrective surgery of the gums, making dentures and crowns, and providing instruction in diet, brushing, flossing, and the use of fluorides. Most dentists are general practitioners while others practice in one of eight specialty areas: orthodontists, oral and maxillofacial surgeons, pediatric dentistry, periodontics, prosthodontics, endodontics, dental public health, and oral pathology.

➤ **WORKING CONDITIONS:** The average dentist works a 40-hour week in dental offices that are open 4 to 5 days a week. Most dentists own their own business and work alone or with a small staff. Dentists wear masks, gloves, and safety glasses for protection against infectious diseases such as hepatitis and AIDS.

➤ **EDUCATION, TRAINING, QUALIFICATIONS:** All states require dentists to be licensed, graduated from an accredited dental school, and to have passed both written and practical examinations. Most dental schools require at least 2 years of college-level predental education or a bachelor's degree. Most dental school programs last 4 academic years and include classroom instruction and laboratory work in anatomy, microbiology, biochemistry, and physiology.

➤ **EARNINGS:** In 1998 the net median income for dentists in private practice was $125,000 a year. Specialists made about $185,000 a year whereas those in general practice made about $115,000 a year.

➤ **KEY CONTACTS:** For information on dental careers and accredited dental schools, contact:

- **American Association of Dental Schools:** 1625 Massachusetts Ave., NW, Washington, DC 20036, Tel. 202/667-9433 Web site: *http://www.ada.org*

- **American Dental Association:** 211 E. Chicago Ave., Chicago, IL 60611, Tel. 312/440-2500

DIETITIANS & NUTRITIONISTS

➤ **EMPLOYMENT OUTLOOK:** Employment for dietitians and nutritionists should grow about average for all occupations, from 60,000 jobs in 1998 to 68,000 jobs in 2006—a 13 percent increase. This growth responds to expanding needs for such health services in nursing homes, hospitals, schools, prisons, community health programs, and health clubs as well as increased interest in preventing disease by improved health habits and the need for improved dietary education.

➤ **NATURE OF WORK:** Dietitians and nutritionists plan nutrition programs and supervise the preparation and serving of meals. They promote healthy eating habits by evaluating diets and suggesting courses of action for improving diet and nutrition.

➤ **WORKING CONDITIONS:** Dietitians and nutritionists work 40 hours a week in a variety of work settings—clinics, food service systems in hospitals and schools, administrative offices, and kitchens. Nearly one in five dietitians work part time. Many spend most of their time on their feet rather than sitting behind desks.

➤ **EDUCATION, TRAINING, QUALIFICATIONS:** Dietitians and nutritionists need a bachelor's degree in dietetics, foods and nutrition, or food service systems management. They take such courses as foods, nutrition, institutional management, chemistry, biology, microbiology, physiology, business, math, statistics, computer science, psychology, sociology, and economics.

➤ **EARNINGS:** Dietitians and nutritionists earn in the range of $31,000 to $45,000 a year, depending on their level of work experience and where they work. Those in education, research, and consulting earn the most.

➤ **KEY CONTACTS:** For information on education programs and careers in dietetics, contact:

- **American Dietetic Association:** 216 West Jackson Blvd., Suite 800, Chicago, IL 60606-6995
  Web site: *http://www.eatright.org*

★   # ELECTRONEURODIAGNOSTIC TECHNOLOGISTS

➤ **EMPLOYMENT OUTLOOK:** Employment of electroneuro-diagnostic technologists (also known as EEG technologists) is expected to rise faster than average—from 6,500 in 1998 to 9,700 in 2006, a 50% increase—in response to increased demand for neurodiagnostic tests.

➤ **NATURE OF WORK:** EEG technologists, which include electron-eurodiagnostic or neurophysiologic technologists (electric brain scan operators), operate electroencephalograph (EEG) machines that help neurologists diagnose brain tumors, strokes, toxic-metabolic disorders, and epilepsy as well as detect infectious diseases and organic impairments affecting the brain.

➤ **WORKING CONDITIONS:** Most EEG technologists work a standard 40-hour week in hospitals or clinics and are often on call for evening, weekend, and holiday work. Their work involves a great deal of bending and lifting; half of their time is spent on their feet.

➤ **EDUCATION, TRAINING, QUALIFICATIONS:** Most EEG technologists acquire on-the-job training, although some complete formal training. Employers increasingly prefer 1 to 2 year formal postsecondary training offered by hospitals and community colleges. Most hospital trainee positions require a high school diploma.

➤ **EARNINGS:** The median annual base salary of full-time EEG technologists in 1998 was $27,200. The middle 50 percent earned between $23,600, and $30,500.

➤ **KEY CONTACTS:** For additional information on these jobs, contact the following organizations:

- **American Society of Electroneurodiagnostic Technologists, Inc.**
  204 W. 7th, Carroll, IA 51401
  Web site: *http://www.aset.org/*

- **Joint Review Committee on Electroneurodiagnostic Technology:** Route 1, Box 63A, Genoa, WI 54632

- **American Board of Registration For Electroencephalographic Technologists and Evoked Potential Technologists:** P.O. Box 916633, Longwood, FL 32791-6633

- **American Society of Electrodiagnostic Technologists:** 35 Hallett Lane, Chatham, MA 02633-2408

EMERGENCY MEDICAL TECHNICIANS

➤ **EMPLOYMENT OUTLOOK:** Job growth for emergency medical technicians will be rapid—from 155,000 jobs in 1998 to 210,000 jobs in 2006, a 35% increase—as more and more paid emergency medical technicians replace unpaid volunteers. Opportunities will be especially good with hospitals and private ambulance services where pay and benefits are generally lower than with higher paying and more competitive fire, police, and rescue squads.

➤ **NATURE OF WORK:** Yes, you've seen them on television and in the movies as emergency lifesavers. Responding to automobile accident injuries, heart attacks, near drownings, unscheduled childbirths, poisonings, and gunshot wounds, emergency medical technicians (EMT's)—also known as paramedics—provide immediate medical care and transport the sick or injured to medical facilities. Two-fifths of EMT's work with private ambulance services; one-third work with municipal fire, police, or rescue squad departments; one-fourth work with hospitals.

➤ **WORKING CONDITIONS:** The work of EMT's is both physically strenuous and stressful, involving indoor and outdoor work and in all kinds of weather. Much of their work involves standing, kneeling, bending, and lifting. EMT's may be exposed to Hepatitus-B and AIDS as well as violent drug overdose victims.

➤ **EDUCATION, TRAINING, QUALIFICATIONS:** EMT's must receive formal classroom and internship training. EMT-Basic training involves 110-120 hours of classroom work plus 10 hours of internship experience in a hospital or emergency room. EMT-Intermediate training includes 35-55 hours of additional instruction. The basic entry requirement for training programs is a high school diploma. Training programs for EMT-Paramedics lasts between 750 and 2,000 hours.

➤ **EARNINGS:** Average starting salaries in 1998 were $26,000 for EMT-Ambulance or Basic and $31,000 for EMT-Paramedic. The highest paid EMT's work in fire departments (EMT-Paramedic averages $34,000 a year). Many ETM workers in small cities, towns, and rural areas serve as volunteers.

➤ **KEY CONTACTS:** For information on EMT careers and training programs, contact your State Emergency Medical Service Director. For general information on EMT's, contact:

- **National Association of Emergency Medical Technicians:** 408 Monroe, Clinton, MS 39056

- **National Registry of Emergency Medical Technicians:** P.O. Box 29233, Columbus, OH 43229

★ ★ HOMEMAKER—HOME HEALTH AIDES

➤ **EMPLOYMENT OUTLOOK:** Compared to most occupations in the coming decade, this job category is expected to experience explosive growth through the year 2006, from 780,000 in 1998 to 1,150,000 in 2005—a 47 percent increase.

➤ **NATURE OF WORK:** If you have limited education and training, desire to help others, and your financial needs are not significant, this can be a very rewarding job. Homemaker-home health aides help elderly, disabled, and ill persons live at home rather than receive care in institutions. They provide housekeeping services, personal care, and emotional support for their clients.

➤ **WORKING CONDITIONS:** Work routines and environments vary depending on the particular need of clients. Some jobs require working in the same home each day whereas others may involve working in several homes for a few hours each day. Some clients may require a great deal of physical assistance and may be angry and abusive whereas others require minimal assistance and may be very pleasant and cooperative.

➤ **EDUCATION, TRAINING, QUALIFICATIONS:** Federal law requires home health aides to pass a competency test in 12 areas and complete at least 75 hours of classroom and practical training supervised by a registered nurse.

➤ **EARNINGS:** Wages in this field are relatively low, just above minimum wage and with little possibility of moving beyond $10.00 an hour. The average starting hourly wage in 1998 for homemakers who work with Medicare-certified agencies range from $5.40 to $7.15; the average starting hourly wage for home health aides ranged from $6.15 to $8.45.

➤ **KEY CONTACTS:** For information on opportunities for homemaker-home health aides, contact:

- **National Association For Home Care:** 228 7th Street, SE, Washington, DC 20003.

- **National Association of Health Career Schools:** 750 First St., NE, Suite 940, Washington, DC 20002, Fax 202/842-1565. Email: NAHCS@aol.com

LICENSED PRACTICAL NURSES

➤ **EMPLOYMENT OUTLOOK:** Employment is expected to grow much faster than average—from 719,000 in 1998 to 920,000 in 2006, a 28 percent increase, due to long-term health care needs of an aging population and the overall growth in health care needs and services.

➤ **NATURE OF WORK:** Licensed practical nurses (L.P.N.'s) care for the sick, injured, convalescing, and handicapped under the direction of physicians and registered nurses. Most provide basic bedside care—take temperature, blood pressure, pulse, and respiration; treat bedsores; prepare and give injections and enemas; apply dressings; give alcohol rubs and massages; apply ice packs and hot water bottles; insert catheters; feed patients and help them with bathing, dressing, and personal hygiene. Some States allow L.P.N.'s to administer prescribed medicines, start intravenous fluids, and help deliver, care for, and feed infants. Thirty-two percent work in hospitals, 27 percent work in nursing homes, and 13 percent work in doctors' offices and clinics.

➤ **WORKING CONDITIONS:** Most L.P.N's work a 40-hour week, but some work nights, weekends, and holidays. They spend a great deal of time on their feet, helping move patients and equipment. Many L.P.N's are exposed to caustic chemicals, radiation, and infectious diseases such as AIDS and hepatitis. L.P.N.'s in nursing homes and private homes often have heavy workloads and long hours.

➤ **EDUCATION, TRAINING, QUALIFICATIONS:** Most L.P.N.'s complete a one-year State-approved practical nursing program. They must pass a State licensing examination. Approximately 1,100 State-approved programs are operated by trade, technical and vocational schools; community and junior colleges; and high schools, hospitals, and colleges and universities.

➤ **EARNINGS:** In 1998 the median annual earnings of full-time, salaried L.P.N.'s were $25,876. The middle 50 percent earned between $21,148 and $28,948. L.P.N's working in chain nursing homes averaged an annual salary of $23,900. Those working in hospitals and medical centers earned a median annual salary of $25,360.

➤ **KEY CONTACTS:** For information on practical nursing careers, contact:

- **National Association for Practical Nurse Education and Service, Inc.:** 1400 Spring St., Suite 310, Silver Spring, MD 20910, Fax 301/588-2839, Email: napnes@aol.com

- **National League of Nursing:** Communications Department, 350 Hudson St., New York, NY 10014, Fax 212/989-2272

★ MEDICAL ASSISTANTS

➤ **EMPLOYMENT OUTLOOK:** This is one of the 10 fastest growing occupations through the year 2006. Expect rapid growth in opportunities for medical assistants—from 247,000 in 1998 to 322,000 in 2006. Growth in job opportunities reflects the overall expansion of the health care industry in response to an aging population as well as major advances in medical technology.

➤ **NATURE OF WORK:** Seven in 10 jobs are in physicians' offices. Medical assistants help physicians examine and treat patients and conduct routine office tasks. They perform numerous clerical duties, from answering telephones and greeting patients to completing insurance forms and scheduling appointments. Many arrange examining room instruments and equipment, handle supplies, and maintain waiting and examining rooms.

➤ **WORKING CONDITIONS:** Medical assistants work a regular 40-hour week in medical offices. They constantly interact with patients and perform multiple responsibilities.

➤ **EDUCATION, TRAINING, QUALIFICATIONS:** This is one of the few health occupations open to individuals with no formal training. Applicants normally need a high school diploma or equivalent. High school courses in mathematics, health, biology, typing, bookkeeping, computers, and office skills are helpful.

➤ **EARNINGS:** Earnings vary widely depending on experience, skill level, and location. Average starting salary for graduates of medical assistant programs is about $18,200. The average annual salary for medical assistants is $22,600. Those with fewer than 2 years experience average around $18,000; those with 11 years experience or more average around $26,800.

➤ **KEY CONTACTS:** For information on medical assistant careers, contact these organizations:

- **American Association of Medical Assistants:** 20 North Wacker Dr., Suite 1575, Chicago, IL 60606-2903

- **American Society of Podiatric Medical Assistants:** 2124 S. Austin Blvd., Cicero, IL 60650

- **Registered Medical Assistants of American Medical Technologists:** 710 Higgins Rd., Park Ridge, IL 60068-5765

★ MEDICAL RECORD TECHNICIANS

➤ **EMPLOYMENT OUTLOOK:** Excellent job outlook due to greater use of medical records for financial management and quality control. Expect the number of jobs to increase from 98,000 in 1998 to 127,000 in 2006.

➤ **NATURE OF WORK:** Medical record technicians organize and evaluate medical records for completeness and accuracy. They ensure that medical charts are complete and all forms are properly identified, signed, and on file.

➤ **WORKING CONDITIONS:** Most medical record technicians work a 40-hour week in pleasant and comfortable office settings. Their jobs require accuracy, attention to detail, and concentration.

➤ **EDUCATION, TRAINING, QUALIFICATIONS:** Medical record technicians normally complete a 2-year associate degree program at a community or junior college. Some receive training through an Independent Study Program in Medical Record Technology offered by the American Medical Record Association. Most employers prefer hiring Accredited Record Technicians (ART) which are accredited by passing a written examination offered by the American Medical Record Association.

➤ **EARNINGS:** Medical record technicians with ART status can expect to start earning between $20,000 and $25,000 a year. The average salary for an ART is about $36,000. Experienced and specialized ARTs can earn $47,000 a year. Technicians with advanced degrees can earn as much as $80,000 a year.

➤ **KEY CONTACTS:** For more information on careers in medical record technology, including the Independent Study Program, contact:

- **American Medical Association:** Division of Allied Health Education & Accreditation, 515 N. State St., Chicago, IL 60610, Tel. 312/464-5000

- **American Health Information Management Association:** 919 N. Michigan Ave., Suite 1400, Chicago, IL 60611, Tel. 312/787-2672

★ # NURSING AIDES AND PSYCHIATRIC AIDES

➤ **EMPLOYMENT OUTLOOK:** Job opportunities are excellent, increasing from 1,490,000 jobs in 1998 (1,380,000 nursing aids and 110,000 psychiatric aides) to 2,050,000 in 2006. These increases reflect greater emphasis on rehabilitation and long-term care for a rapidly growing population aged 75 years old and older. Many of these people will require mental health services. Turnover is high because of modest entry requirements, low pay, and limited advancement opportunities.

➤ **NATURE OF WORK:** Nursing aids and psychiatric aids help care for physically or mentally ill, injured, disabled, or infirm individuals confined to hospitals, nursing or residential care facilities, and mental health settings. Nursing aids, also known as nursing assistants or hospital attendants, answer patients' call bells, deliver messages, serve meals, make beds, and feed, dress, and bathe patients. Psychiatric aides—also known as mental health assistants, psychiatric nursing assistants, or ward attendants—help patients dress, bathe, groom, eat, socialize, and engage in educational and recreational activities.

➤ **WORKING CONDITIONS:** Aids normally work a 5-day, 40-hour week, although many work evenings, nights, weekends, and holidays, and part-time. Much of their work involves standing and helping patients move, stand, and walk. Nursing aids often have unpleasant duties— empty bed pans, change soiled bed linens, and care for disoriented and irritable patients. Psychiatric aids are often confronted with violent patients.

➤ **EDUCATION, TRAINING, QUALIFICATIONS:** These positions offer young people and those without a high school diploma or previous work experience entry into the work world. Only a few employers require some training or experience. Most health facilities provide on-the-job training.

➤ **EARNINGS:** These are generally low paying jobs with little or no advancement opportunities. Median annual earnings of full-time nursing and psychiatric aides in 1998 were $15,600. The top 10% earned more than $27,000; the lowest 10 percent earned less than $11,500. The median annual earnings for nursing aides in chain nursing homes was $14,000.

➤ **KEY CONTACTS:** For information on nursing careers in hospitals, contact:

- **National Association of Health Career Schools:** 750 First St., NE, Suite 940, Washington, DC 20005, Fax 202/842-1565, Email: NAHCS@aol.com

OPTOMETRISTS

➤ **EMPLOYMENT OUTLOOK:** Employment is expected to increase as fast as the average for all occupations through the year 2006, from 42,000 jobs in 1998 to 45,000 in 2006, due to the growing demand for eye care from a larger and older population.

➤ **NATURE OF WORK:** Optometrists (doctors of optometry) provide primary vision care to nearly one half of the population that wears glasses or contact lens. Optometrists examine eyes, diagnose vision problems and eye diseases, analyze test results, and prescribe treatments such as eyeglasses, contact lenses, vision therapy, and low-vision aids. Many provide post-operative care to cataract patients.

➤ **WORKING CONDITIONS:** Most optometrists work as either private practitioners in clean and comfortable offices or operate franchise optical stores. Most work a 40-hour week but many work Saturdays and evenings to accommodate the schedules of patients.

➤ **EDUCATION, TRAINING, QUALIFICATIONS:** All states require optometrists to be licensed. Licensing requirements include having a Doctor of Optometry degree from an accredited optometry school (16 institutions in the U.S.) and passing a written and clinical State board examination. Most optometrists acquire 7-8 years of higher education—2-3 years of undergraduate study or bachelor's degree and graduation from a 4-year program at an accredited optometry school.

➤ **EARNINGS:** In 1998 earnings of optometrists averaged $84,000 a year. The average starting salary for new graduates was $60,000.

➤ **KEY CONTACTS:** For information on optometry careers and accredited optometric education institutions, contact:

- **American Optometric Association:** Educational Services, 243 North Lindbergh Blvd., St. Louis, MO 63141-7881
  Web site: *http://www.aoanet.org/aoanet*

- **Association of Schools and Colleges of Optometry:** 6110 Executive Blvd., Suite 510, Rockville, MD 20852
  Web site: *http://www.opted.org*

PHARMACISTS

➤ **EMPLOYMENT OUTLOOK:** Opportunities for pharmacists will be as fast as average, increasing from 175,000 jobs in 1998 to 213,000 jobs in 2006. This growth in jobs is largely in response to a larger and older population and the increasing use of drugs in medical treatment. Most of the job growth will take place in community pharmacies.

➤ **NATURE OF WORK:** Pharmacists measure, count, mix, and dispense drugs and medicines prescribed by physicians, podiatrists, and dentists. They answer customers' questions about prescription and over-the-counter drugs as well as give advice about durable medical equipment and home health care supplies.

➤ **WORKING CONDITIONS:** Pharmacists spend a great deal of time on their feet and many work evenings, nights, weekends, and holidays. They work in clean and well-lighted areas in community pharmacies (independently owned, drug store, chain, grocery, department store), hospitals, health maintenance organizations (HMO's), clinics, and the federal government.

➤ **EDUCATION, TRAINING, QUALIFICATIONS:** All States require pharmacists to be licensed. This requirement is met by graduating from an accredited college of pharmacy, passing a State board examination, and accumulating a certain amount of practical experience. Degrees in pharmacy usually require 5-6 years of study beyond high school in accredited pharmaceutical education programs.

➤ **EARNINGS:** In 1998 the medium annual income for full-time, salaried pharmacists was $62,000. Pharmacists working in chain drug stores had an average base salary of $64,000; those working in independent drug stores averaged $55,000; those in discount stores averaged $53,200; and hospital pharmacists averaged $63,000.

➤ **KEY CONTACTS:** For information on opportunities in pharmacy, contact:

- **American Association of Colleges of Pharmacy:** 1426 Prince St., Alexandria, VA 22314

★ PHYSICAL THERAPISTS

➤ **EMPLOYMENT OUTLOOK:** This is one of the fastest growing and best paying occupations in the decade ahead. Employment for physical therapists is expected to increase from 124,000 jobs in 1998 to 175,000 jobs in 2006. The increase is due to the expansion of rehabilitation and long-term care services in response to public needs.

➤ **NATURE OF WORK:** Physical therapists improve the mobility, relieve the pain, and prevent or limit the permanent physical disabilities of patients suffering from injuries or disease. Their patients include accident victims and individuals disabled with multiple sclerosis, cerebral palsy, nerve injuries, burns, amputations, head injuries, fractures, low back pain, arthritis, and heart disease. Their treatments include exercise, electricity, heat, ultrasound, traction, and deep-tissue massage. Many physical therapists specialize in areas such as pediatrics, geriatrics, orthopedics, sports medicine, neurology, and cardiopulmonary physical therapy.

➤ **WORKING CONDITIONS:** Most physical therapists work a 40-hour week in hospitals, clinics, and therapists' offices. Some work in homes and schools. Their work can be physically demanding because they often stoop, kneel, crouch, lift, and stand for long periods of time as well as move heavy equipment and lift patients or help them turn, stand, or walk. About 25 percent work part time.

➤ **EDUCATION, TRAINING, QUALIFICATIONS:** You need a college education for this occupational field. All States require physical therapists to pass a licensure exam after graduating from an accredited physical therapy program. Over 170 accredited programs offer bachelor's degrees (46) and master's degrees (116). By the year 2001 all physical therapy programs will be at the master's degree level and above.

➤ **EARNINGS:** In 1998 the median annual earnings of full-time, salaried physical therapists were $41,000. The top 10 percent earned at least $67,000; the bottom 10 percent earned less than $22,000. Full-time physical therapists working in hospitals and medical centers earned a median yearly income of $50,000. Physical therapists in private practice tend to earn more than salaried workers.

➤ **KEY CONTACTS:** For information on careers in this field, contact:

- **American Physical Therapy Association:** 1111 North Fairfax St., Alexandria, VA 22314-1488
  Web site: *http://www.apta.org/*

PHYSICIANS

➤ **EMPLOYMENT OUTLOOK:** Despite a reputed oversupply of physicians, employment for physicians is expected to grow faster than average—from 570,000 jobs in 1998 to 755,000 in 2006. The best job prospects will be in internal medicine, general and family practice, general pediatrics, and preventive medicine.

➤ **NATURE OF WORK:** Physicians practice in numerous specialties. They perform medical examinations, diagnose illnesses, and treat people suffering from injury or disease. They advise patients on diet, hygiene, and preventive health care. Most M.D.'s specialize, with the following specialties employing the largest number of physicians: general and family practice (10.5%), internal medicine (16.0%), pediatrics (7.0%), general surgery (5.2%), psychiatry (5.3%), obstetrics and gynecology (5.2%), and anesthesiology (4.6%).

➤ **WORKING CONDITIONS:** Physicians often work long, irregular hours. Nearly half work more than 60 hours a week.

➤ **EDUCATION, TRAINING, QUALIFICATIONS:** All States require physicians to be licensed. Physicians must graduate from an accredited medical school (usually 4 years), complete a licensing exam, and acquire 1-6 years of graduate medical education.

➤ **EARNINGS:** Salaries vary for physicians, depending on their specialty. In general, they are one of the highest paid occupational groups. In 1998 the average net income of M.D.s after expenses was

All physicians	**$175,000**
Surgery	240,000
Radiology	230,000
Anesthesiology	216,000
Obstetrics/gynecology	205,000
Pathology	165,000
Internal medicine	149,000
Pediatrics	141,000
Psychiatry	135,000
General practice/family practice	139,000

➤ **KEY CONTACTS:** For information on premedical education, financial aid, and medical careers, contact:

- **American Medical Association:** 515 N. State St., Chicago, IL 60610

- **Association of American Medical Colleges:** Section for Student Services, 2450 N St., NW, Washington, DC 20037-1131
  Web site: *http://www.aamc.org*

- **American Osteopathic Association:** Department of Public Relations, 142 East Ontario St., Chicago, IL 60611
  Web site: *http://www.am-osteo-assn.org*

- **American Association of Colleges of Osteopathic Medicine:** 5550 Friendship Blvd., Suite 310, Chevy Chase, MD 20815-7321
  Web site: *http://www.aacom.org*

PODIATRISTS

➤ **EMPLOYMENT OUTLOOK:** A relatively small occupation, employment is expected to grow as fast as average, increasing from 12,000 jobs in 1998 to 14,000 jobs in 2006. The increase is due to rising demand for podiatric services from older people and fitness enthusiasts.

➤ **NATURE OF WORK:** Podiatrists diagnose and treat disorders and diseases of the foot and lower leg. They treat major foot conditions such as corns, calluses, ingrown toenails, bunions, hammertoes, and ankle and foot injuries. They order X-rays and laboratory tests, prescribe drugs, perform surgery, and order physical therapy.

➤ **WORKING CONDITIONS:** Most podiatrists work independently in their own general practice. They work an average work week of 38 hours. Some podiatrists work in hospitals and clinics where they work nights and weekends.

➤ **EDUCATION, TRAINING, QUALIFICATIONS:** All States require podiatrists to be licensed which includes graduating from an accredited college of podiatric medicine and passing written and oral examinations. Colleges of podiatric medicine offer a 4-year program with a core curriculum similar to other schools of medicine. Most graduates also complete a 1-3 year residency program after receiving their DPM (Doctor of Podiatric Medicine) degree.

➤ **EARNINGS:** In 1998 the average net income of podiatrists was $97,000. Those with 1 to 2 years experience netted $48,000; those with 16 to 30 years of experience netted $150,000.

➤ **KEY CONTACTS:** For information on careers in podiatric medicine, contact:

- **American Association of Colleges of Podiatric Medicine:** 1350 Piccard Dr., Suite 322, Rockville, MD 20850-4307 Web site: *http://www.aacpm.org*

- **American Podiatric Medical Association:** 9312 Old Georgetown Rd., Bethesda, MD 20814-1621. Web site: *http://www.apma.org*

OCCUPATIONAL THERAPISTS

➤ **EMPLOYMENT OUTLOOK:** Occupational therapy is one of the fastest growing occupations that also offers excellent compensation. The demand for such services is largely driven by an increasing number of middle-aged and elderly individuals requiring therapeutic services. In 1998 occupational therapists occupied 59,000 jobs. This number should increase to 80,000 by 2006.

➤ **NATURE OF WORK:** Occupational therapists help individuals who are mentally, physically, developmentally, or emotionally disabled lead more independent, productive, and satisfying lives. They assist clients with all types of activities, from using a computer to taking care of daily needs such as dressing, cooking, and eating. Occupational therapists often work with individuals in a particular age group or those with a specific type of disability.

➤ **WORKING CONDITIONS:** Occupational therapists working in hospitals and other health care and community settings usually put in a 40-hour work week. About one-third of occupational therapists work part-time. The work can be very tiring since therapists are on their feet much of the time and they are often lifting and moving clients and equipment.

➤ **EDUCATION, TRAINING, QUALIFICATIONS:** The minimal requirement for entry into this field is a bachelor's degree in occupational therapy. All states regulate this occupation, requiring licences and certification. Individuals must graduate from an accredited educational program and pass a national certification examination in order to receive a licence to practice. Occupational therapists need patience and strong interpersonal skills in working with clients.

➤ **EARNINGS:** The medium annual income for full-time salaried occupational therapists in 1998 was $41,000. The middle 50 percent earned between $32,000 and $52,000. The lowest 10 percent earned less than $25,000 a year; the top 10 percent earned more than $58,000 a year.

➤ **KEY CONTACTS:** For information on opportunities in occupational therapy, contact:

- **American Occupational Therapy Association:** 4720 Montgomery Lane, P. O. Box 31220, Bethesda, MD 20824-1220
  Web site: *http://www.aota.org*

★ # RADIOLOGIC TECHNOLOGISTS

➤ **EMPLOYMENT OUTLOOK:** Employment for radiologic technologists will be highly competitive in the decade ahead as hospitals merge radiologic with nuclear medicine technology departments. Expect fewer job opportunities in hospitals. However, employment of radiological technologists should be faster than the average for all occupations through 2006 as the population grows and ages and places increased demand on diagnostic imaging and therapeutic technology. Radiologic technologists held 178,000 jobs in 1998; their numbers should increase to 240,000 by 2006.

➤ **NATURE OF WORK:** Radiologic technologists perform a variety of jobs related to the use of X-ray equipment. Radiographers produce X-ray films (radiographs) of parts of the human body for use in diagnosing medical problems. Radiation therapy technologists prepare cancer patients for treatment and administer prescribed doses of ionizing radiation to specific body parts. Sonographers, also known as ultrasound technologists, use non-ionizing, ultrasound equipment to transmit high frequency sound waves into patients' bodies to form images for diagnostic purposes.

➤ **WORKING CONDITIONS:** Most radiologic technologists work a 40-hour week. They spend a great deal of time on their feet and may lift or turn disabled patients.

➤ **EDUCATION, TRAINING, QUALIFICATIONS:** Most radiological technologists attend 1-4 year training programs offered in hospitals, colleges and universities, vocational-technical institutes, and the Armed Forces. Many States require radiographers and radiation therapy technologists to be licensed.

➤ **EARNINGS:** The median annual earnings for full-time radiologic technologists in 1998 were $30,000; 10 percent earned less than $17,000; 10 percent earned more than $45,000. For hospitals and medical centers, the median annual salary was $29,500. For radiation therapy technologists, the median was $38,500 and for ultrasound technologists, $37,500.

➤ **KEY CONTACTS:** For information on opportunities for radiologic technologists, contact:

- **American Healthcare Radiology Administrators:** 111 Boston Rd., Suite 105, P.O. Box 334, Sudbury, MA 01776

- **American Society of Radiologic Technologists:** 15000 Central Ave. SE, Albuquerque, NM 87123-3917

- **Society of Diagnostic Medical Sonographers:** 12770 Coit Rd., Suite 708, Dallas, TX 75251

RECREATIONAL THERAPISTS

➤ **EMPLOYMENT OUTLOOK:** Employment of recreational therapists should increase rapidly in the decade ahead as demand increases for physical and psychiatric rehabilitative services and services for the disabled. Recreational therapists held 40,000 jobs in 1998. The number of jobs should increase to 60,000 by 2006.

➤ **NATURE OF WORK:** Recreational therapists provide a variety of treatment services to individuals with illnesses or disabilities. These include the use of arts and crafts, animals, sports, games, dance and movement, drama, music, and community outings to help reduce depression, stress, and anxiety and to build confidence and independence.

➤ **WORKING CONDITIONS:** Recreational therapists work in a variety of settings—hospitals, rehabilitation centers, park and recreation departments, special education programs of school districts, and programs for older adults and people with disabilities. Their work usually takes place in special activity rooms and may involve travel to parks, playgrounds, swimming pools, restaurants, and theaters.

➤ **EDUCATION, TRAINING, QUALIFICATIONS:** The basic entry-level requirement for recreational therapists is a bachelor's degree in therapeutic recreation. Paraprofessional positions require an associate degree in recreational therapy or a health care related field. Most employers want to hire individuals who are certified therapeutic recreation specialists (CTRS). Such individuals must have a bachelor's degree, pass a written certification examination, and complete an internship of at least 360 hours under the supervision of a certified therapeutic recreation specialist.

➤ **EARNINGS:** The average annual salary for therapeutic recreation specialists in 1998 was $35,000. The average annual salary for consultants, supervisors, administrators, and educators was approximately $43,000. Recreational therapists with the Federal government earned $40,000 a year.

➤ **KEY CONTACTS:** For information on careers in recreational therapy, contact:

- **American Therapeutic Recreation Association:** P.O. Box 15215, Hattiesburg, MS 39402-5215
  Web site: *http://www.atra-tr.org*

- **National Therapeutic Recreation Society:** 22377 Belmont Ridge Rd., Ashburn, VA 20148, Email: NTRSNRPA@aol.com
  Web site: *http://www.nrpa.org/branches/htrs.htm*

- **National Council for Therapeutic Recreation Certification:** P.O. Box 479, Thiells, NY 10984-0479

★ ★   # REGISTERED NURSES
(R.N.s)

► **EMPLOYMENT OUTLOOK:** Registered Nurses constitute the largest health care occupation with nearly 2 million jobs. Jobs for registered nurses will grow much faster than for most other occupational groups, increasing from 2 million jobs in 1998 to 2.6 million jobs in 2006. This increase responds to the overall growth in health care and the increased demand for new nurses in home health, long-term, and ambulatory care.

► **NATURE OF WORK:** Registered nurses provide for the physical, mental, and emotional needs of sick and injured patients. They observe, assess, and record symptoms, reactions, and progress; assist physicians during treatments and examinations; administer medications; assist in convalescence and rehabilitation; instruct patients and their families in proper care; and help individuals and groups take steps to improve or maintain their health.

► **WORKING CONDITIONS:** Registered nurses work in a variety of settings as hospital nurses, nursing home nurses, public health nurses, private duty nurses, office nurses, occupational health or industrial nurses, and head nurses or nurse supervisors.

► **EDUCATION, TRAINING, QUALIFICATIONS:** All States require nurses to be licensed. This requirement includes graduation from an accredited nursing school and passing a national licensing examination. Individuals can acquire a nursing education through three types of programs. Nursing graduates can earn an associate degree (A.D.N.), diploma, and bachelor of science degree in nursing (B.S.N.). The A.D.N. program takes 2 years and is offered by community and junior colleges. B.S.N. programs take 4-5 years and are offered by colleges and universities. Diploma programs are offered by hospitals and last 2-3 years. Licensed graduates of these three programs qualify for entry level positions as staff nurses.

► **EARNINGS:** Median annual earnings of full-time salaried registered nurses were $36,500 in 1998. The lowest 10 percent earned less than $22,500; the top 10 percent earned more than $54,500. The median annual base salary of full-time nurse practitioners was $68,000 in 1998. The median annual base salary of full-time nurse anesthetists was $83,000.

➤ **KEY CONTACTS:** For information on nursing careers, contact:

- **American Association of Colleges of Nursing:** 1 Dupont Circle, Suite 530, Washington, DC 20036, Fax 202/785-8320

- **American Nurses Association:** 600 Maryland Ave., SW, Washington, DC 20024-2571, Tel. 202/651-7000

- **National League for Nursing:** Communications Department, 350 Hudson Street, New York, NY 10014, Tel. 212/989-9393

★ RESPIRATORY THERAPISTS

➤ **EMPLOYMENT OUTLOOK:** Employment is expected to grow faster than average. The number of jobs is expected to increase from 86,000 in 1998 to 115,000 in 2006. This increase responds to growing demand from an increasingly middle-aged and elderly population. Older people are more likely to suffer from cardiopulmonary diseases such as pneumonia, chronic bronchitis, emphysema, and heart disease.

➤ **NATURE OF WORK:** Respiratory therapists treat all sorts of patients, from infants with lung problems to elderly people suffering from lung disease. They provide temporary relief to patients with chronic asthma or emphysema and emergency care for heart failure, stroke, drowning, or shock victims. They most commonly use oxygen or oxygen mixtures, chest physiotherapy, and aerosol medications. They apply oxygen masks, connect patients to ventilators, and regularly check on patients and equipment.

➤ **WORKING CONDITIONS:** Respiratory therapists usually work 35-40 hours per week in hospital departments of respiratory care, anesthesiology, or pulmonary medicine. About 10 percent work with home health agencies, respiratory therapy clinics, and nursing homes.

They may work evenings, nights, or weekends. Much of their work involves standing and walking.

➤ **EDUCATION, TRAINING, QUALIFICATIONS:** Entry into this field requires postsecondary formal training which is provided by hospitals, medical schools, colleges and universities, trade schools, vocational-technical institutes, and the Armed Forces. Most of the 210 Commission on Accreditation of Allied Health Education Programs (CAAHEA)-accredited therapist programs last 2 years and lead to an associate degree. Some are 4-year bachelor's degree programs. Technician programs last about 1 year and award certificates.

➤ **EARNINGS:** Median annual earnings for full-time respiratory therapists in 1998 were $33,600. The lowest 10 percent earned less than $20,000; the top 10 percent earned more than $52,000.

➤ **KEY CONTACTS:** For information on respiratory therapist careers, contact:

- **American Association for Respiratory Care:** 11030 Ables Lane, Dallas, TX 75229, Tel. 214/243-2272

- **The National Board for Respiratory Care, Inc.:** 8310 Nieman Rd., Lenexa, KS 66214, Tel. 913/599-4200

- **Joint Review Committee for Respiratory Therapy Education:** 1701 W. Euless Blvd., Suite 300, Euless, TX 76040, Tel. 817/283-2835

★ # SPEECH-LANGUAGE PATHOLOGISTS/AUDIOLOGISTS

➤ **EMPLOYMENT OUTLOOK:** Jobs will grow faster than average—from 88,000 in 1998 to 112,000 in 2006—due to the overall rapid growth of the health care industry and the increased incidence of stroke-induced hearing and speech loss in an aging population.

➤ **NATURE OF WORK:** Speech-language pathologists assess and treat persons with speech, language, voice, and fluency disorder. They work with people who are unable to make speech sounds, or make them clearly; those with speech rhythm and fluency problems, such as stuttering; people with speech quality problems, such as inappropriate pitch or harsh voice; and those with problems understanding and producing language. Audiologists assess and treat those with hearing and related disorders. They use audiometers and other testing devices to measure the loudness at which a person begins to hear sounds, their ability to distinguish between sounds, and other tests of the nature and extent of their hearing loss.

➤ **WORKING CONDITIONS:** Speech-language pathologists and audiologists work in clean comfortable surroundings. Nearly 50 percent provide services in preschools, elementary and secondary schools, or colleges and universities. Others work in hospitals and offices of physicians and with home health care agencies. Some also have their own private practices. Audiologists tend to be employed in independent healthcare offices while speech-language pathologists more often work in school settings. Working from desks or tables, their jobs are not physically demanding.

➤ **EDUCATION, TRAINING, QUALIFICATIONS:** Most speech-language pathologists and audiologists have master's degrees. All 39 States that require speech-language pathologists to be licensed also require a master's degree or equivalent; 275 to 300 hours of supervised clinical experience; a passing score on a national examination; and 9 months of post-graduate professional experience. About 230 colleges and universities offer relevant master's degrees.

➤ **EARNINGS:** The median annual earnings of full-time salaried speech-language pathologists and audiologists were $36,500 in 1998. The median annual salary for certified speech-language pathologists with 1-3 years experience in 1998 was $39,000. Certified audiologists averaged $33,000. Speech-language pathologists with 22+ years experience earned a median annual salary of $53,000. Experienced audiologists earned $56,000 a year.

➤ **KEY CONTACTS:** For information on speech-language pathology and audiology careers, contact:

- **American Speech-Language-Hearing Association:** 10801 Rockville Pike, Rockville, MD 20852, Tel. 301/897-5700
  Web site: *http://www.asha.org*

- **American Academy of Audiology:** 8201 Greensboro Dr., Suite 300, McLean, VA 22102

- **American Auditory Society:** 1966 Inwood Road, Dallas, TX 75235, Tel. 602/789-0755

- **National Student Speech, Language, and Hearing Association:** 10801 Rockville Pike, Rockville, MD 20852, Tel. 301/897-5700

VETERINARIANS

➤ **EMPLOYMENT OUTLOOK:** Employment of veterinarians will grow faster than average—from 59,000 in 1998 to 76,000 in 2006—in response to the growing animal population and the willingness of pet owners to pay for more intensive care. Job prospects are especially good for those specializing in farm animals because fewer graduates prefer working in rural and isolated settings.

➤ **NATURE OF WORK:** Veterinarians care for pets, livestock, sporting and laboratory animals, and protect humans against diseases carried by animals. Veterinarians diagnose medical problems, dress wounds, set broken bones, perform surgery, prescribe and administer medicines, and vaccinate animals against diseases. They also advise owners on care and breeding.

➤ **WORKING CONDITIONS:** Most veterinarians treat pets in hospitals and clinics. Those with large animal practices work out of mobile clinics and drive long distances to farms and ranches. They are exposed to disease and infection and may be kicked, bitten, or scratched. Those in private practice tend to work long hours.

➤ **EDUCATION, TRAINING, QUALIFICATIONS:** All States require veterinarians to be licensed. They must have a Doctor of Veterinary Medicine from an accredited college of veterinary medicine and pass a

State board examination. The degree requires a minimum of 6 years of college—2 years of preveterinary study and a 4-year veterinary program—and clinical experience. Most applicants have completed 4 years of college.

➤ **EARNINGS:** Beginning salaries for recent graduates in private practice averaged $37,000 in 1998. The average income of veterinarians in private practice was $58,000 in 1998. Those employed by the federal government in nonsupervisory, supervisory, and managerial positions earned an average of $58,000 a year in 1998.

➤ **KEY CONTACTS:** For information on veterinarian careers, contact:

- **American Veterinary Medical Association:** 1931 N. Meacham Rd., Suite 100, Schaumburg, IL 60173-4360, Tel. 800/248-2862 Web site: *http://www.avma.org*

- **Association of American Veterinary Medical Colleges:** 1101 Vermont Ave., NW, Suite 710, Washington, DC 20005

- **National Association of Federal Veterinarians:** 1101 Vermont Ave., NW, Suite 710, Washington, DC 20005

8

Computer and Internet Careers

The computer and Internet industries will generate a large number of jobs during the next 10 years. Indeed, according to the U.S. Department of Labor's most recent occupational projections to the year 2006, the fastest growing occupations—increasing the number of jobs by over 100 percent—will be in the computer industry: database administrators, computer support specialists, computer scientists, computer engineers, and systems analysts. Requiring at least a bachelor's degree, entry into these high demand occupational fields should result in long-term job security, career advancement, job mobility, and relatively high salaries and generous benefits. Computer engineers and computer systems analysts in particular rank at the very top on most lists of the 10 or 25 hottest jobs in the decade ahead. If you want to fast track your career, make good money, and experience long-term job security, these are the fields to be in for the coming decade.

The Internet is one of today's newest, hottest, most innovative, and adventuresome occupational frontiers. We include it with computer occupations because of this emerging field's affinity to the computer industry. But the Internet industry involves numerous occupations and jobs that go beyond just computers and high-tech. When viewed as an electronic form of commerce, the Internet encompasses a broad spectrum of occupations with a high tech and electronic communication emphasis: engineering, software development, graphic arts, sales, marketing, advertising, writing, and publishing. Because of the multi-dimensional aspect of the Internet, we're not sure how to best classify Internet-related occupations. What we do know is that this will be a "hot" job and career arena in the coming decade.

Expanding at an exponential rate, Internet activity is generating a whole new occupational vocabulary reflecting the evolution of the Internet industry and related commerce. Straddling both the computer and Internet worlds, Webmasters occupy one of today's most envious positions in both the computer and Internet worlds. Their skills are in great demand and they command high salaries—the perfect combination for one of the best jobs for the 21st century.

As more and more businesses and homes use computers and the Internet, as well as adapt new applications to work processes, the computer field will experience steady growth. Many of the best paying jobs that also lead to career advancement will be in the computer field.

While fewer jobs will be available at the manufacturing end of the industry—due to the export of low wage computer manufacturing jobs to developing countries—the largest growth in jobs will take place at the service and application ends of the computer industry—computer engineers, programmers, operations research analysts, and computer systems analysts. We expect continued growth within the field for computer programmers, consultants, salespeople, marketers, educators, technicians, and repairers. New generations of computers will come on line and provide increased job opportunities for such computer specialists.

Not all computer jobs will survive the winds of change in this highly volatile field. As the use of computers becomes more widespread at all levels in organizations, many jobs will decline in number, especially for computer operators, word processors, and data entry people.

We also expect the computer field will remain volatile given the highly competitive nature of the computer industry and the large number of small start-up firms challenging the market shares of medium to large computer companies. Jobs in computer manufacturing will be most volatile. Expect strong performance from Microsoft, Intel, Hewlett Packard, Compaq, IBM, Dell, and Gateway. Apple and Netscape will most likely face difficult times and be bought out by other firms. Software producers will continue to face an extremely competitive market increasingly dominated by Microsoft. New jobs will continue to

173

be created in multimedia and on the information highway through commercial on-line services and the Internet.

Given the highly volatile nature of the computer field, individuals working directly in this field should be prepared to change jobs frequently as firms go out of business, downsize, and start up. Surviving and prospering in this field requires constant learning and retraining in the face of short product cycles, many lasting only a few months! This is the classic example of a highly entrepreneurial field that rewards education, hard work, and initiative. Individuals need to be fast on their feet and love what they are doing. Many individuals in this field may eventually start their own computer companies.

COMPUTER AND OFFICE MACHINE REPAIRERS

➤ **EMPLOYMENT OUTLOOK:** Overall employment is expected to increase faster than average (3.7% each year) due to the increased use of computers in offices and homes. However, employment growth will be slower than the growth in equipment due to the increased reliability of computer and office machines and the ease of repair. Organizations throughout the economy will continue to further automate in order to achieve greater productivity and improved service. More repairers will be needed to install, maintain, and repair machines. Employment is expected to increase from 143,000 in 1998 (81,000 computer repairers and 62,000 office machine repairers) to 180,000 (100,000 computer repairers and 80,000 office machine repairers) in 2006.

➤ **NATURE OF WORK:** Computer and office machine repairers install new machines, do preventive maintenance, and correct emergency problems. Computer equipment repairers work on computers (mainframes, minis, and micros), peripheral equipment, and word processing systems; office machine repairers work on photocopiers, cash registers, mail processing equipment, fax machines, and typewriters.

➤ **WORKING CONDITIONS:** Computer and office machine repairers normally work a 40-hour week. Daily work routines vary from working in shops to servicing machines in clients' offices.

➤ **EDUCATION, TRAINING, QUALIFICATIONS:** Formal education and training is acquired through post secondary vocational-technical schools, private vocational schools and technical institutes, and junior and community colleges. Given the rapidly changing technology of computer and office machines, individuals in these occupations receive a great deal of on-the-job training as well as participate in numerous training courses to update their skills.

➤ **EARNINGS:** In 1998 the median annual earnings for computer and office machine repairers were $30,000.

➤ **KEY CONTACTS:** For information on career opportunities for computer and office machine repairers, contact your local junior and community college or vocational-technical school.

COMPUTER PROGRAMMERS

➤ **EMPLOYMENT OUTLOOK:** The growth of computer programmer jobs will be faster than average, from 575,000 jobs in 1998 to 725,000 jobs in 2006. While this growth is faster than average, it is not as fast as in the past. New software and techniques have simplified or eliminated some programming tasks, and more and more users are able to write their own programs. Job opportunities will be especially good with data processing services firms, software houses, and computer consulting businesses. Individuals experienced in working with a variety of programming languages, especially C++, Java, Smalltalk, Visual Basic, and Ada, as well as domain-specific languages for computer networking, data base management, and Internet applications, will be in the greatest demand.

➤ **NATURE OF WORK:** Computer programmers write, update, and maintain the detailed instructions (called programs or software) that list in a logical order the steps that computers must execute. Computer programmers tend to be the "technicians" of the computer field in contrast to the "theoreticians" who occupy positions as computer scientists, computer engineers, and systems analysts. Applications programmers primarily work with software designed for business, engineering, or science. They write software to handle specific applications in their fields as well as modify existing programs. Systems programmers maintain the software that controls the operation of an entire computer system. They often help applications programmers diagnose and resolve related programming problems. The largest number of computer programmers are employed by computer and data processing companies that write and sell software. Others work in a variety of industries and occupational settings, including educational institutions, government agencies, insurance companies, financial institutions, and engineering and management services.

➤ **WORKING CONDITIONS:** Programmers usually work a 40-hour week in clean and comfortable offices. They sometimes work longer hours in order to meet deadlines. Given the nature of the technology, many programmers telecommute, working from remote locations via modems. Since they spend most of their time at computer screens and using keyboards, computer programmers are more likely to experience physical problems relating to eyestrain, back aches, and hand and wrist discomfort, such as carpal tunnel syndrome.

➤ **EDUCATION, TRAINING, QUALIFICATIONS:** While many programmers have 4-year college degrees, others primarily have high school, community and junior college, or public and private vocational school educations. However, the trend is toward higher levels of formal education and training with a bachelor's degree considered a basic entry-level education requirement. Employers using computers for business applications prefer individuals with college course work in programming and business as well as experience in accounting, management, and other business skills. Programmers need to think logically, demonstrate a high level of analytic skills, and be familiar with several different programming languages rather than specialized in only one language.

➤ **EARNINGS:** The median earnings of computer programmers in 1998 were $42,000 a year. The lowest 10% earned less than $25,000; the highest 10% earned more than $68,000.

➤ **KEY CONTACTS:** For information on certification of computer programmers, contact:

- **Institute for the Certification of Computer Professionals:** 2200 East Devon Ave., Suite 268, Des Plains, IL 60018
  Web site: http://www.iccp.org

- **The Association for Computing:** 1515 Broadway, New York, NY 10036

- **IEEE Computer Society:** 1730 Massachusetts Ave., NW, Washington, DC 20036-1992

★★ COMPUTER SCIENTISTS COMPUTER ENGINEERS, AND SYSTEMS ANALYSTS

➤ **EMPLOYMENT OUTLOOK:** Expect explosive growth in what are definitely three of the decade's hottest career fields involved in designing and developing computer hardware and software. Computer scientists (216,000), computer engineers (220,000), and systems analysts (515,000) held 950,000 jobs in 1998; this number should increase to 1,050,000 in 2006. This growth reflects the overall growth in the application of computer technology throughout the economy, especially as organizations continue to network their computer systems.

➤ **NATURE OF WORK:** *Computer systems analysts* use computers to define and resolve business, scientific, and engineering problems. This may involve planning and developing new computer systems or devising new ways to apply existing systems to on-going manual operations. They may design entirely new systems, including hardware and software, or add a single new software application to harness more of the computer's power. *Computer engineers* apply scientific and mathematical theories and principles in designing computer hardware, software, networks, and processes and in solving technical problems. *Computer scientist* is a generic occupational title encompassing numerous computer professionals involved in designing computer hardware and software, developing information technologies, and applying computers to new uses. Unlike many other computer professionals, computer scientists tend to work at a higher theoretical level as researchers, inventors, and designers. Other related computer professionals include database administrators and computer support specialists.

➤ **WORKING CONDITIONS:** Computer scientists, computer engineers, and systems analysts usually work 40-hour weeks in comfortable offices. Many telecommute as well as operate as independent computer consultants.

➤ **EDUCATION, TRAINING, QUALIFICATIONS:** Most computer scientists, computer engineers, and systems analysts are college graduates; they often have graduate degrees. Many have previous training and work experience in related fields, such as computer programming, engineering, or accounting. Given the rapid changes taking place with both computer software and hardware, these computer specialists must continuously acquire additional education and training. These professionals must think logically, have good communication skills, and like working with ideas and people.

➤ **EARNINGS:** Median annual earnings for full time computer systems analysts and scientists in 1998 were $48,000. The middle 50 percent earned between $36,000 and $62,000 a year. The lowest 10 percent earned less than $26,000 and the highest 10 percent earned more than $78,000 a year. Computer scientists with advanced degrees usually make more than systems analysts. Given the high demand for such computer professionals, starting salaries for new college graduates tend to be high: $40,000 a year for computer engineers with a bachelor's degree and $45,000 for those with a master's degree. New Ph.Ds start around $64,000 a year. The Federal government pays poorly for such expertise—about 60 percent of what the private sector pays!

➤ **KEY CONTACTS:** For more information on these and other related computer careers, contact:

- **Association for Computing:** 1515 Broadway, New York, NY 10036

- **IEEE Computer Society:** 1730 Massachusetts Ave., NW, Washington, DC 20036-1992

- **Institute for the Certification of Computer Professionals:** 2200 East Devon Ave., Suite 268, Des Plaines, IL 60018 Web page: *http://www.iccp.org*

★ # OPERATIONS RESEARCH ANALYSTS

➤ **EMPLOYMENT OUTLOOK:** Between 1996 and 2006 employment is expected to increase a little below average for operations research analysts—from 52,000 to 68,000 jobs. This increase responds to the overall trend toward increasing the efficiency of organizations through the application of operations research to decision-making. Expect good job prospects with manufacturing, trade, and service firms.

➤ **NATURE OF WORK:** Operations research analysts, also known as management science analysts, help organizations coordinate and operate in the most efficient manner by applying scientific methods and mathematical principles to organizational problems. They help managers select alternative courses of action for organizing operations and solving problems. Much of their data gathering and analytic work involves the use of computers.

➤ **WORKING CONDITIONS:** While operations research analysts normally work a 40-hour week, their hours may vary depending on the nature of a project and the pressure to meet deadlines. Most of their work takes place in offices and is sedentary in nature.

➤ **EDUCATION, TRAINING, QUALIFICATIONS:** Employers prefer applicants with at least a master's degree in operations research or management science, mathematics, statistics, business administration, computer science, industrial engineering, or other quantitative disciplines. Individuals working in this field need a high level of computer skills and the ability to think logically and work well with people.

➤ **EARNINGS:** In 1998 the median salary of operations and systems researchers and analysts was $44,000 a year. The middle 50 percent earned between $34,000 and $56,000. The lowest 10 percent earned less than $25,000; the highest 10 percent earned over $66,000 a year.

➤ **KEY CONTACTS:** For information on career opportunities for operations research analysts, contact:

- **The Institute for Operations Research and the Management Science:** 901 Elkridge Landing Rd., Suite 400, Linthicum, MD 21090

- **Military Operations Research Society:** 101 South Whiting St., Suite 202, Alexandria, VA 22304

- **American Mathematical Society:** P.O. Box 6248, Providence, RI 02940, Tel. 401/455-4000
  Web site: *http://www.ams.org*

- **Mathematical Association of America:** 1529 18th Street, NW, Washington, DC 20036, Tel. 202/387-5200
  Web site: *http://www.maa.org*

★   # WEBMASTER

➤ **EMPLOYMENT OUTLOOK:** As the number of World Wide Web sites expand dramatically and as more and more corporations develop Intranets, the relatively new position of Webmaster has been in great demand. We expect the demand for Webmasters will be very great in the coming decade as more and more businesses, nonprofit organizations, and government agencies develop their own Internet and Intranet sites.

➤ **NATURE OF WORK:** Webmasters are literally the "persons in charge" of designing, operating, and maintaining the World Wide Web sites of organizations. Because webmaster is a very new position in a rapidly changing industry, the exact nature of a webmaster's work is difficult to define. In general, webmasters are responsible for developing web pages which are formatted in HTML (HyperText Markup Language). They design sites so they can be easily viewed and used for communicating with the organization. Much of their work is technical in nature (selecting and importing graphics, coding text, and using software) and involve a great deal of troubleshooting to resolve a variety of web-related problems. Many webmasters also are involved with marketing questions which may involve team efforts and working closely with marketing experts and coordinating web site efforts of various departments within the organization. They also may be responsible for receiving and answering e-mail.

➤ **WORKING CONDITIONS:** Webmasters work in a variety of computer settings that primarily put them behind computer terminals and in meeting rooms where they coordinate work with writers, graphic designers, marketing specialists, and department personnel.

➤ **EDUCATION, TRAINING, QUALIFICATIONS:** Since this is a relatively new occupational frontier, it's difficult to identify specific educational backgrounds and qualifications leading to a webmaster position. Webmasters come from a variety of technical backgrounds— computer science, mathematics, and engineering. Others may have backgrounds in graphic arts and marketing. All tend to be very familiar with computer operating systems, programming languages, and computer graphics. Many have bachelor's degrees but others may only have a high school diploma, some college, or a two-year degree. Most are self-taught on the operation of the World Wide Web. They constantly must keep current on the rapid changes taking place in their field.

➤ **EARNINGS:** Salary ranges for Webmasters vary greatly, from $40,000 to $100,000 a year. Many are promoted from computer posi-tions and thus may retain their previous salary level. Since this is a very high demand position at present, it can command a very high salary, depending on the organization and responsibilities involved.

➤ **KEY CONTACTS:** For more information on the work of web-masters, contact:

- **Web Designers and Developers Association**
  Web site: *http://www.wdda.org*

- **Webmasters' Guild**
  Web site: *http://www.webmaster.org/*

- **Webmaster Magazine:** 492 Old Connecticut Path, P.O. Box 9208, Framingham, MA 01701, Tel. 800/788-4605
  Web site: *http://www.web-master.com/*

9

Science and Engineering Careers

While the U.S. economy is by no means experiencing a shortage of scientists and engineers, nonetheless, job opportunities for scientists and engineers should be good to excellent throughout the coming decade. Like others, we assume the U.S. economy will continue to move in the direction of more scientific and high tech areas. More and more money is expected to be invested by both government and private industry in research and development in order to develop a more internationally competitive economy.

While decreased defense spending in the 1990s did have an adverse affect on some scientific and engineering jobs tied to defense industries, the overall picture for the coming decade looks good, especially for those in the biological sciences, chemistry, mathematics, geology, meteorology, and civil, electronics, and mechanical engineering. As more public money is spent on developing the national infrastructure of roads, bridges, airports, tunnels, rapid transit, and water supply and sewage systems, opportunities for civil engineers should improve considerably. Assuming manufacturing industries will continue to grow in the decade ahead, opportunities for mechanical engineers should be good. The future especially looks good for electronics and environmental engineers.

BIOLOGICAL AND MEDICAL SCIENTISTS

➤ **EMPLOYMENT OUTLOOK:** Job opportunities for biological and medical scientists will grow at a faster rate than most jobs in the decade ahead. They should increase from 120,000 jobs in 1998 to 140,000 jobs in 2006. Much of this increase will be in response to increased demand for genetic and biological research as well as efforts to preserve and clean up the environment.

➤ **NATURE OF WORK:** Biological scientists study living organisms and their relationship to the environment. Most specialize in some area of biology such as ornithology (study of birds) or microbiology (study of microscopic organisms). The field includes aquatic biologists, marine biologists, biochemists, botanists, microbiologists, physiologists, zoologists, ecologists, and agricultural scientists. About two-fifths of all biological scientists work in research and development. One of the fastest growing fields today is biotechnology.

➤ **WORKING CONDITIONS:** Most biological scientists work a normal 40-hour week in offices, laboratories, and classrooms. Some work with dangerous organisms or toxic substances. Botanists, ecologists, and zoologists often participate in field trips which may involve strenuous physical activity and primitive living conditions.

➤ **EDUCATION, TRAINING, QUALIFICATIONS:** The Ph.D. degree is required for most college teaching and independent research positions. A master's degree is required for some jobs in applied research, management, inspection, sales, and service. A bachelor's degree is adequate for some nonresearch jobs, such as testing, inspection, and technical sales.

➤ **EARNINGS:** Median annual earnings for biological and life scientists in 1998 were $38,000. The bottom 10 percent earned less than $23,000 a year; the top 10 percent earned more than $67,000 a year. Beginning salaries in private industry averaged $26,000 a year for graduates with bachelor's degrees in biological science. Those employed with the Federal government in nonsupervisory, supervisory and managerial positions averaged $53,000 a year.

➤ **KEY CONTACTS:** For information on careers in biological science, contact:

- ■ **American Institute of Biological Sciences:** 1444 I St., NW, Suite 200, Washington, DC 20005
  Web site: *http://www.aibs.org*

- ■ **American Physiological Society:** Membership Services Department, 9650 Rockville Pike, Bethesda, MD 20814
  Web site: *http://www.faseb.org/aps*

- ■ **American Society for Biochemistry and Molecular Biology:** 9650 Rockville Pike, Bethesda, MD 20814

- ■ **American Society for Microbiology:** Office of Education and Training—Career Information, 1325 Massachusetts Ave., NW, Washington, DC 20005
  Web site: *http://www.asmusa.org*

CHEMICAL ENGINEERS

➤ **EMPLOYMENT OUTLOOK:** Employment growth for chemical engineers should be about average for all occupations as chemical companies develop new chemicals and improve the efficiency of producing existing chemicals. However, since the number of chemical engineering graduates will exceed the number of jobs available, expect above average competition for jobs in this field. Much of the employment growth will be with nonmanufacturing service industries. Opportunities should be especially good in the areas of specialty chemicals, pharmaceuticals, and plastics materials. The number of jobs should increase from 50,000 in 1998 to 58,000 in 2006.

➤ **NATURE OF WORK:** Chemical engineers apply the principles of chemistry and engineering to solve problems. Many work in the production of chemicals and chemical products. They design equipment and develop processes for manufacturing chemicals in chemical plants, plan, and test methods of manufacturing the products, and supervise production. Two-thirds work in chemical, petroleum refining, paper, and related industries. The remainder work for engineering services, research and testing services, or consulting firms that design chemical plants.

➤ **WORKING CONDITIONS:** Chemical engineers work a normal 40-hour week in laboratory and industrial plants. Many work with dangerous chemicals which require special precautions.

➤**EDUCATION, TRAINING, QUALIFICATIONS:** Most chemical engineers have a bachelor's, master's, or Ph.D. degree. Employers prefer graduate degrees.

➤ **EARNINGS:** In 1998 the starting salary for chemical engineers with a bachelor's degree was $39,000. Many experienced chemical engineers earn more than $85,000 a year.

➤ **KEY CONTACTS:** For information on chemical engineering careers, contact:

- **American Chemical Society:** Career Services, 1155 16th St., NW, Washington, DC 20036

- **American Institute of Chemical Engineers:** 345 East 47th St., New York, NY 10017

CHEMISTS

➤ **EMPLOYMENT OUTLOOK:** Employment of chemists is expected to grow about as fast as the average for all occupations in the decade ahead. The increases will especially take place in drug manufacturing and research, development, and testing services firms. Demand for new consumer goods such as better pharmaceuticals, personal care products, and specialty chemicals designed to address specific problems support such employment increases. Employment is expected to increase from 91,000 in 1998 to 105,000 in 2006.

➤ **NATURE OF WORK:** Chemists conduct research and apply chemical knowledge to developing synthetic fibers, paints, adhesives, drugs, electronic components, lubricants, and other products. They develop processes for saving energy, reducing pollution, and advancing medicine and agriculture. Chemists work in several fields as analytical chemists, organic chemists, inorganic chemists, physical chemists, and biochemists.

➤ **WORKING CONDITIONS:** Most chemists work a 40-hour week in offices and laboratories. Some are exposed to health or safety hazards related to handling certain chemicals.

➤ **EDUCATION, TRAINING, QUALIFICATIONS:** The minimum education requirement for a position as chemist is a bachelor's degree. However, most research and college teaching jobs require a master's or Ph.D. degree.

➤ **EARNINGS:** In 1998 the median starting salary for chemists with a recent bachelor's degree was $26,000; with a master's degree, $33,000; with a Ph.D., $48,000. In 1998 the median salary for members of the American Chemical Society with a bachelor's degree was $50,000; with a master's degree, $57,000; with a Ph.D., $72,000.

➤ **KEY CONTACTS:** For information on career opportunities for chemists, contact:

- **American Chemical Society:** Education Division, 1155 16th St., NW, Washington, DC 20036

CIVIL ENGINEERS

➤ **EMPLOYMENT OUTLOOK:** Employment for civil engineers should grow faster than average in response to population and economic growth as well as the need to design, construct, and rebuild transportation systems, water resource and disposal systems, large buildings, and other structures in the decade ahead. Expect employment to increase from 198,000 in 1998 to 225,000 in 2006.

➤ **NATURE OF WORK:** Civil engineers design and supervise the construction of roads, airports, tunnels, bridges, water supply and sewage systems, and buildings. They specialize in structural, water resources, environmental, construction, transportation, and geotechnical engineering.

➤ **WORKING CONDITIONS:** Civil engineers work a normal 40-hour week. Their work environments vary from office settings to field locations. Many spend much of their time at construction sites.

➤ **EDUCATION, TRAINING, QUALIFICATIONS:** Civil engineers normally require bachelor's degrees.

➤ **EARNINGS:** The average starting salaries for civil engineers with bachelor's degrees was $37,000 in 1998.

➤ **KEY CONTACTS:** For information on civil engineering careers, contact:

- **American Society of Civil Engineers:** 345 E. 47th St., New York, NY 10017

ELECTRICAL AND ELECTRONICS ENGINEERS

➤ **EMPLOYMENT OUTLOOK:** Expect faster than average growth in employment opportunities for electrical and electronics engineers in the decade ahead. Fastest growth is anticipated outside manufacturing. Most of the growth will be due to increased demand for computers, electronic consumer goods, communications equipment, and other electrical and electronic products. Jobs should increase from 370,000 in 1998 to 445,000 in 2006.

➤ **NATURE OF WORK:** Electrical and electronics engineers design, develop, test, and supervise the manufacture of electrical and electronic equipment. Electrical equipment includes power generating and transmission equipment used by electric utilities, and electric motors, machinery controls, and lighting and wiring in buildings, automobiles, and aircraft. Electronic equipment includes radar, computer hardware, and communications and video equipment.

➤ **WORKING CONDITIONS:** Electrical and electronics engineers work a normal 40-hour week. Their work environments include offices, workshops, plants, and other field locations.

➤ **EDUCATION, TRAINING, QUALIFICATIONS:** Most electrical and electronics engineers require a bachelor's degree.

➤ **EARNINGS:** In 1998 the starting salary for electrical and electronic engineers was $39,000 a year.

➤ **KEY CONTACTS:** For information on careers for electrical and electronic engineers, contact:

- **Institute of Electrical and Electronics Engineers/United States Activities Board:** 1828 L St. NW, Suite 1202, Washington, DC 20036-5104

GEOLOGISTS & GEOPHYSICISTS

➤ **EMPLOYMENT OUTLOOK:** Job opportunities for geologists and geophysicists should grow as fast as average for most occupations, increasing from 48,000 jobs in 1998 to 56,000 in 2006. Although employment prospects are uncertain in the petroleum industry, given the cyclical fluctuations in oil and gas exploration and production, demand for these professionals in environmental protection, reclamation, and regulation is expected to be strong.

➤ **NATURE OF WORK:** Geologists and geophysicists study the physical aspects and history of the earth. They examine surface rocks and buried rocks recovered by drilling, study information collected by satellites, conduct geological surveys, construct maps, and use instruments to measure the earth's gravity and magnetic field. They also study earthquakes, design and monitor waste disposal sites, preserve water, and search for oil, natural gas, minerals, and underground water.

➤ **WORKING CONDITIONS:** Geoscientists work a normal 40-hour week. They work in offices, laboratories, and field locations. Many travel abroad as well as work in remote areas and spend time at sea.

➤ **EDUCATION, TRAINING, QUALIFICATIONS:** A bachelor's degree is required for entry into some lower level geology jobs. Jobs with good advancement potential require at least a master's degree in geology or geophysics. A Ph.D. is required for most research and college or university teaching positions.

➤ **EARNINGS:** Recent graduates with bachelor's degrees in geological sciences earned an average of $31,500 a year in 1998. However, starting salaries can vary widely depending on the particular industry (i.e., average salary in the oil and gas industry for geoscientists with less than 2 years experience was $49,000 in 1998).

➤ **KEY CONTACTS:** For information on career opportunities for geologists and geophysicists, contact:

- **American Geological Institute:** 4220 King St., Alexandria, VA 22302-1507
  Web site: *http://www.agiweb.org*

- **American Geophysical Union:** 2000 Florida Ave., NW, Washington, DC 20009

- **Geological Society of America:** P.O. Box 9140, Boulder, CO 80301
  Web site: *http://www.geosociety.org*

- **Marine Technology Society:** 1828 L St., NW, Suite 906, Washington, DC 20036

INDUSTRIAL ENGINEERS

➤ **EMPLOYMENT OUTLOOK:** Employment is expected to grow about average, from 117,000 jobs in 1998 to 130,000 jobs in 2006. The increase is due to the increased complexity of business operations, increased interest in efficiency by businesses, and greater use of automation in factories and offices. Their skills will be readily sought by manufacturing firms seeking to reduce costs and increase productivity through scientific management and safety engineering.

➤ **NATURE OF WORK:** Industrial engineers, serving as a bridge between management and operations, assist organizations in determining how to best use the basic factors of production—people, machines, materials, information, and energy. They design data processing systems, use operations research, develop management control systems for financial planning and cost analysis, design production planning and control systems, design or improve systems for the physical distribution of goods and services, and develop wage and salary administration systems and job evaluation programs.

➤ **WORKING CONDITIONS:** Industrial engineers work a normal 40-hour week in office and plant settings.

➤ **EDUCATION, TRAINING, QUALIFICATIONS:** Industrial engineers have at least a bachelor's degree; many have graduate degrees.

➤ **EARNINGS:** In 1998 the average starting salary for industrial engineers with a bachelor's degree was $38,000.

➤ **KEY CONTACTS:** For information on careers for industrial engineers, contact:

- **Institute of Industrial Engineers, Inc.:** 25 Technology Park/Atlanta, Norcross, GA 30092

MECHANICAL ENGINEERS

➤ **EMPLOYMENT OUTLOOK:** The employment growth for mechanical engineers will be about average for most occupations in the decade ahead, increasing from 230,000 jobs in 1998 to 265,000 jobs in 2006. This employment increase will be in response to expected growth in demand for machinery and machine tools. Although many mechanical engineering jobs are in defense-related industries and reductions will probably continue in these industries, rapid growth in other industries should make job opportunities favorable overall. Employment in manufacturing is expected to decline. Employment of mechanical engineers in business and engineering services firms is expected to grow faster than average as firms out-source engineering problems to these firms.

➤ **NATURE OF WORK:** Mechanical engineers specialize in the production, transmission, and use of mechanical power and heat. They design and develop power-producing machines such as internal combustion engines, steam and gas turbines, and jet and rocket engines. They also design and develop power-using machines such as refrigeration and air-conditioning equipment, robots, machine tools, materials handling systems, and industrial production equipment.

➤ **WORKING CONDITIONS:** Most mechanical engineers work a normal 40-hour week in office, laboratory, and plant settings. Many work in production operations, maintenance, and technical sales.

➤ **EDUCATION, TRAINING, QUALIFICATIONS:** The minimum educational requirement for mechanical engineers is a bachelor's degree. Many have graduate degrees in mechanical engineering.

➤ **EARNINGS:** The average starting salary for mechanical engineers with a bachelor's degree in 1998 was $39,000.

➤ **KEY CONTACTS:** For information on career opportunities for mechanical engineers, contact:

- **American Society of Mechanical Engineers:** 345 E. 47th St., New York, NY 10017

- **The American Society of Heating, Refrigerating, and Air-Conditioning Engineers, Inc.:** 1791 Tullie Circle NE, Atlanta, GA 30329

METEOROLOGISTS

➤ **EMPLOYMENT OUTLOOK:** Employment of meteorologists is expected to slow in the coming decline, increasing from 7,500 jobs in 1998 to 8,100 jobs in 2006. This slow increase is largely due to the decline in employment with the National Weather Service which employs nearly one-third of all meteorologists. Most employment growth will be found with colleges and universities, private consulting firms, and companies analyzing emissions to improve air quality.

➤ **NATURE OF WORK:** Meteorology is the study of the atmosphere, the air that surrounds the earth. Meteorologists study the atmosphere's physical characteristics, motions, and processes, and the way the atmosphere affects the rest of the environment. The best-known application of this knowledge is in forecasting the weather. Weather information and meteorological research also are applied in air-pollution control, agriculture, air and sea transportation, and the study of trends in the earth's climate such a global warming or ozone depletion.

➤ **WORKING CONDITIONS:** Meteorologists not doing forecasting work regular office hours. Those working in weather stations often work at night and do shift work. Weather stations are located at airports, in or near cities, and in isolated and remote areas. Meteorologists in small weather offices often work alone.

➤ **EDUCATION, TRAINING, QUALIFICATIONS:** The minimum educational requirement for meteorologists is a bachelors' degree with a major in meteorology or a clearly related field. A master's degree is necessary for conducting research and development; a Ph.D. is usually required for college teaching.

➤ **EARNINGS:** The average salary of meteorologists in nonsupervisory, and managerial positions with the Federal government in 1998 was $57,500. Meteorologists in the federal government with a bachelor's degree and no experience received starting salaries between $20,000 and $24,700 a year in 1998, depending on their college grades. Those with a master's degree started at $24,800 or $30,000; those with a Ph.D. degree started at $40,000 or $43,300.

➤ **KEY CONTACTS:** For information on career opportunities for meteorologists, contact:

- **American Meteorological Society:** 45 Beacon St., Boston, MA 02108
  Web site: *www.ametsoc.org/AMS*

- **National Weather Service:** Personnel Branch, 1335 East West Hwy., SSMC1, Silver Spring, MD 20910

SCIENCE TECHNICIANS

➤ **EMPLOYMENT OUTLOOK:** Job opportunities for science technicians are expected to increase as fast as the average for all occupations, from 232,000 jobs in 1998 to 280,000 jobs in 2006. Expect continued growth in scientific and medical research and the development and production of technical products to stimulate job growth for science technicians in all areas. Opportunities for biological technicians will grow faster than for other science technicians due to the continuing development of agricultural and medicinal products through biotechnology techniques. Employment growth also will be related to the increased demand for technicians to help regulate waste products, collect air, water, and soil samples to measure levels of pollutants, monitor compliance with environmental regulations, and clean up contaminated sites.

➤ **NATURE OF WORK:** Science technicians use the principles and theories of science and mathematics to solve problems in research and development and to investigate, invent, and help improve products. Their jobs are more practically oriented than those of scientists. They make extensive use of computers, computer-interfaced equipment, robotics, and high-technology industrial applications such as biological engineering. They encompass a variety of occupations such as agricultural technicians, biological technicians, chemical technicians, nuclear technicians, and petroleum technicians.

➤ **WORKING CONDITIONS:** Science technicians work in a variety of settings. Many work indoors, usually in laboratories, and have regular hours. Others, such as agricultural and petroleum technicians, work outdoors, sometimes in remote locations, and may be exposed to hazardous conditions. Chemical technicians sometimes work with toxic chemicals, nuclear technicians may be exposed to radiation, and biological technicians sometimes work with disease-causing organisms or radioactive agents.

➤ **EDUCATION, TRAINING, QUALIFICATIONS:** Science technicians have at least two years of specialized training. Many junior and community colleges offer associate degrees in specific technology or a more general education in science and mathematics. Many science technicians have a bachelor's degree in science or mathematics, or have had science and math courses in 4-year colleges. Some companies offer formal or on-the-job training for science technicians.

➤ **EARNINGS:** The median annual earnings for science technicians were about $28,000 in 1998. Ten percent earned over $50,000 a year.

➤ **KEY CONTACTS:** For information on career opportunities for chemical technicians, contact:

- **American Chemical Society:** Education Division, Career Publications, 1155 16th St., NW, Washington, DC 20036 Web site: *http://www.acs.org*

10

Business and Financial Careers

Opportunities in business and financial careers should be excellent in the decade ahead as long as the economy continues to grow at a healthy rate. New businesses will be created at a rate of 700,000 to 800,000 firms a year. While most of these businesses will be small (fewer than 500 employees), they will require the services of accountants, auditors, actuaries, cashiers, clerks, financial managers, management analysts and consultants, personnel specialists, and underwriters.

As many large corporations continue to downsize, middle management ranks will shrink further during the next decade. Large firms will rely more on fundamental personnel such as accountants, auditors, financial managers, and personnel specialists as well as use more outside management analysts and consultants. Most of these jobs require individuals who are well educated and trained in the nuts and bolts of business. Numerous opportunities will also be available for such entry-level positions as clerks and cashiers. But many of these jobs will be low paying and offer few advancement opportunities.

Enterprising job seekers are well advised to set their sights on new and growing businesses that provide products and services for tomorrow's economy. They should also acquire fundamental business skills that will make them more marketable for the jobs in business and finance in the decade ahead.

ACCOUNTANTS AND AUDITORS

➤ **EMPLOYMENT OUTLOOK:** More accountants and auditors will be needed to set up books and prepare taxes as the number of businesses increase and the complexity of financial information required grows. Fast as average job growth is expected with the number of jobs expected to increase from 1,100,000 in 1998 to 1,250,000 in 2006.

➤ **NATURE OF WORK:** Accountants and auditors prepare, analyze, and verify financial reports that are used by management to make business decisions as well as comply with government regulations. Computers are widely used but the accounting programs are easily learned and greatly reduce the amount of tedious manual work associated with figures and records.

➤ **WORKING CONDITIONS:** Accountants and auditors work in offices—either their own or their client's. Those that are self-employed may be able to do part of their work at home. The majority work a 40-hour week, but many work longer—particularly during the tax season or if they are self-employed.

➤ **EDUCATION, TRAINING, QUALIFICATIONS:** Most public accounting and business firms require at least a bachelor's degree in accounting or a related field. Some employers prefer hiring someone with a master's degree in accounting or business administration with a concentration in accounting. Familiarity with computer applications in accounting and internal auditing is often necessary.

➤ **EARNINGS:** In 1998 starting salaries for those holding bachelor's degrees averaged $30,000; starting salaries with a master's degree averaged $34,000. Experienced accountants earn between $40,000 and $80,000 a year, with some earning over $100,000 a year (mainly directors of accounting and auditing). The most experienced public accountants have a median annual income of $50,000.

➤ **KEY CONTACTS:** For information on accounting and auditing careers contact:

- **American Institute of Certified Public Accountants:** Harborside Financial Center, 201 Plaza III, Jersey City, NJ 07311-3881
  Web site: *http://www.aicpa.org*

- **The Information Systems Audit and Control Association:** 3701 Algonquin Rd., Suite 101, Rolling Meadows, IL 60008
  Web site: *http://www.isaca.org*

- **The Institute of Internal Auditors:** 249 Maitland Ave., Altamonte Springs, FL 32701-4201
  Web site: *http://www.theiia.org*

- **Institute of Management Accountants:** 10 Paragon Drive, Montvale, NJ 07645
  Web site: *http://www.imanet.org*

- **National Society of Public Accountants and the Accreditation Council for Accountancy and Taxation:** 1010 North Fairfax St., Alexandria, VA 22314
  Web site: *http://www.nspa.org*

ACTUARIES

➤ **EMPLOYMENT OUTLOOK:** Slower than average employment growth due to slower growth in the insurance industry. However, employment growth for consulting actuaries will be faster because investment firms and large corporations will turn to consultants to provide actuarial services previously performed in-house. Actuaries will face competition for jobs because the number of workers entering the occupation has increased substantially in recent years. The number of jobs is expected to increase from 17,000 in 1998 to 20,000 in 2006.

➤ **NATURE OF WORK:** Actuaries assemble and analyze statistics to calculate the probability of death, sickness, injury, disability, unemployment, retirement or property loss. They use this information to calculate the probability of claims to ensure that the price charged for insurance will enable the company to pay all claims yet remain competitive with other insurance companies. They answer questions about future risk, make pricing decisions, and formulate investment strategies. Some design insurance, financial, and pension plans and make sure these are maintained on a sound financial basis. Most actuaries specialize in life, health, or property and casualty insurance; others specialize in pension plans.

➤ **WORKING CONDITIONS:** Actuaries have desk jobs in offices that are generally comfortable. They usually work a 40 hour week. Consulting actuaries may travel to meet with clients and may be expected to work longer than 40 hours per week.

➤ **EDUCATION, TRAINING, QUALIFICATIONS:** Actuaries need a bachelor's degree in a mathematical or business related discipline, such as actuarial science, mathematics, statistics, economics, finance, or accounting. Opportunities will be best for college graduates who have passed at least two actuarial exams while still in school and have a strong background in mathematics and statistics.

➤ **EARNINGS:** Starting salaries for actuaries averaged about $39,000 in 1998 for those with a bachelor's degree. Associate Actuaries, who direct and provide leadership in the design and pricing of products received an average salary of $80,000. Actuaries with additional experience earned substantially more.

➤ **KEY CONTACTS:** For information about actuarial careers contact:

- **American Academy of Actuaries:** 1100 17th St., NW, 7th Floor, Washington, DC 20036

- **American Society of Pension Actuaries:** 4350 N. Fairfax Dr., Suite 820, Arlington, VA 22203

- **Casualty Actuarial Society:** 1100 N. Glebe Rd., Suite 600, Arlington, VA 22201
  Web site: *http://www.casact.org*

- **Society of Actuaries:** 475 N. Martingale Rd., Suite 800, Schaumburg, IL 60173-2226

Cashiers

➤ **EMPLOYMENT OUTLOOK:** Average growth is expected in response to increased demand for goods and services by a growing population. Given the large size of this occupation with a higher turnover rate, both full-time and part-time job opportunities will be good to excellent. The number of jobs should increase from 3,200,000 jobs in 1998 to 3,700,000 in 2006.

➤ **NATURE OF WORK:** Most cashiers total bills, receive money, make change, fill out charge forms and give receipts. They may also wrap or bag the purchase. Cashiers may also handle returns and exchanges.

➤ **WORKING CONDITIONS:** Many cashiers work a 40-hour week; however, more than one-half of all cashiers are on part-time schedules. Generally, cashiers are expected to work week-ends, evenings, and holidays to accommodate customer's needs. The work of cashiers can be very repetitive and dealing with angry customers can be taxing, but the job can be rewarding for those who like working with people.

➤ **EDUCATION, TRAINING, QUALIFICATIONS:** Cashier jobs tend to be entry level positions requiring little or no work experience. Although there are no specific educational requirements, employers filling full-time jobs often prefer applicants with a high school diploma.

➤ **EARNINGS:** Cashiers have earnings ranging from the minimum wage to significantly more than that amount. In 1998, the median annual earnings for full-time cashiers were $13,500. Ten percent earned less than $10,000; and 10 percent earned about $26,000 a year.

➤ **KEY CONTACTS:** For information about employment opportunities as a cashier, contact:

- **National Association of Convenience Stores:** 1605 King St., Alexandria, VA 22314-2792

- **National Retail Federation:** 325 7th St., NW, Suite 1000, Washington, DC 20004
  Web site: *http://www.nrf.com*

- **Food Marketing Institute:** 800 Connecticut Avenue, NW, Washington, DC 20006

- **Service Station Dealers of America:** 9420 Annapolis Rd., Suite 307, Lanham, MD 20706

COUNTER AND RENTAL CLERKS

➤ **EMPLOYMENT OUTLOOK:** Faster than average employment growth is expected due to the anticipated increase in employment in business services, automotive rentals, and amusement and recreation services. Both part-time and full-time opportunities will be excellent. Jobs should increase from 390,000 in 1998 to 450,000 in 2006.

➤ **NATURE OF WORK:** Counter and rental clerks are responsible for answering questions, taking orders, receiving payments, and accepting returns. Counter and rental clerks may explain what is available, its cost, the rental provisions, and any promotions that are in effect. In some businesses they may write out tickets or order forms, but computers and bar code scanners are quickly becoming the norm.

➤ **WORKING CONDITIONS:** Working conditions are usually pleasant; however, clerks are on their feet much of the time and may be confined behind a small counter area. Because firms employing such clerks operate for the convenience of their customers, they often work nights and weekend hours. This job requires constant interaction with the public and this can be taxing—especially when things go wrong.

➤ **EDUCATION, TRAINING, QUALIFICATIONS:** Counter and rental clerk jobs are primarily entry level and require little or no experience and little formal education. Many employers prefer high school graduates for these positions. In most companies counter and rental clerks receive on the job training under the observation of a more experienced worker.

➤ **EARNINGS:** Counter and rental clerks typically start at the minimum wage. Some may receive commissions based on the number of contracts they complete or services they sell. Retail counter clerks earned a median annual income of $16,600 in 1998. The top 10 percent earned more than $33,500 a year.

➤ **KEY CONTACTS:** For more information about opportunities as counter and rental clerks contact:

- **Association of Progressive Rental Organizations:** 1900 19th Street, Moline, IL 61265

FINANCIAL MANAGERS

➤ **EMPLOYMENT OUTLOOK:** Expect employment growth for financial managers to be as fast as average for all occupations in the decade ahead. The increasing variety and complexity of financial services, increased interstate and international banking, and changing laws regarding taxes and other financial matters will promote a greater demand for the services of financial managers. The number of jobs should increase from 825,000 jobs in 1998 to 900,000 jobs in 2006. Competition for these attractive jobs should be keen since the number of applicants will exceed the number of openings.

➤ **NATURE OF WORK:** Financial managers prepare the financial reports necessary for the firm to conduct its operations and to satisfy tax and regulatory requirements. Financial managers, who may be the treasurer, controller, credit manager, cash manager or vice-president of finance, also oversee the flow of cash and financial instruments and develop information to assess the present and future financial status of the firm. Besides supervising financial services, they may advise individuals and businesses on financial planning.

➤ **WORKING CONDITIONS:** Financial managers work in comfortable offices, often close to top managers and to departments which develop financial data managers need. Although overtime may sometimes be required, financial managers typically work a 40-hour week.

➤ **EDUCATION, TRAINING, QUALIFICATIONS:** A bachelor's degree in accounting or finance, or in business administration with an emphasis on accounting or finance is expected for most financial managers. A Master of Business Administration (MBA) degree is increasingly valued by employers.

➤ **EARNINGS:** In 1998 the median annual salary of financial managers was $41,500. The top ten percent earned over $82,000 and some experienced financial managers earned substantially higher salaries. Chief financial officers averaged $145,000; treasurers $123,000; controllers $86,000; senior analysts $56,000; cash managers $52,000; and analysts $41,000.

➤ **KEY CONTACTS:** For information about careers in finance management, contact:

- **American Bankers Association:** 1120 Connecticut Ave., NW, Washington, DC 20036

- **National Association of Credit Management:** Credit Research Foundation, 8815 Centre Park Dr., Columbia, MD 21045-2117
  Web site: *http://www.nacm.org/*

HUMAN RESOURCES, TRAINING, AND LABOR RELATIONS SPECIALISTS AND MANAGERS

➤ **EMPLOYMENT OUTLOOK:** Faster than average growth is expected for human resources, training, and labor relations specialists and managers as legislation and court rulings have increased the amount of recordkeeping, analysis, and report writing required of employers. In addition, employers are expected to devote more resources to recruiting qualified personnel as well as training and retraining existing personnel. However, the job market is likely to remain competitive in view of the abundant supply of college graduates and experienced workers with suitable qualifications. The number of jobs should increase from 560,000 in 1998 to 680,000 in 2006.

➤ **NATURE OF WORK:** Human resources specialists and managers recruit, interview, and hire employees based on policies and requirements they have established in conjunction with top management. Although some jobs in this field require only limited contact with people outside one's office, most involve frequent contact. Training specialists plan, organize and direct a wide range of training activities. Labor relations specialists prepare information for management to use during collective bargaining negotiations and interpret and administer the contract negotiated with the union.

➤ **WORKING CONDITIONS:** Most personnel work is office work; however, some positions involve travel. Many human resources, training, and labor relations specialists work a 35-40 hour week. However, some may work longer hours—for example, labor relations specialists—when contract agreements are being prepared and negotiated.

➤ **EDUCATION, TRAINING, QUALIFICATIONS:** In filling entry level jobs, firms generally seek college graduates. Some employers prefer applicants who have majored in human resources, personnel administration, or industrial or labor relations, while others look for graduates with a technical or business background. Others think a well-rounded liberal arts education is best. Some experience through an internship program or on-the-job experience is an asset for specialists.

➤ **EARNINGS:** Starting salaries in 1998 for college graduates with a bachelor's degree in human resources averaged $27,000; those with master's degrees averaged $40,000. The median earnings of personnel supervisors/managers with limited experience were $60,000 a year. Personnel specialists in the Federal government average $53,400 a year. Salaries for selected personnel and labor relations occupations range from $35,000 to $110,000.

➤ **KEY CONTACTS:** For general information on careers in personnel, training, or labor relations management contact:

- **American Society for Training and Development:** 1640 King St., Box 1443, Alexandria, VA 22313

- **American Arbitration Association:** 140 West 51st St., New York, NY 10020, Tel. 800/778-7879

- **American Compensation Association:** 14040 Northsight Blvd., Scottsdale, AZ 85260

- **International Personnel Management Association:** IPMA Center for Personnel Research, 1617 Duke St., Alexandria, VA 22314

- **Society for Human Resource Management:** 1800 Duke Street, Alexandria, VA 22314

INFORMATION CLERKS

➤ **EMPLOYMENT OUTLOOK:** Overall employment is expected to increase much faster than average due to the rapid growth of industries such as business, professional, and other services. In 1998 over 1.7 million information clerks were employed in the following occupations:

■ Receptionists and information clerks	1,135,000
■ Interviewing and new accounts clerks	225,000
■ Reservation and transportation ticket agents and travel clerks	180,000
■ Hotel and motel desk clerks	160,000

The jobs should increase from 1,700,000 in 1998 to 1,950,000 in 2006.

➤ **NATURE OF WORK:** Information clerks gather information from and provide information to the public. Although duties vary, many information clerks greet customers and other visitors, determine their needs, and either assist them or refer the individuals to the person who can help. Others elicit information from the public.

➤ **WORKING CONDITIONS:** Information clerks who greet the public usually work in pleasant surroundings. Reservation agents generally work away from the public, and their work space can be noisy if a number of agents work in limited space. Although most information clerks work a standard 40-hour week, a sizable number work irregular schedules—especially those in the transportation industry, hospitals, hotels and banks.

➤ **EDUCATION, TRAINING, QUALIFICATIONS:** Although hiring requirements vary by industry, a high school diploma is usually required. For some jobs such as airline reservation and ticket agents, some college education is preferred. With the exception of airline reservation and other passenger transportation agents, orientation and training is usually given on the job.

➤ **EARNINGS:** In 1998, average annual earnings of full-time information clerks were $18,500. The bottom 10 percent earned less than $12,000; the top 10 percent earned more than $30,000. Salaries of reservation and ticket agents tend to be significantly higher than for other clerks, while hotel/motel desk clerks tend to earn less.

➤ **KEY CONTACTS:** For more information on information clerks in the hotel and motel industry contact:

- **The Educational Institute of the American Hotel and Motel Association:** P.O. Box 1240, East Lansing, MI 48826

★ # MANAGEMENT ANALYSTS AND CONSULTANTS

➤ **EMPLOYMENT OUTLOOK:** This is one of the hottest career fields today and in the decade ahead. Competitive pressures on organizations will contribute to much faster than average growth for management analysts and consultants. The number of jobs is expected to increase from

258,000 in 1992 to 300,000 in 2006. Nearly 45 percent are self-employed.

➤ **NATURE OF WORK:** Management analysts and consultants collect, review, and analyze information relating to organizational problems; develop solutions and make recommendations; and often assist in the implementation of their proposal.

➤ **WORKING CONDITIONS:** Management analysts and consultants usually divide their time between their offices and their client's operation. Although much of their time is spent in clean, well-lighted offices, they may have to visit a client's production facilities where conditions may not be so favorable. Typically, analysts and consultants work at least 40 hours a week. Overtime is common, especially when deadlines must be met. Because they must spend a significant portion of their time with clients, they may travel frequently.

➤ **EDUCATION, TRAINING, QUALIFICATIONS:** Employers prefer to hire those with a master's degree in business administration or a discipline related to the firms' area of specialization. Those individuals hired straight out of school with only a bachelor's degree are likely to work as research associates or junior consultants, rather than full-fledged management consultants.

➤ **EARNINGS:** Salaries for management analysts and consultants vary widely by experience, education, and employer. In 1998, those who were wage and salary workers had median annual earnings of $41,000. The top 10 percent earned more than $82,000 a year. Senior partners in management consulting firms earned an average of $168,000. The annual average salary for management analysts in the Federal government in nonsupervisory, supervisory, and managerial positions was $56,000.

➤ **KEY CONTACTS:** Information about career opportunities in management consulting is available from:

- **The Association of Management Consulting Firms:** 521 Fifth Ave., 35th Floor, New York, NY 10175-3598

MARKETING, ADVERTISING, AND PUBLIC RELATIONS MANAGERS

➤ **EMPLOYMENT OUTLOOK:** Intensifying domestic and foreign competition—requiring greater marketing, promotional, and public relations efforts—should result in much faster than average growth for jobs in marketing, advertising, and public relations. The number of jobs should increase from 490,000 jobs in 1998 to 580,000 in 2006. These jobs are well represented across numerous industries.

➤ **NATURE OF WORK:** Marketing managers work with advertising and promotion managers to best promote the firm's products and services and to attract potential users. Except in the largest firms, advertising and promotion staffs are generally small and serve as a liaison between the firm and the advertising agency that performs many advertising functions. Promotion managers direct programs which combine advertising with purchase incentives to increase sales of products or services.

➤ **WORKING CONDITIONS:** Marketing, advertising, and public relations managers are provided with offices close to top managers. Long hours, including evenings and weekends, are not uncommon. Working under pressure is unavoidable as deadlines must be met. Substantial travel may be involved to meet with clients, dealers, distributors or attend conferences.

➤ **EDUCATION, TRAINING, QUALIFICATIONS:** Requirements vary, but a bachelor's degree is generally expected. Some employers prefer a broad liberal arts background; whereas others prefer a marketing, advertising, or public relations major. For all specialties, courses in management and completion of an internship while in school are highly recommended. Familiarity with computerized word processing and data base applications is also important for many positions.

➤ **EARNINGS:** Starting salaries for marketing majors in 1998 averaged $30,000; advertising majors averaged $28,000. The median annual salary of marketing, advertising, and public relations managers was $47,000. The top 10% earned $100,000+; the lowest 10 percent earned $25,000 or less. Many also earned bonuses equal to 10% or more of their salaries.

➤ **KEY CONTACTS:** For information about careers in sales and marketing management contact:

- **American Marketing Association:** 250 S. Wacker Dr., Chicago, IL 60606

- **American Association of Advertising Agencies:** 666 Third Ave., 13th Floor, New York, NY 10017

- **American Advertising Federation:** 1101 Vermont Ave., NW, Suite 500, Washington, DC 20005

- **Council of Sales Promotion Agencies:** 750 Summer St., Stamford, CT 06901

- **Promotion Marketing Association of America Inc.:** 322 Eighth Ave., Suite 1201, New York, NY 10001

- **Public Relations Society of America:** 33 Irving Place, New York, NY 10003-2376

PROPERTY AND REAL ESTATE MANAGERS

➤ **EMPLOYMENT OUTLOOK:** Fast as average job growth is expected to result from increases in the number of office buildings, retail properties, and apartment complexes requiring management. Overbuilding and subsequent concern for profitable management should also stimulate employment growth. Employment growth is projected from 275,000 jobs in 1998 to 345,000 in 2006.

➤ **NATURE OF WORK:** Property managers administer income-producing commercial and residential properties and manage the communal property and services of condominium and community associations. Some real estate managers are employed by businesses to locate, acquire, and develop real estate needed for their operations and to dispose of property no longer suited to their uses.

➤ **WORKING CONDITIONS:** Property and real estate managers work in clean, well lighted offices, but many spend a major portion of their time away from their desks. They often must attend meetings in the evening with property owners, community association boards, or civic groups. Many put in long work weeks and may have to be available at night or on weekends for which they usually receive time off

➤ **EDUCATION, TRAINING, QUALIFICATIONS:** Most employers prefer to hire college graduates for property and real estate management positions. Degrees in business administration, finance, real estate, public administration, or related fields are preferred, but persons with degrees in liberal arts are often accepted. Good speaking and writing skills and an ability to deal tactfully with people are essential.

➤ **EARNINGS:** Median annual earnings of property and real estate managers were $30,000 in 1998. The top 10 percent earned more than $62,000 a year. Property managers with regional shopping malls made more than $85,000 a year.

➤ **KEY CONTACTS:** General information about careers in property and real estate management is available from:

- **Apartment Owners and Managers Association of America:** 65 Cherry Plaza, Watertown, CT 06795, Tel. 860/274-2589

- **Building Owners and Managers Institute International:** 1521 Ritchie Hwy., Arnold, MD 21012

- **Building Owners and Managers Association:** 720 Light Street, Baltimore, MD 21230, Tel. 410/752-3318 Web site: *http://www.bom.org*

- **Community Associations Institute:** 1630 Duke St., Alexandria, VA 22314, Tel. 703/548-8600 Web site: *http://www.caionline.org*

- **Institute of Real Estate Management:** 430 N. Michigan Ave., Chicago, IL 60611, Tel. 312/329-6000 Web site: *http://www.irem.org*

- **National Apartment Association:** 201 N. Union St., Suite 200, Alexandria, VA 22314, Tel. 703/518-6141

- **National Association of Home Builders:** 1201 15th St., NW, Washington, DC 20005
  Web site: *http://www.nahb.com/multi.html*

UNDERWRITERS

➤ **EMPLOYMENT OUTLOOK:** Employment growth of insurance underwriters is expected to be slower than average in the decade ahead. The expected rise in the volume, complexity, and variety of insurance products will be offset by the trend toward self-insurance and the increased use of artificial intelligence. Jobs are projected to increase from 100,000 in 1998 to 120,000 by 2006. These are broken down into six groups of underwriters: fire, marine, and casualty insurance carriers (37%); insurance agents, brokers, and service personnel (33%); life insurance carriers (15%); pension funds and miscellaneous insurance carriers (4%); medical service and health insurance carriers (4%); and underwriters in other industries (7%)

➤ **NATURE OF WORK:** Underwriters appraise and select the risks their company will insure. The underwriter must analyze information in insurance applications, reports from loss control consultants, medical reports, and actuarial studies and then decide whether to issue a policy. They use computer programs to analyze and rate applications and then recommend acceptance or denial of a risk. Most underwriters specialize in one of three major categories of insurance—life, property and casualty, or health—as well as group or individual policies.

➤ **WORKING CONDITIONS:** Underwriters have desk jobs and offices are usually pleasant. Although some overtime may be required, the normal workweek is 35-40 hours. Some travel may be required.

➤ **EDUCATION, TRAINING, QUALIFICATIONS:** Many large insurance companies prefer college graduates who have a degree in business administration or finance with courses or experience in accounting. However, a degree in almost any field plus courses in business law and accounting provide a good general background. Some companies hire persons without a college degree for underwriter trainee positions. Some high school graduates who begin as underwriting clerks may be trained as underwriters after they demonstrate an aptitude for the work.

➤ **EARNINGS:** In 1998 the median annual earnings of full-time wage and salary underwriters were $33,000. The bottom 10 percent earned less than $20,000; the top 10 percent earned more than $54,000.

➤ **KEY CONTACTS:** General information about a career as an insurance underwriter is available from the home offices of many life insurance and property and liability insurance companies. Information may also be obtained from:

- **American Institute for Chartered Property and Casualty Underwriters, and the Insurance Institute of America:** 720 Providence Rd., P.O. Box 3016, Malvern, PA 19355-0716

11

Education, Government, & Legal Careers

C areer opportunities in education, government, and law should be good to excellent in the coming decade. Within education, population increases and demands for a better educated and retrained workforce should result in good job prospects for educators at all levels, but especially at the high school and adult education levels. Opportunities will also be excellent for kindergarten and elementary teachers, education administrators, and counselors.

While government at all levels will experience some cutbacks in personnel, the trend is to expand the public service in response to population growth. As the federal government continues to cutback by devolving programs to state and local government in the form of block grants, state and local governments will grow accordingly. Within government at the state and local level, opportunities will be especially good for individuals in criminal justice (police officers, corrections officers) and human and social services. At the federal level, we expect opportunities to expand in the areas of health services and criminal justice.

Opportunities also should be good for lawyers, judges, and paralegals in the decade ahead as American society continues to become more litigious. However, optimistic projections for major job growth in the legal field may be tempered by the continuing glut of law graduates and the high costs of legal services. While opportunities may continue to grow, we expect they will not grow at the high rates projected by the Department of Labor.

ADULT EDUCATION TEACHERS

➤ **EMPLOYMENT OUTLOOK:** Employment opportunities for adult education teachers should grow faster than the average for all occupations, increasing from 570,000 jobs in 1998 to 680,000 jobs in 2006. Many openings will be for replacement of workers who leave the occupation, particularly given the large number of part-time workers and high turnover in the occupation.

➤ **NATURE OF WORK:** Adult education teachers work in adult vocational technical, adult basic, and adult continuing education. They lecture in classrooms and provide students with hands-on experience. Similar to other teachers, they prepare lessons and assignments, grade papers and do related paperwork, attend faculty and professional meetings, and stay abreast of developments in their field.

➤ **WORKING CONDITIONS:** Adult education teachers work either full-time or part-time in classroom and workshop settings. Many courses are offered at night or on weekends and range from 2 to 4-hour workshops and 1-day mini-sessions to semester-long courses. Since adult education teachers work with adult students, they do not experience many of the behavioral or social problems sometimes found when teaching younger students.

➤ **EDUCATION, TRAINING, QUALIFICATIONS:** Education and training requirements vary greatly from state to state. Most states require teachers to have work or other experience in their field, and a license or certificate in fields where these usually are required for full professional status. In some cases, particularly at educational institutions, a bachelor's master's, or doctoral degree is required. In other cases an acceptable portfolio of work is required. Adult education teachers update their skills through continuing education by participating in seminars, conferences, or graduate courses in adult education, training and development, or human resources development.

➤ **EARNINGS:** In 1998, adult education teachers working full time had median earnings of $32,000 a year. The top 10 percent earned more than $58,000 a year; the bottom 10 percent averaged $14,000 a year. Part-timers are generally paid hourly wages and do not receive benefits or pay for preparation time outside of class.

➤ **KEY CONTACTS:** For information on career in adult education, contact:

- **American Association for Adult and Continuing Education:** 1200 19th St., NW, Suite 300, Washington, DC 20036

- **American Vocational Association:** 1410 King St., Alexandria, VA 22314

- **ERIC Clearinghouse on Adult, Career, and Vocational Education:** 1900 Kenny Rd., Columbus, OH 43210-1090

★ CORRECTIONAL OFFICERS

➤ **EMPLOYMENT OUTLOOK:** No doubt about it—crime is a growth industry. Rapid growth in correctional facilities and continuing turnover of jobs should result in a much faster than average growth rate in job opportunities for correctional officers. We expect the number of jobs to increase from 335,000 in 1998 to 450,000 in 2006.

➤ **NATURE OF WORK:** Correction officers supervise individuals who have been arrested, are awaiting trial, or who have been convicted of a crime and sentenced to serve time in a correctional institution. Their work involves inspecting facilities, reporting orally and in writing on inmate conduct and work, escorting inmates to and from cells, admitting and accompanying visitors, and counseling and helping inmates with problems.

➤ **WORKING CONDITIONS:** Correction officers may work indoors or outdoors, depending on their specific duties. Working in a correctional institution can be stressful and hazardous, and occasionally correction officers are injured or killed during inmate disturbances.

➤ **EDUCATION, TRAINING, QUALIFICATIONS:** Most institutions require correctional officers to have at least a high school education or its equivalent. Most correctional institutions seek correctional officers with postsecondary education in psychology, criminology, and related fields emphasizing personal counseling and rehabilitation of inmates.

➤ **EARNINGS:** In 1998, the average earnings for State correctional officers were $27,000 a year. These averages ranged from a low of $17,700 in South Carolina to a high of $42,200 in Rhode Island. The annual average salary for correctional officers with the Federal government was $34,000.

➤ **KEY CONTACTS:** For information on corrections careers, as well as information about schools offering criminal justice education, financial assistance, and job listings, contact:

- **American Correctional Association:** 8025 Laurel Lakes Ct., Laurel, MD 20707

- **American Probation and Parole Association:** P.O. Box 201, Lexington, KY 40584

- **International Association of Correctional Officers:** Box 53, 1333 South Wabash Ave., Chicago, IL 60605

COUNSELORS

➤ **EMPLOYMENT OUTLOOK:** Employment opportunities for counselors will be as fast as the average for all occupations in the decade ahead due to increased school enrollments, greater use of third party payments to counselors, and the expanded responsibilities of counselors. The number of jobs should increase from 180,000 in 1998 to 215,000 in 2006.

➤ **NATURE OF WORK:** Counselors assist people with personal, family, social, educational, and career decisions, problems, and concerns. Their work varies depending on whom they serve and their different work settings. The major occupational groups include school and college counselors, college career planning and placement counselors, rehabilitation counselors, employment counselors, and mental health counselors.

➤ **WORKING CONDITIONS:** Most school counselors work the traditional 9- to 10-month school year with a 2- to 3-month vacation, although an increasing number are employed on 10½- to 11-month contracts. They generally have the same hours as teachers. Rehabilitation and employment counselors generally work a standard 40-hour week. College career planning and placement counselors may work long and irregular hours during recruiting periods.

➤ **EDUCATION, TRAINING, QUALIFICATIONS:** Most counselors have a master's degree in college student affairs, elementary or secondary school counseling, gerontological counseling, marriage and family counseling, substance abuse counseling, rehabilitation counseling, agency or community counseling, mental health counseling, counseling psychology, career counseling, or a related field. As of 1998, 43 States and the District of Columbia had some form of counselor credentialing legislation—licensure, certification, or registry—for practice outside schools. Requirements vary from State to State with some requiring mandatory and others specifying voluntary credentialing.

➤ **EARNINGS:** Median earnings for full-time educational and vocational counselors were about $36,300 a year in 1998. The top 10 percent earned over $61,000 a year; the bottom 10 percent earned less than $20,000 a year. The average salary of school counselors in 1998 was about $46,000.

➤ **KEY CONTACTS:** For information on counseling careers, contact:

- **American Counseling Association:** 5999 Stevenson Avenue, Alexandria, VA 22304

- **American School Counselor Association:** 5999 Stevenson Ave., Alexandria, VA 22304

- **Council on Rehabilitation Counselor Certification:** 1835 Rohlwing Rd., Suite E, Rolling Meadows, IL 60008

- **National Board for Certified Counselors:** 3 Terrace Way, Suite D, Greensboro, NC 27403
  Web site: *http://www.nbcc.org/*

- **National Council on Rehabilitation Education:** Department of Special Education, Utah State University, Logan, UT 84322

- **National Rehabilitation Counseling Association:** 1910 Association Dr., Reston, VA 22091

EDUCATION ADMINISTRATORS

➤ **EMPLOYMENT OUTLOOK:** Employment of education administrators is expected to grow as fast as average—from 390,000 jobs in 1998 to 430,000 in 2006—due to increased school enrollments. Expect a great deal of competition for principal, assistant principal, and central office jobs because many teachers and other staff meet the requirements for these jobs and seek promotion.

➤ **NATURE OF WORK:** Education administrators provide direction, leadership, and day-to-day management of educational activities in schools, colleges and universities, businesses, correctional institutions, museums, and job training and community service organizations. They set educational standards and goals, develop academic programs, train and motivate teachers, manage guidance and other student services, administer recordkeeping, prepare budgets, and handle relations with parents, prospective students, employers, or others outside of education.

➤ **WORKING CONDITIONS:** Education administrators hold management positions with significant responsibility. Coordinating and interacting with faculty, parents, and students can be fast-paced and stimulating, but also stressful and demanding. Some jobs include travel. Most education administrators work more than 40 hours a week, including many nights and weekends when school activities take place. Unlike teachers, they usually work year round.

➤ **EDUCATION, TRAINING, QUALIFICATIONS:** Most education administrators begin their careers in related occupations, often moving from teaching positions. In public schools, principals, assistant principals, and school administrators in central offices generally need a master's degree in education administration or educational supervision, and a State teaching certificate. Some principals and central office administrators have a doctorate in education administration. In private schools, they often have a master's or doctoral degree, but may hold only a bachelor's degree since they are not subject to State certification requirements. Academic deans usually have a doctorate in their specialty. A Ph.D. or Ed.D. is usually necessary for top student affairs positions.

➤ **EARNINGS:** Salaries of education administrators vary according to position, level of responsibility and experience, and the size and location of the institution. In 1998 the average salaries for principals in elementary schools was $64,000; in junior high/middle schools, $68,000; and in senior high schools, $73,000. Average salaries for academic deans in higher education were as follows: medicine, $203,000; law, $143,000; engineering, $114,000; arts and sciences, $84,000; business, $83,000; education, $81,000; social sciences, $63,000; mathematics, $61,000. Student services directors averaged the following: admissions and registrar, $52,000; student financial aid, $47,000; and student activities, $35,000.

➤ **KEY CONTACTS:** For information on education administration careers, contact:

- **American Association of Collegiate Registrars and Admissions Officers:** One Dupont Circle NW, Suite 330, Washington, DC 20036-1171

- **American Association of School Administrators:** 1801 North Moore St., Arlington, VA 22209

- **American Federation of School Administrators:** 1729 21st St., NW, Washington, DC 20009

- **National Association of Elementary School Principals:** 1615 Duke St., Alexandria, VA 22341-3483

- **National Association of Secondary School Principals:** 1904 Association Dr., Reston, VA 22091

- **National Association of Student Personnel Administrators:** 1875 Connecticut Ave. NW, Suite 418, Washington, DC 20009-5728

★ # GUARDS

➤ **EMPLOYMENT OUTLOOK:** Job opportunities for guards will be plentiful in the decade ahead. Jobs should increase faster than average due to increased concern about crime, vandalism, and terrorism. The number of jobs is expected to increase from 970,000 in 1998 to 1,200,000 in 2006. Opportunities should be best for those who work for contract security agencies. Competition will be greatest for in-house guard jobs, which generally pay higher salaries, provide more benefits and greater job security, and offer greater potential for advancement.

➤ **NATURE OF WORK:** Guards patrol and inspect property to protect against fire, theft, vandalism, and illegal entry. Their duties vary with the size, type, and location of their employer. Guards work in office buildings, banks, hospitals, department stores, ports, airports, railroads, public buildings, factories, laboratories, data processing centers, and military bases as well as attend social affairs, sports events, conventions, and other public gatherings. Some drive armored cars and serve as personal bodyguards.

➤ **WORKING CONDITIONS:** Guards work indoors and outdoors patrolling buildings, industrial plants, and grounds. Many work alone at night; the usual shift lasts 8 hours. Guards usually eat on the job rather than take a regular break.

➤ **EDUCATION, TRAINING, QUALIFICATIONS:** Most employers prefer guards who are high school graduates. Applicants with less than a high school education also can qualify if they pass reading and writing tests and demonstrate competence in following written and oral instructions. Some jobs require a driver's license. Applicants are expected to have good character references, no police record, good health, and good personal habits such as neatness and dependability. All States have licensing or registration requirements for guards who work for contract security agencies.

➤ **EARNINGS:** Median annual earnings for full-time guards in 1998 were $18,200. The lowest 10 percent earned less than $11,000; the top 10 percent earned more than $36,000. Guards working in 160 urban areas with the least responsibility and training averaged $6.65 an hour in 1998. Guards with more specialized training and experience had median hourly earnings of $12.00. Guards employed by industrial security and guard agencies generally started at or slightly above the minimum wage. Newly hired guards in the Federal government earned between $16,000 and $18,000 a year in 1998. The average federal guard earned $23,500 a year.

➤ **KEY CONTACTS:** For information on work opportunities for guards, contact local detective and guard firms and the nearest State employment service office.

INSPECTORS AND COMPLIANCE OFFICERS
(Except Construction)

➤ **EMPLOYMENT OUTLOOK:** Job opportunities are expected to be slower than average because of the recent trend toward fewer government regulations and smaller government. Nonetheless, the number of jobs should increase from 165,000 in 1998 to 185,000 in 2006. Most of the increase will take place in State government and within private industry which does a great deal of self-enforcement of government regulations and company policies.

➤ **NATURE OF WORK:** Inspectors and compliance officers enforce adherence to a wide range of laws, regulations, policies, and procedures that protect the public on matters such as health, safety, food, immigration, licensing, interstate commerce, and international trade. Depending upon their employer, inspectors vary widely in title and responsibilities. The major categories of inspectors include health inspectors (consumer safety, food, agricultural quarantine, environmental health, and agricultural commodity graders) and regulatory inspectors (immigration, customs, postal, aviation safety, railroad, motor vehicle, traffic, occupational safety and health, mine safety and health, wage-hour compliance, alcohol, tobacco, firearms, securities, logging operations, and quality control inspectors and securities compliance examiners, revenue officers, attendance officers, dealer compliance representatives, and travel accommodations raters).

➤ **WORKING CONDITIONS:** Inspectors and compliance officers' work may be active; they meet many people and work in a variety of environments. Their jobs often involve considerable field work, and some inspectors travel frequently. They are furnished with an automobile or are reimbursed for travel expenses.

➤ **EDUCATION, TRAINING, QUALIFICATIONS:** The qualifications for inspector and compliance officer jobs vary greatly given the diversity of functions. Requirements are a combination of education, experience, and examinations. Employers generally prefer applicants with college training, including courses related to the job.

➤ **EARNINGS:** The median annual salary of inspectors and compliance officers, except construction, was $36,500 in 1998. The highest 10 percent earned over $64,000 a year. Average annual salaries for inspectors varied substantially in 1998 for federal employers—from $29,500 (environmental protection assistants) to $67,000 (air safety inspectors).

➤ **KEY CONTACTS:** For information on inspector and compliance officer jobs in the federal government, contact the State employment service, area offices of the U.S. Office of Personnel Management (or call 912/757-3000 or access OPM's web site: *http://www.usajobs.opm.gov/*). The State civil service commission or a local government office will have information on jobs at the state and local level. Information about jobs in private industry is available from the State Employment Service and is listed under "Job Service" or "Employment" in the State government section of local telephone directories.

LAWYERS AND JUDGES

➤ **EMPLOYMENT OUTLOOK:** The demand for legal services should continue to increase in response to population growth and economic expansion in the decade ahead. We expect the number of lawyers and judges will increase from 720,000 (640,000 lawyers and 80,000 judges) in 1998 to 900,000 in 2006.

➤ **NATURE OF WORK:** Lawyers act as both advocates and advisors. As advocates, they represent one of the opposing parties in criminal and civil trials by presenting arguments that support their client in court. As advisors, lawyers counsel their clients as to their legal rights and obligations and suggest particular courses of action in business and personal matters. Many lawyers specialize on a particular branch of law, such as admiralty, probate, or international law. Much of their work is devoted to conducting legal research, writing reports or briefs, and counseling clientele. Judges preside over cases touching on virtually every aspect of society, from traffic offenses to disputes over management of professional sports, from the rights of huge corporations to questions of disconnecting life support equipment for terminally ill persons. They are responsible for ensuring that trials and hearings are conducted fairly and that justice is administered in a manner that safeguards the legal rights of all parties involves. Judges preside over trials or hearings and listen as attorneys representing the parties present and argue their cases.

➤ **WORKING CONDITIONS:** Although many lawyers work for government, corporations, and nonprofit groups, the largest single category of lawyers are in private practice where they may concentrate on civil law, areas such as litigation, wills, trusts, contracts, mortgages, titles, and leases. Lawyers and judges do most of their work in offices, law libraries, and courtrooms. Lawyers sometimes meet in clients' homes or places of business and, when necessary, in hospitals or prisons. Lawyers often work long hours, and about half regularly work 50 hours or more per week. They are under particularly heavy pressure, for example, when a case is being tried. Many judges work a standard 40-hour week, but the caseload of some judges requires that they work over 50 hours per week.

➤ **EDUCATION, TRAINING, QUALIFICATIONS:** To practice law in the courts of any State or other jurisdiction, a person must be licensed, or admitted to its bar, under rules established by the jurisdiction's highest court. Nearly all require that applicants for admission to the bar pass a written bar examination. To qualify for the bar examination in most States, an applicant must complete at least 3 years of college and graduate from a law school approved by the American Bar Association or the proper State authorities.

➤ **EARNINGS:** The median annual salary of all lawyers in 1998 was $62,000. Median salaries for beginning lawyers 6 months after graduation varied by the type of work, ranging from $32,000 for public interest lawyers to $52,000 for lawyers in private practice. The median annual salary for all recent graduates (6 months experience) was $42,000. The highest paid lawyers tend to be partners in law firms, with some major partners in high powered corporate law firms making over $1 million a year. Lawyers with the Federal government averaged $62,000 per year. Federal district court judges averaged $135,000 in 1998. Circuit court judges earned $143,000 a year. Full-time Federal administrative law judges averaged $96,000 a year. Associate justices of State supreme courts averaged $103,000. Salaries of State intermediate appellate court judges average $93,000.

➤ **KEY CONTACTS:** The American Bar Association publishes an annual *Review of Legal Education in the United States* which provides detailed information on each of the 179 law schools approved by the ABA, State requirements for admission to legal practice, a directory of State bar examination administrators, and other information on legal education. Single copies are free. For information on the bar examination, financial aid for law students, and law as a career, contact:

- **American Bar Association:** 750 North Lake Shore Dr., Chicago, IL 60611

- **Law School Admission Council:** Box 40, Newtown, PA 18940 Web site: *http://www.usajobs.opm.gov*

★ PARALEGALS

➤ **EMPLOYMENT OUTLOOK:** Paralegal job opportunities will be one of the fastest growing job areas in the decade ahead. Paralegal jobs should increase from 115,000 in 1998 to 180,000 in 2006.

➤ **NATURE OF WORK:** Paralegals assist lawyers in doing legal work, much of which is background work. A paralegal is often allowed to perform all the functions of a lawyer other than accepting clients, setting legal fees, giving legal advice, or presenting a case in court. Most of this work involves conducting legal research and preparing written reports. Some paralegals coordinate the activities of the law office employees and keep the financial records for the office.

➤ **WORKING CONDITIONS:** Paralegals do most of their work at desks in offices and law libraries. Occasionally, they travel to gather information and perform other duties. Paralegals employed by corporations and government work a standard 40-hour week. Paralegals employed by law firms sometimes work very long hours when they are under pressure to meet deadlines.

➤ **EDUCATION, TRAINING, QUALIFICATIONS:** Employers generally require formal paralegal training, although some employers prefer to train their paralegals on the job, promoting experienced legal secretaries or hiring persons with college education but no legal experience. Over 800 formal paralegal training programs are offered by 4-year colleges and universities, law schools, community and junior colleges, business schools, and proprietary schools; 214 are approved by the American Bar Association.

➤ **EARNINGS:** Earnings of paralegals vary greatly. Salaries depend on the education, training, and experience the paralegal brings to the job, the type and size of employer, and the geographic location of the job. In 1998 the average annual salary for paralegals was $35,500. Starting salaries of paralegals with one year or less of experience averaged $31,000. Many paralegals also receive annual bonuses which average around $2,000. The average annual salary of paralegals with the Federal government in 1998 was $45,000.

➤ **KEY CONTACTS:** For information on paralegal careers, contact:

- **American Association for Paralegal Education:** P.O. Box 40244, Overland Park, KS 66204

- **American Bar Association:** Standing Committee on Legal Assistants, 750 North Lake Shore Dr., Chicago, IL 60611

- **National Association of Legal Assistants, Inc.:** 1516 South Boston St., Suite 200, Tulsa, OK 74119
  Web site: *http://www.nala.org*

- **National Federation of Paralegal Association:** P.O. Box 33108, Kansas City, MO 64114

★ # POLICE, DETECTIVES, AND SPECIAL AGENTS

➤ **EMPLOYMENT OUTLOOK:** Employment of police, detectives, and special agents is expected to increase from 710,000 in 1998 to 780,000 in 2006. This increase reflects an increase in population, the need for police protection, and growing concern about drugs and drug-related crimes. Competition should be keen for higher paying jobs in large police departments and federal law enforcement agencies, such as the FBI, Drug Enforcement Administration, and the Secret Service.

➤ **NATURE OF WORK:** Police officers, detectives, and special agents are responsible for the safety of the Nation's cities, towns, and highways. Police officers and detectives in small communities and rural areas have numerous duties. In the course of a day's work, they may direct traffic at the scene of a fire, investigate a burglary, and give first aid to an accident victim. In a large police department, officers usually are assigned to a specific type of duty. Most officers are detailed either to patrol or to traffic duty; smaller numbers are assigned to special work such as accident prevention. Others are experts in chemical and microscopic analysis, firearms identification, and handwriting and fingerprint identification. Detectives and special agents are plainclothes investigators who gather facts and collect evidence for criminal cases. They conduct interviews, examine records, observe the activities of suspects, and participate in raids or arrests. Federal Bureau of Investigation (FBI) special agents investigate violations of federal laws in connection with bank robberies, theft of Government property, organized crime, espionage, sabotage, kidnaping, and terrorism. Special agents employed by the U.S. Department of Treasury work for the U.S. Customs Service; the Bureau of Alcohol, Tobacco, and Firearms; the U.S. Secret Service; and the Internal Revenue Service.

➤ **WORKING CONDITIONS:** Police, detectives, and special agents usually work 40 hours a week. Some officers work weekends, holidays, and nights. They are subject to call any time their services are needed and may work overtime, particularly during criminal investigations. The jobs of some special agents such as U.S. Secret Service agents, require extensive travel. Police, detectives, and special agents may have to work outdoors for long periods in all kinds of weather. The injury rate among these law officers is higher than in many occupations and reflects the risks taken in pursuing speeding motorists, apprehending criminals, and dealing with public disorders. Police work can be very dangerous and stressful.

➤ **EDUCATION, TRAINING, QUALIFICATIONS:** Civil service regulations govern the appointment of police and detectives in most States and large cities and in many small ones. Candidates must be U.S. citizens, usually at least 20 years of age, and must meet rigorous physical and personal qualifications. Eligibility for appointment depends on performance in competitive written examinations as well as on education and experience. Physical examinations often include tests of vision, strength, and agility. Qualifications for many jobs in law enforcement with the federal government require college degrees.

➤ **EARNINGS:** In 1998, the median salary of nonsupervisory police officers and detectives was $36,000 a year. Police officers in supervisory positions had a median salary of $42,500 a year. Sheriffs, bailiffs, and other law enforcement officers had a median annual salary of $27,800. In 1998, FBI agents started at $35,000 a year, while Treasury Department agents started at $26,000 or $32,000 a year. Salaries of Federal agents progress to $57,000 a year; supervisory agents start at $67,500 a year.

➤ **KEY CONTACTS:** For information on law enforcement careers, contact the appropriate federal, state, or local law enforcement agency. In the case of the federal government, contact any Federal Employment Information Center for pamphlets providing general information and instructions for submitting an application for jobs as Treasury special agents, drug enforcement agents, FBI special agents, or U.S. marshals. For information about law enforcement careers in general, contact:

- **International Union of Police Associations:** 1421 Prince Street, Suite 330, Alexandria, VA 22314, Tel. 703/549-7473

- **American Police Academy:** 1000 Connecticut Avenue, NW, Suite 9, Washington, DC 20036, Tel. 202/293-9088

- **National Police Officers Association of America:** P.O. Box 22129, Louisville, KY 40252-0129, Tel. 800/467-6762

- **National United Law Enforcement Association:** 256 East McLemore Avenue, Memphis, TN 38106, Tel. 901/774-1118

★ # PSYCHOLOGISTS

➤ **EMPLOYMENT OUTLOOK:** Job opportunities for psychologists should slow in the decade ahead. The number of job opportunities is expected to increase from 144,000 in 1996 to 170,000 in 2006. This increase is due to increased attention being paid to the expanding elderly population, the maintenance of mental health, and the testing and counseling of children. Job opportunities also should increase with businesses, nonprofit organizations, and research firms. Ph.D.'s with training in applied areas, such as clinical or counseling psychology, and in quantitative research methods, should have the best prospects.

➤ **NATURE OF WORK:** Psychologists study human behavior and mental processes to understand, explain, and change people's behavior. Research psychologists investigate the physical, cognitive, emotional, or social aspects of human behavior. Psychologists in applied fields counsel and conduct training programs; do market research; or provide mental health services in hospitals, clinics, or private settings. Over two-fifths of all psychologists are self-employed.

➤ **WORKING CONDITIONS:** A psychologist's specialty and place of employment determine working conditions. For example, clinical, school, and counseling psychologists in private practice have pleasant, comfortable offices and set their own hours. However, they often have evening hours to accommodate clients. Some employed in hospitals, nursing homes, and other health facilities often work evenings and weekends, while others in schools and clinics work regular hours. Psychologists employed by academic institutions divide their time among teaching, research, and administration responsibilities. Psychologists in government and private industry have more structured schedules.

➤ **EDUCATION, TRAINING, QUALIFICATIONS:** Ph.D.'s with training in applied areas, such as clinical or counseling psychology, and in quantitative research methods, should have the best prospects. Among master's degree holders, specialists in school psychology should have the best prospects, while bachelor's degree holders will have very few opportunities in this field.

➤ **EARNINGS:** The median annual salary of psychologists with a doctoral degree and 5-9 years experience in 1998 was $57,000 in counseling psychology in individual private practice; $56,000 in private research organizations; $53,000 in clinical psychology in private psychiatric hospitals; and $61,000 in school psychology. The median annual salary of master's degree holders was $39,000 in counseling psychology; $44,000 in clinical psychology; $43,000 in research positions; $62,000 in school psychology; and $57,000 in industrial-organizational psychology. Many psychologists in private practice earn much more.

➤ **KEY CONTACTS:** For information on careers, educational requirements, financial assistance, and licensing in the field of psychology, contact:

- **American Psychologist Association:** Education in Psychology and Accreditation Offices, Education Directorate, 750 1st St., NE, Washington, DC 20002
  Web site: *http://www.apa.org/*

■ **Association of State and Provincial Psychology Boards:** P.O. Box 4389, Montgomery, AL 36103-4389

■ **National Association of School Psychologists:** 4030 East West Highway, Suite 402, Bethesda, MD 20814

★ # SCHOOL TEACHERS
(Kindergarten, Elementary, and Secondary)

➤ **EMPLOYMENT OUTLOOK:** Employment growth for kindergarten, elementary, and secondary school teachers is expected to be faster than average for jobs in general, increasing from 3.2 million jobs in 1998 to 4.4 million jobs in 2006. Projected growth will vary for different teaching occupations. Employment of special education teachers is expected to increase much faster than average as will employment of math and science teachers. Employment of secondary school teachers is expected to grow faster than average, while average employment growth is projected for kindergarten and elementary school teachers, reflecting population trends and corresponding student enrollment. However, ongoing legislative initiatives to fundamentally reform American education with smaller teacher-student ratios may have a very significant impact on increasing the number of teachers at all levels to achieve smaller class sizes.

➤ **NATURE OF WORK:** Kindergarten and elementary school teachers introduce children to numbers, language, science, and social studies. They often work with an entire class, but also provide individual attention. They assign lessons, give tests, hear oral presentations, and oversee special projects. They maintain classroom order and instill good study habits and appreciation for learning. Secondary teachers help students delve more deeply into subjects.

➤ **WORKING CONDITIONS:** School teachers spend most of their time moving about the classroom. While most teachers work a 40-hour week, some may work more than 40 hours both inside and outside the classroom. Most school teachers work a traditional 10-month school year with a 2-month vacation during the summer.

➤ **EDUCATION, TRAINING, QUALIFICATIONS:** All States require public school teachers to be certified. This normally includes a bachelor's degree and completion of an approved teacher training program with a prescribed number of education credits. Most States require applicants for certification to be tested for competency in basic skills, teaching skills, or subject matter. Most require continuing education for renewing certification—some require a master's degree.

➤ **EARNINGS:** The average annual salary for all public elementary and secondary school teachers in 1998 was $39,000. Secondary school teachers tend to make about $1,300 a year more than elementary teachers. Earnings in private schools generally are lower. Many public school teachers belong to unions, such as the American Federation of Teachers and the National Education Association.

➤ **KEY CONTACTS:** For information on teaching careers, accreditation, certification, and unions, contact:

- **American Federation of Teachers:** 555 New Jersey Ave., NW, Washington, DC 20001

- **National Council for Accreditation of Teacher Education:** 2010 Massachusetts Ave., NW, Suite 500, Washington, DC 20036

- **National Education Association:** 1201 16th St., NW, Washington, DC 20036

★ SOCIAL AND HUMAN SERVICE ASSISTANTS

➤ **EMPLOYMENT OUTLOOK:** Expect an explosive growth in employment for social and human service assistants, growing from 185,000 jobs in 1996 to 385,000 jobs in 2006. This expected growth rate is due to the expansion of facilities and programs for the elderly and disabled, greater services for families in crisis, and programs for those with substance-abuse problems, the homeless, pregnant teenagers, and the mentally ill.

➤ **NATURE OF WORK:** The work of human services workers is relatively demanding, the pay is relatively low, and job turnover tends to be high—key characteristics leading to a large number of job opportunities for human services workers in the decade ahead. Human services workers come under a variety of job titles such as social service technicians, case management aide, social work assistant, residential counselor, alcohol or drug abuse counselor, mental health technicians, child abuse worker, community outreach worker, and gerontology aide. They work in group homes and halfway houses; correctional, mental retardation, and community mental health centers; family, child, and youth service agencies; and programs concerned with alcoholism, drug abuse, family violence, and aging. Working under the supervision of social workers or psychologists, they help clients obtain benefits or services.

➤ **WORKING CONDITIONS:** Working conditions of human services workers vary. Many spend part of their time in an office or residential facility and the rest in the field—visiting clients, taking them on trips, or meeting with people who provide services to their clients. Most work a regular 40-hour week. The work, while satisfying, can be emotionally draining. Understaffing and lack of equipment may add to the pressure.

➤ **EDUCATION, TRAINING, QUALIFICATIONS:** While some employers hire high school graduates, most prefer applicants with some college preparation in human services, social work, or one of the social or behavioral sciences. Some prefer those with a 4-year college degree.

➤ **EARNINGS:** Starting salaries for social and human services assistants ranged from $16,000 to $25,000 a year in 1998. Experienced workers earned between $21,000 and $32,000 a year, depending on their education, experience, and employer.

➤ **KEY CONTACTS:** For information on programs and careers in human services, contact your State employment service office; city, county, or State department of health, mental health and mental retardation, and human resources; or the following organizations:

- **Council for Standards in Human Service Education:** Northern Essex Community College, Haverhill, MA 01830

- **National Organization for Human Service Education:** Brookdale Community College, Lyncroft, NJ 08837

SOCIAL WORKERS

➤ **EMPLOYMENT OUTLOOK:** Employment opportunities for social workers should increase faster than average, from 590,000 in 1998 to 690,000 in 2006. This increase will be in response to the needs of a growing and aging population, as well as increasing concern about services for the mentally ill, the mentally retarded, and families in crisis.

➤ **NATURE OF WORK:** Social workers help individuals and families cope with problems such as homelessness or inadequate housing, unemployment, lack of job skills, financial mismanagement, serious illness, handicaps, substance abuse, unwanted pregnancy, or antisocial behavior. They also work with families that have serious conflicts, including those involving child or spousal abuse or divorce. Most social workers specialize in one field such as child welfare and family services, mental health, medical social work, school social work, community organization, clinical social work, or gerontological services.

➤ **WORKING CONDITIONS:** Most social workers work a standard 40-hour week. However, some work evenings and weekends to meet with clients, attend community meetings, and handle emergencies. Some, particularly in voluntary nonprofit agencies, work part time. They may spend most of their time in an office or residential facility, but may also travel locally to visit clients or meet with service providers. The work, while satisfying, can be stressful and emotionally draining. Understaffing and large caseloads add to the pressure of some agencies. Nearly 40 percent of the jobs are held with State, country, or municipal government agencies and are found in departments of health and human resources, mental health, child welfare, education, corrections, social services, housing, and welfare.

➤ **EDUCATION, TRAINING, QUALIFICATIONS:** A bachelor's degree is the minimum requirement for most positions. Besides the bachelor's in social work (BSW), undergraduate majors in psychology, sociology, and related fields satisfy hiring requirements in some agencies,

especially small community agencies. A master's degree in social work
(MSW) is necessary for positions in health and mental health settings.
College and university teaching positions and most research appointments normally require a doctorate in social work. In 1990, 48 States had
licensing, certification, or registration laws regarding social work practice
and the use of professional titles.

➤ **EARNINGS:** In 1998, the median earnings of social workers with
MSW degrees were $36,000. For those with BSW degrees, median
earnings were $26,000. Social workers with a master's degree working
full-time in acute care hospitals averaged $36,000. Social workers in
nonsupervisory, supervisory, and managerial positions with the Federal
government averaged $47,500.

➤ **KEY CONTACTS:** For information about career opportunities in
social work, contact:

- **Council on Social Work Education:** 1600 Duke St., Alexandria,
  VA 22314-3421

- **National Association of Social Workers:** Career Information, 750
  First St., NE, Suite 700, Washington, DC 20002-4241

- **National Network for Social Work Managers, Inc.:** 1316 New
  Hampshire Ave., NW, Suite 602, Washington, DC 20036

Art, Media, and Entertainment Careers

Highly sensitive to business cycles, the arts, entertainment, and media industries offer numerous and exciting opportunities for talented and enterprising job seekers. After experiencing a major recession and significant downturns during the early 1990s, these industries experienced a major comeback during much of the 1990s. They should continue to do well in the decade ahead.

Opportunities in major sectors of the arts, entertainment, and media industries should be good to excellent in the decade ahead. While numerous opportunities will be available, we expect keen competition in what are some of the most sought-after, glamorous, and high turnover occupations.

The proliferation of cable television stations, home movie rental establishments, and television syndication should lead to a greater demand for television and movie productions. In addition to increased demand for actors, directors, and producers, these industries will require more creative production personnel and technicians.

The growth in small businesses and advertising will also require the services of more artists, illustrators, and designers skilled in using the latest technology. Graphic artists skilled in computer-based design and working in advertising agencies, publishing firms, and art and design studios should do very well in the decade ahead.

The publishing industry should continue to experience major growth in the decade ahead. As desktop and electronic publishing play central roles in restructuring this industry, more and more opportunities will be available for individuals using the latest publishing technology.

★   ACTORS, DIRECTORS, AND PRODUCERS

➤ **EMPLOYMENT OUTLOOK:** Employment is expected to grow much faster than average as cable television, home movie rentals, television syndication, and growing foreign markets for American films fuel a growing demand for productions. However, competition for jobs will remain keen because large numbers of people seek these careers which do not require formal preparation. Jobs are expected to grow from 110,000 in 1998 to 185,000 in 2006.

➤ **NATURE OF WORK:** Actors entertain and communicate with people through their interpretation of dramatic roles. Directors interpret plays or scripts, audition performers, select the cast, and conduct rehearsals. Producers are entrepreneurs: they arrange financing; oversee the budget; hire directors, principal cast and production members; and coordinate the activities of writers, directors, managers and other personnel.

➤ **WORKING CONDITIONS:** Actors work long and frequently irregular hours. They often travel—sometimes to locations with adverse weather and living conditions. Directors and producers often work under stress as they try to meet schedules, stay within budgets, and resolve personnel problems.

➤ **EDUCATION, TRAINING, QUALIFICATIONS:** Formal dramatic training or acting experience is generally necessary, although some people enter the field without it. Training can be obtained at dramatic arts schools in New York and Los Angeles, and at colleges and universities throughout the country offering degrees in dramatic and theater arts. There are no specific training requirements for directors and producers.

Talent, experience, and business acumen are very important. Actors, writers, film editors, and business managers often become directors or producers. Formal training is available at some colleges.

➤ **EARNINGS:** Most actors belong to unions or guilds which set daily and weekly rates. Average salaries can easily be skewed in these professions where the majority earn very little, but a few earn extremely high salaries. According to Actors' Equity Association, 80 percent of their members make less than $5,000 a year from acting; therefore, most actors must supplement their income with other jobs. Fewer than 1,000 members make more than $40,000 a year. In 1998, actors in Broadway stage productions received a minimum weekly salary of $1,040. Those in old Broadway productions received weekly minimums of $400 to $625. Small regional theaters pay $375-$600 a week. Motion picture and television actors with speaking parts receive a minimum daily rate of $560 or nearly $2,000 for a 5-day week. Stage directors for summer theaters usually make $2,500 to $8,000 for a three to four-week run of a production. The highest paid directors work on Broadway; they are usually paid around $80,000 plus royalties for a production. Producers seldom get a set fee; instead, they get a percentage of a show's earnings or ticket sales.

➤ **KEY CONTACTS:** For information on relevant associations and recent publications, send a self addressed stamped envelope to:

- **Associated Actors and Artists of America (AFL-CIO):** 165 West 46th St., New York, NY 10036, Tel. 212/869-0358

Information about opportunities in regional theaters may be obtained from:

- **Theatre Communications Group, Inc.:** 355 Lexington Ave., New York, NY 10017

For information on actors, directors, and producers, contact:

- **Screen Actors Guild:** 5757 Wilshire Blvd., Los Angeles, CA 90036-3600

- **Association of Independent Video and Filmmakers:** 304 Hudson Street, 6th Floor, New York, NY 10013

- **American Federation of Television and Radio Artists:** Screen Actors Guild, 4340 East-West Hwy., Suite 204, Bethesda, MD 20814-4411

★ DANCERS & CHOREOGRAPHERS

➤ **EMPLOYMENT OUTLOOK:** Employment is expected to grow much faster than average. However, competition will remain keen as the number of dancers seeking professional careers will continue to exceed the job openings. The number of jobs should increase from 24,000 in 1998 to 27,000 jobs in 2006.

➤ **NATURE OF WORK:** Dancers express ideas, stories, rhythm, and sound with their bodies in diverse musical forms from modern dance to classical ballet. Many dancers sing and act as well as dance. Choreographers create original dances as well as new interpretations of traditional dances.

➤ **WORKING CONDITIONS:** Dancing is strenuous. Rehearsals require long hours and usually take place daily, including weekends and holidays. Most performances take place in the evening, so dancers must become accustomed to working late hours.

➤ **EDUCATION, TRAINING, QUALIFICATIONS:** Training depends on the type of dance. Early ballet training begins at 5 to 8 years of age and is usually given by private teachers and independent ballet schools. Most dancers have their professional auditions by age 17 or 18.

➤ **EARNINGS:** Earnings of many professional dancers are largely governed by union contracts. Dancers in ballet and modern dance corps belong to the American Guild of Musical Artists, Inc., AFL-CIO; those on live or videotaped television are affiliated with the American Federation of Television and Radio Arts; and those who perform in films and on TV belong to the Screen Actors Guild. In 1998 the minimum weekly salary for dancers in ballet and modern productions was $693.

The minimum performance rate for dancers in theatrical motion pictures was $500 per day of filming. Earnings of choreographers vary greatly. Earnings from fees and performance royalties ranged from $1,000 a week in small professional theaters to over $30,000 for an eight- to ten-week rehearsal period for a Broadway production. Choreographers with high budget films can earn $3,500 a week; in television they may make between $8,000 and $12,500 for 14 work days.

➤ **KEY CONTACTS:** You can purchase directories of dance study and degree programs from:

- **National Association of Schools of Dance:** 11250 Roger Bacon Dr., Suite 21, Reston, VA 22090

- **The National Dance Association:** 1900 Association Dr., Reston, VA 20191

DESIGNERS

➤ **EMPLOYMENT OUTLOOK:** Continued emphasis on the quality and visual appeal of products will prompt faster than average growth for designers, especially industrial designers. However, competition may remain keen because of an abundant supply of qualified people. Jobs are expected to grow from 350,000 in 1998 to 400,000 in 2006.

➤ **NATURE OF WORK:** Designers organize and design articles, products, and materials in such a way that they not only serve the purpose for which they were intended but are visually pleasing as well. Designers usually specialize in one particular area of design, for example, automobiles, clothing, furniture, industrial equipment, interiors, movie and theater sets, or floral arrangements.

➤ **WORKING CONDITIONS:** Designers employed by manufacturing firms generally work regular hours in well-lighted and comfortable settings. Self-employed designers tend to work longer hours. Designers frequently adjust their workday to suit their clients, meeting with them evenings or on weekends when necessary. They may transact business in clients' homes or offices, in their own offices, or in showrooms.

➤ **EDUCATION, TRAINING, QUALIFICATIONS:** Educational requirements vary. Some design occupations such as industrial design, require a bachelor's degree. Interior designers also generally need a college education, preferably a 4-year degree in fine arts. In fashion design too, a 2 or 4 year degree is almost always needed to land a job. Graduates of 2 year programs generally qualify as assistants to designers. Floral design is taught in private trade and technical schools.

➤ **EARNINGS:** Median annual earnings of experienced full-time designers in all design specialties were about $33,000 in 1998. The top 10% earned more than $70,000. Floral designers earned less, averaging approximately $16,500 a year. Industrial designers in managerial or executive positions earned up to $145,000.

➤ **KEY CONTACTS:** For more information on careers in design contact:

- **American Society of Furniture Designers:** P.O. Box 2688, High Point, NC 27261

- **American Society for Interior Designers:** 608 Massachusetts Ave., NE, Washington, DC 20002-6006

- **Foundation for Interior Design Education Research:** 60 Monroe Center, NW, Grand Rapids, MI 49503
  Web site: *http://www.fider.org*

- **Industrial Designers Society of America:** 1142-E Walker Rd., Great Falls, VA 22066
  Web site: *http://www.idsa.org*

- **National Association of Schools of Art and Design:** 11250 Roger Bacon Dr., Suite 21, Reston, VA 22090

PHOTOGRAPHERS AND
CAMERA OPERATORS

➤ **EMPLOYMENT OUTLOOK:** Average overall growth is expected because of growing importance of visual images in education, communications, and entertainment. Faster than average growth is expected for camera operators. Jobs are expected to expand from 158,000 in 1998 to 195,000 in 2006. Four out of ten photographers are self-employed.

➤ **NATURE OF WORK:** Photographers and camera operators use a variety of photo and electronic equipment to film in a variety of specialty areas—portrait, commercial, and news photography. Some specialize in aerial, police, medical, or scientific photography which requires specialization in such fields as engineering, medicine, biology, or chemistry. They also make films for TV news and film private ceremonies and special events. Photojournalists photograph newsworthy events, places, people and things for publication in newspapers, journals, and magazines. Taking quality pictures and movies is both a technical and a creative process. Major technological changes have had an important impact on this field as more and more photographers use digital cameras, scanners, and computers to process and transmit their images.

➤ **WORKING CONDITIONS:** Working conditions vary considerably. Photographers in government, commercial studios, and advertising agencies usually work a 5 day 35-40 hour week. Newspaper photographers and camera operators may work long and irregular hours and must be available on short notice. Press and commercial photographers and camera operators may frequently travel locally or overnight. Their work may put them in uncomfortable or even dangerous surroundings. This is especially true for photojournalists assigned to cover natural disasters or military conflicts. They may stand long hours carrying heavy equipment and may face deadlines that create stress.

➤ **EDUCATION, TRAINING, QUALIFICATIONS:** Many entry level jobs require little formal preparation in photography. However, entry level positions in photojournalism and in scientific or technical photography are likely to require a college degree. Learning on the job is a good approach for fashion, commercial and portrait photography.

Camera operators also generally acquire their skills through on-the-job training. Many schools offer courses in photography; there are relatively few academic programs in cinematography. Most schools do not offer degrees in photography or cinematography.

➤ **EARNINGS:** The median annual earnings for salaried photographers and camera operators who worked full time were about $31,500 in 1998. The top 10 percent earned more than $76,000, while the lowest 10 percent earned less than $15,000.

➤ **KEY CONTACTS:** For more information on careers for photographers and camera operators, contact:

- **American Society of Media Photographers:** 14 Washington Road, Suite 502, Princeton Junction, NJ 08550-1033, Tel. 609-799-8300

- **National Press Photographers Association:** 3200 Croasdaile Dr., Suite 306, Durham, NC 27705

- **Newspaper Guild:** Education Department, 8611 Second Avenue, Silver Springs, MD 20910, Tel. 301/585-2990

- **Professional Photographers of America, Inc.:** 57 Forsyth St., Suite 1600, Atlanta, GA 30303, Tel. 404/522-8600

RADIO AND TV NEWS ANNOUNCERS AND NEWSCASTERS

➤ **EMPLOYMENT OUTLOOK:** Employment is expected to remain flat or decline slightly as few new radio and TV stations are licensed and the number of cable TV stations remains stable. Competition for entry jobs will be strong because the glamorous broadcasting field attracts many more jobseekers than there are jobs. Jobs will be easier to find in radio than in television because more radio stations hire beginners. The number of radio and television announcers and newscasters will remain around the 1998 employment figure of 52,000.

➤ **NATURE OF WORK:** Radio announcers, often called disk jockeys, select and introduce recorded music. Both radio and TV announcers present news, sports, weather and commercials; interview guests; and report on community activities—public service announcements and programming. At small radio stations they may operate the control board and sell commercial time to advertisers. Announcers at large stations usually specialize in sports, weather, or general news. Some are news analysts and present commentaries that interpret how events may affect the Nation or listeners personally.

➤ **WORKING CONDITIONS:** Announcers and newscasters usually work in well lighted, air-conditioned, soundproof studios. The broadcast day is long—some are on the air 24-hours—so announcers can expect to work long hours. Working on tight schedules and meeting deadlines can be stressful.

➤ **EDUCATION, TRAINING, QUALIFICATIONS:** Entry to this occupation is highly competitive. While formal training in broadcast journalism from a college or technical school is valuable, station officials consider taped auditions that show an applicant's delivery and in television, appearance and style. Those hired by television stations usually begin as production secretaries, production assistants, researchers, or reporters. A beginner's chance of landing an on-air job is remote except possibly for a small radio station. Students may gain experience at campus TV or radio facilities. On-the-job training in the form of an internship is especially valuable.

➤ **EARNINGS:** Salaries vary widely depending on the type and size of station. They are higher in television than in radio and higher in commercial than in public broadcasting. The median salary for radio news announcers in 1998 was $32,000. Salaries ranged from $7,500 in the smallest markets to $103,000 in the largest markets for on-air personalities. Sports announcers averaged $45,000, ranging from $11,000 in the smallest to $108,000 in the largest markets. In television, news anchors' median salary was $67,000, ranging from $26,000 in the smallest to just over $200,000 in the largest markets. Weathercasters' median was $54,600. Sportscasters' median was $50,000, ranging from $23,000 to $130,000.

➤ **KEY CONTACTS:** Additional information can be requested from:

- **Broadcast Education Association:** 1771 N St. NW, Washington, DC 20036

- **National Association of Broadcasters:** 1771 N St. NW, Washington, DC 20036

- **Radio-Television News Directors Association:** 1000 Connecticut Avenue, NW, Washington, DC 20036.

VISUAL ARTISTS

➤ **EMPLOYMENT OUTLOOK:** Strong demand for art, illustration, and design by advertising agencies, publishing firms, and other businesses will stimulate faster than average growth for graphic artists. Competition for jobs among fine artists will continue to be keen. The number of jobs is expected to increase from 278,000 in 1998 to 325,000 in 2006.

➤ **NATURE OF WORK:** Visual artists generally fall into one of two categories—graphic artists and fine artists—depending not so much on the medium but on the artist's purpose in creating the work. Graphic artists put their artistic skills at the service of commercial clients, such as major corporations, retail stores, and advertising, design or publishing firms. They create promotional displays and marketing brochures, design corporate literature, develop logos for products and businesses, and layout and design magazines, newspapers, journals, and other publications. Fine artists usually work independently, choosing the subject matter and medium that allows them to express themselves and may display their work in museums, art galleries, and homes.

Painters generally work in two dimension with any of a variety of materials: oils, watercolors, acrylics, pastels, magic markers, pencils, pen and ink, silkscreen, plaster, clay, or any of a number of other media. Sculptors design three-dimensional art—either molding and joining materials such as clay, wire, plastic, or metal, or cutting and carving forms from a block of plaster, wood or stone. Some sculptors combine materials such as concrete, metal, wood, plastic, and paper. Printmakers create printed images from designs cut into wood, stone, or metal, or from computer driven data.

Graphic artists use a variety of print and film media to create art that meets a client's needs. Most graphic artists use computer software and CD-ROMs to produce their work. Many are involved in designing the graphic elements of Internet sites. Cartoonists draw political, advertising, social and sports cartoons. Animators work in the motion picture and television industries drawing the large series of pictures which, when transferred to film or tape, form animated cartoons.

➤ **WORKING CONDITIONS:** Graphic and fine artists usually work in art and design studios located in office buildings or their own homes. While their surroundings are usually well lighted and ventilated, odors from glues, paint, ink or other materials may be present.

Graphic artists employed by businesses and art and design studios generally work a 40 hour week. During busy periods, they may work overtime to meet deadlines. Self employed graphic artists can set their own hours, but may spend much time and effort marketing their services to potential clients.

➤ **EDUCATION, TRAINING, QUALIFICATIONS:** In the fine arts field, formal training requirements do not exist, but it is difficult to become skilled enough to make a living without some basic training. Bachelor's and graduate degree programs in fine arts are offered in many colleges and universities. In the graphic arts field, demonstrated ability and appropriate training are needed for success. Evidence of talent and skill shown in the "portfolio" is an important factor used by art directors and others in deciding whether to hire or contract out work to an artist. Assembling a successful portfolio requires skills generally developed in a postsecondary art school program.

➤ **EARNINGS:** Median earnings for salaried visual artists who usually work full time were about $28,000 a year in 1998. The top 10 percent earned in excess of $44,000. Entry-level graphic designers earned between $23,000 and $27,000. Many are self-employed.

➤ **KEY CONTACTS:** For additional information about careers in graphic arts or illustration contact:

- **The American Institute of Graphic Arts:** 164 Fifth Ave., New York, NY 10010, Tel. 800/548-1634

- **The National Association of Schools of Art and Design:** 11250 Roger Bacon Dr., Suite 21, Reston, VA 20190, Tel. 703/437-0700

- **The Society of Publication Designers:** 60 East 42nd St., Suite 721, New York, NY 10165-1416, Tel. 212/983-8585

WRITERS AND EDITORS

➤ **EMPLOYMENT OUTLOOK:** Increased demand for salaried writers in publishing, public relations, communications, and advertising should cause employment to rise faster than average. Keen competition is expected to continue. We expect employment to increase from 288,000 in 1998 to 345,000 in 2006.

➤ **NATURE OF WORK:** Writers develop original fiction and nonfiction for books, magazines, trade journals, newspapers, technical studies and reports, company newsletters, radio and television broadcasts, and advertisements. Editors supervise writers and select and prepare material for publication or broadcasting.

➤ **WORKING CONDITIONS:** Working conditions for writers and editors vary with the kind of publication they work on and the kind of articles they produce. Some work in comfortable offices; others must travel and visit diverse places to gather data for their writing. The work week usually is 35-40 hours. Night and weekend work is required of those who prepare morning or weekend publications or broadcasts. Some work overtime to develop a late-breaking story.

➤ **EDUCATION, TRAINING, QUALIFICATIONS:** A college degree is generally required. Although some employers look for a broad liberal arts background, most prefer to hire people with degrees in communication, journalism, or English. Technical writing requires a degree or knowledge about a specialized field such as engineering, business or one of the sciences. Word processing skills may be required; familiarity with electronic publishing, graphics and video production equipment is increasingly needed. Writers must be proficient at doing research and in presenting material.

High school and college newspapers, literary magazines, and community newspapers and radio and television stations all provide valuable —sometimes unpaid—practical writing experience. College internships can give on-the-job experience.

➤ **EARNINGS:** In 1998, beginning salaries for writers and editorial assistants averaged $22,000 annually. Those with at least 5 years experience averaged more than $31,000 and senior editors at the largest newspapers earned over $68,000 a year. Technical writers and editors in the federal government averaged $48,000; other writers and editors averaged $47,000.

➤ **KEY CONTACTS:** For information and careers in journalism contact:

- **American Society of Magazine Editors:** 919 3rd Avenue, New York, NY 10022

- **Society for Technical Communication, Inc.:** 901 N. Stuart St., Suite 904, Arlington, VA 22203

13

Travel and Hospitality Careers

The travel and hospitality industries are expected to experience major growth during the coming decade. Given an aging population with more disposable income as well as increased domestic and international business activity, Americans are expected to travel with increased frequency in the decade ahead for both business and pleasure. This is good news for the complex of interrelated industries that define the travel and hospitality industries—airlines, rental car companies, hotels, motels, resorts, cruise lines, incentive groups, wholesalers, meeting planners, restaurants, and travel agencies.

The bad news is that many jobs in the travel and hospitality industries are low paying jobs. Although they receive numerous travel perks, travel agents, for example, receive near minimum wages. While flight attendants may appear to be in a glamorous occupation, the work can be stressful and the pay low. On the other hand, airline pilots tend to be well paid, and many people in the travel and hospitality industries make a very good living.

The travel and hospitality industries do offer some of the most interesting and exciting careers available today. People working in the travel and hospitality industries report some of the highest levels of job satisfaction found in any career field. If you enjoy travel and working with people, you'll discover numerous appealing jobs in these industries. Entry into many of these jobs is relatively easy. Many jobs require few educational credentials and little experience. Advancement and rewards tend to go to those who perform.

AIRCRAFT PILOTS

➤ **EMPLOYMENT OUTLOOK:** While employment is expected to increase as fast as average for most other occupations—increasing from 115,000 jobs in 1998 to 125,000 jobs in 2006—competition for these jobs will be keen. The number of applicants is expected to exceed the number of jobs available as the military, which is the major source for commercial pilots, continues to downsize.

➤ **NATURE OF WORK:** Pilots are highly trained people who fly airplanes and helicopters to carry out a wide variety of tasks. Most pilots transport passengers, cargo, and mail, while others dust crops, spread seed for reforestation, test aircraft, and take photographs. Helicopter pilots are involved in firefighting, police work, offshore exploration for natural resources, evacuation and rescue efforts, logging operations, construction work, and weather station operations.

➤ **WORKING CONDITIONS:** By law, airline pilots cannot fly more than 100 hours a month or more than 1,000 hours a year. Most airline pilots fly an average of 75 hours a month and work an additional 120 hours a month performing non-flying duties. Airlines operate flights at all hours of the day and night, so work schedules often are irregular. Pilots employed outside the airlines often have irregular schedules as well; they may fly 30 hours one month and 90 hours the next.

➤ **EDUCATION, TRAINING, QUALIFICATIONS:** All pilots who are paid to transport passengers or cargo must have a commercial pilot's license with an instrument rating issued by the FAA. To qualify for a license, applicants must be at least 18 years old and have at least 250 hours of flight experience. They also must pass a strict physical examination and a written test on the principles of safe flight, navigation techniques, and FAA regulations. They also must demonstrate their flying ability to FAA examiners. Pilots hired by airlines must be high school graduates; however, most airlines require 2 years of college and prefer to hire college graduates.

➤ **EARNINGS:** Airline pilots earn some of the highest salaries in the Nation. However, starting salaries with small airlines can be low. It's only after a pilot gains a great deal of experience and moves on to the major airlines and flies the largest aircraft that they begin to receive excellent salaries. In 1998, the average starting salary for airline pilots was about $17,000 at the smaller turboprop airlines to $28,000 at the major airlines. Average earnings ranged from $30,000 at the turboprop airlines to $78,000 at the largest airlines. Many senior captains on the largest aircrafts earned as much as $200,000 a year. Commercial helicopter pilots averaged $35,000 to $62,000 a year. Some helicopter pilots earned over $100,000 a year. Most airline pilots are unionized—members of the Airline Pilots Association.

➤ **KEY CONTACTS:** For addresses of airline companies and information about job opportunities and salaries, contact:

- **Airline Pilots Association:** 1625 Massachusetts Avenue, NW, Washington, DC 20036

- **Air Transport Association of America:** 1301 Pennsylvania Ave., NW, Suite 1110, Washington, DC 20006

- **Helicopter Association International:** 1619 Duke St., Alexandria, VA 22314

CHEFS, COOKS, AND OTHER KITCHEN WORKERS

➤ **EMPLOYMENT OUTLOOK:** Faster than average growth is expected due to the increasing size of the population and economy, while higher incomes and increased leisure time allow people to dine out more often. Jobs are expected to increase from 3.5 million in 1998 to 4.2 million in 2006.

➤ **NATURE OF WORK:** Chefs, cooks, and other kitchen workers prepare foods for restaurants, institutions, bakeries, and fast-food outlets. Chefs are the most highly skilled, trained, and experienced kitchen workers. Executive chefs coordinate the work of the kitchen staff and often direct certain kinds of food preparation. They decide the size of servings, sometimes plan menus, and buy food supplies.

➤ **WORKING CONDITIONS:** Many restaurant and institutional kitchens have modern equipment, convenient work areas, and air-conditioning; but others, particularly in older and smaller eating places, are frequently not as well equipped. Workers generally must withstand the pressure and strain of working in close quarters during busy periods, stand for hours at a time, lift heavy pots and kettles, and work near hot ovens and grills. Work hours in restaurants may include late evening, holiday, and weekend work, while hours in cafeterias in factories, schools, or other institutions may be more regular.

➤ **EDUCATION, TRAINING, QUALIFICATIONS:** Most kitchen workers start as fast-food or short-order cooks, or in one of the other less skilled kitchen positions that require little education or training and that allow them to acquire their skills on the job. An increasing number of chefs and cooks obtain their training through high school or post-high school vocational programs and 2- or 4-year colleges. Chefs and cooks may also be trained in apprenticeship programs offered by professional culinary institutes, industry associations, and trade unions. Some large hotels and restaurants operate their own training programs for cooks and chefs.

➤ **EARNINGS:** Wages of chefs, cooks, and other kitchen workers vary depending on where they work. Elegant restaurants and hotels pay the highest wages. Many executive chefs earned over $40,000 a year. Top chefs can earn twice that much. In 1998, median hourly earnings for cooks was around $7.00; assistant cooks averaged $6.75 an hour; bread and pastry bakers averaged $6.60 an hour; and salad preparation workers earned an average of $5.60 an hour.

➤ **KEY CONTACTS:** For information on career opportunities and educational programs for chefs, cooks, and other kitchen workers, contact local employers, local offices of the State employment service, or:

- **American Culinary Federation:** P.O. Box 3466, St. Augustine, FL 32085

- **Council on Hotel, Restaurant, and Institutional Education:** 1200 17th St. NW, Washington, DC 20036-3097

- **National Restaurant Association:** 1200 17th Street, NW, Washington, DC 20036-3097

FLIGHT ATTENDANTS

➤ **EMPLOYMENT OUTLOOK:** Although increases in the number and size of planes will result in faster than average employment growth, competition for jobs is likely to remain keen. Jobs are projected to increase from 135,000 in 1998 to 165,000 in 2006.

➤ **NATURE OF WORK:** Flight attendants are aboard all passenger planes to look after the passengers' flight safety and comfort. Before flights, attendants see that the passenger cabin is in order, that supplies of food, beverages, blankets, and reading material are adequate. As passengers board the plane, attendants greet them, check their tickets, and assist them in sorting coats and carry-on luggage. Before the plane takes off, attendants instruct passengers in the use of emergency equipment and check to see that all passengers have their seat belts fastened and seat backs forward. In the air, they answer questions, distribute magazines and pillows, help care for small children and elderly and handicapped persons, administer first aid, serve cocktails and meals. Upon landing, they assist passengers in leaving the plane.

➤ **WORKING CONDITIONS:** Attendants may work at night and on holidays and weekends. They usually fly 75 to 85 hours a month. In addition, they spend about 75 to 85 hours a month on the ground preparing planes for flight, writing reports following completed flights, and waiting for planes that arrive late. Because of variations in scheduling and limitations on flying time, many attendants have 11 or more days off each month. Attendants may be away from their home bases at least one-third of the time. The combination of free time and discount air fares provides flight attendants the opportunity to travel and see new places.

The work can be strenuous and trying. Flight attendants are susceptible to injury because of the job demands in a moving aircraft.

➤ **EDUCATION, TRAINING, QUALIFICATIONS:** Airlines like to hire poised, tactful, and resourceful people who can deal comfortably with strangers. Applicants must be at least 19 to 21 years old as well as high school graduates. Airlines prefer hiring those with several years of college or experience in dealing with the public. Flight attendants for international airlines must speak an appropriate foreign language fluently. Most large airlines require that newly hired flight attendants complete 4 to 6 weeks of intensive training in their own schools.

➤ **EARNINGS:** Beginning flight attendants in 1998 earned a median annual income of $14,000. Flight attendants with 6 years of flying experience had median annual earnings of about $21,000, while some senior flight attendants earned as much as $40,000 a year.

➤ **KEY CONTACTS:** For information on flight attendant careers, contact the individual airline companies or:

- **Air Line Employees Association:** 6520 South Cicero Avenue, Bedford Park, IL 60638, Tel. 708/563-9999

- **Air Transport Association of America:** 1301 Pennsylvania Avenue, NW, Washington, DC 20004

- **Future Aviation Professionals of America:** 4959 Massachusetts Blvd., Atlanta, GA 30337, Tel. 800-JET-JOBS

FOOD AND BEVERAGE SERVICE WORKERS

➤ **EMPLOYMENT OUTLOOK:** Employment is expected to grow faster than average due to the anticipated increase in the population, personal income, and leisure time. Replacement needs because of high turnover will result in plentiful job openings. Jobs are expected to increase from 4.9 million in 1998 to 5.6 million in 2006.

➤ **NATURE OF WORK:** Waiters and waitresses all take customers' orders, serve food and beverages, prepare itemized checks, and sometimes accept payments. In some establishments waiters and waitresses may perform additional duties such as escorting guests to tables, setting and clearing tables, or cashiering.

Bartenders fill drink orders waiters take from customers seated in the restaurant as well as take orders from customers seated at the bar. Most bartenders must know dozens of drink recipes and be able to mix drinks accurately, quickly and without waste. Bartenders collect payment, operate the cash register, clean up after customers have left, and may also serve food to customers seated at the bar.

Hosts and hostesses welcome guests, direct patrons to where they may leave coats and indicate where they may wait until their table is ready. Hosts and hostesses assign guests to tables, escort them to their seats and provide menus.

Dining room attendants and bartender helpers assist waiters, waitresses, and bartenders by keeping the serving area stocked with supplies, cleaning tables and removing dirty dishes to the kitchen.

Fast-food workers take orders, get the ordered items, serve them to the customer, and accept payment. They may cook and package French fries, make coffee and fill beverage cups.

➤ **WORKING CONDITIONS:** Food and beverage workers are on their feet most of the time and often have to carry heavy trays of food, dishes and glassware. During busy dining periods, they are under pressure to serve customers quickly. Many food and beverage workers are expected to work evenings, weekends and holidays; some work split shifts. Although some food and beverage workers work 40 hours or more per week, the majority are employed part-time.

➤ **EDUCATION, TRAINING, QUALIFICATIONS:** There are no specific educational requirement for food and beverage service jobs. Although many employers prefer to hire high school graduates for waiter, waitress, bartender, host and hostess positions, completion of high school is generally not required for fast food workers, or dining room attendants and bartender helpers. For many persons, these jobs serve as a source of immediate income rather than a career. Most food and beverage workers pick up their skills on the job by observing and working with more experienced workers.

➤ **EARNINGS:** Food and beverage service workers derive their earnings from a combination of hourly wages and customer tips. In 1998, median yearly earnings (including tips) of full-time waiters and waitresses were $14,500. The top 10 percent earned about $25,000 a year. Waiters at some of the very top restaurants are known to make up to $50,000 a year. For most waiters and waitresses, higher earnings are primarily the result of receiving more in tips rather than higher wages. Tips generally average 10-20 percent of the guests' checks, so waiters and waitresses working in busy, expensive restaurants earn the most.

In 1998, full-time bartenders had average yearly earnings (including tips) of $15,000. The top 10 percent earned around $28,000 a year. Average yearly earnings (including tips) of full-time dining room attendants and bartender helpers were about $14,000. Full-time counter attendants and fast-food workers averaged $12,000 a year.

➤ **KEY CONTACTS:** For information on food and beverage service jobs contact:

- **Council on Hotel, Restaurant, and Institutional Education:** 1200 17th St. NW, Washington, DC 20036-3097, Tel. 202/331-5990

- **National Restaurant Association:** 1200 17th Street, NW, Washington, DC 20036-3097

- **The Educational Foundation of the National Restaurant Association:** 250 South Wacker Dr., Suite 1400, Chicago, IL 60606, Tel. 312/715-1010

HOTEL AND MOTEL DESK CLERKS

➤ **EMPLOYMENT OUTLOOK:** Employment is expected to grow as fast as average as the number of hotels, motels, and other lodging establishments increases in response to increased business travel and tourism. Opportunities for part-time work should be plentiful. Jobs are projected to increase 150,000 in 1998 to 180,000 in 2006.

➤ **NATURE OF WORK:** Hotel and motel desk clerks may register guests, assign rooms and answer questions about available services, checkout times, the local community, and other matters. Because most smaller hotels and motels have minimal staffs, the clerk also may function as a bookkeeper, advance reservation agent, cashier, and/or telephone operator.

➤ **WORKING CONDITIONS:** Hotel and motel desk clerks are on their feet most of the time. During holidays and other busy periods, these clerks may find the work hectic due to the large number of guests or travelers who must be served. When service does not flow smoothly, because of mishandled reservations for example, these clerks act as a buffer between the establishment and its customers.

➤ **EDUCATION, TRAINING, QUALIFICATIONS:** A high school diploma or its equivalent usually is required. Hotel and motel desk clerk job orientation is usually brief and includes an explanation of the job duties and information about the establishment, such as room location and available services. They start work on the job under the guidance of a supervisor or experienced clerk. They may need additional training in data processing or office machine operations to use computerized reservation, room assignment, and billing systems.

➤ **EARNINGS:** In 1998, the average annual earnings of full-time hotel and motel clerks was around $15,000. Earnings depend on the location, size and type of establishment in which they work. Large luxury hotels and those located in metropolitan and resort areas generally pay clerks more than less expensive ones and those located in less populated areas. In general, hotels pay higher salaries than motels or other types of lodging establishments.

➤ **KEY CONTACTS:** Information on careers in the lodging industry may be obtained from:

- **The Educational Institute of the American Hotel and Motel Association:** P.O. Box 531126, Orlando, FL 32853-1126 Web site: *http://www.ei-ahma.org*

HOTEL MANAGERS
AND ASSISTANTS

➤ **EMPLOYMENT OUTLOOK:** The growing volume of business and vacation travel and foreign tourism will increase demand for hotels and motels, spurring average employment growth. Jobs are projected to increase from 180,000 in 1998 to 235,000 in 2006.

➤ **NATURE OF WORK:** Hotel managers are responsible for the efficient and profitable operation of their establishments. In a small hotel, motel or inn with a limited staff, a single manager may direct all aspects of operations. However, large hotels may employ hundreds of workers, and the manager may be aided by a number of assistant managers assigned among departments responsible for various aspects of operations. Within guidelines established by the owners of the hotel or executives of the hotel chain, the general manager sets room rates, allocates funds to departments, approves expenditures, and establishes standards for service to guests, decor, housekeeping, food quality, and banquet operations.

➤ **WORKING CONDITIONS:** Since hotels are open around the clock, night and weekend work is common. Many hotel managers work considerably more than 40 hours per week. Managers who live in the hotel usually have regular work schedules, but they may be called for work at any time. Dealing with the pressures of coordinating a wide range of functions as well irate patrons can be stressful.

➤ **EDUCATION, TRAINING, QUALIFICATIONS:** Postsecondary training in hotel or restaurant management is preferred for most hotel management positions, although a college liberal arts degree may be sufficient when coupled with related hotel experience. In the past, many managers were promoted from the ranks of front desk clerks and other positions within the hotel. Increasingly postsecondary education is preferred. However, experience working in a hotel—even part time while in school—is an asset to persons seeking to enter hotel management careers. A bachelor's degree in hotel and restaurant administration provides particularly strong preparation for a career in hotel management. Graduates of hotel or restaurant management programs usually start as trainee assistant managers, or at least advance to such positions more quickly. Large hotel and motel chains may offer better opportunities for advancement than small, independently owned establishments, but relocation every several years often is necessary for advancement.

➤ **EARNINGS:** Salaries of hotel managers varied greatly according to their responsibilities and the size of the hotel in which they worked. In 1998, annual salaries of assistant hotel managers averaged $42,000. Food and beverage managers averaged $44,000 a year. Front office managers averaged $29,000 a year. Salaries of general managers averaged nearly $55,000, but this represented a range of $40,000 to $83,000, depending on the size of the establishment. Managers also may earn bonuses (up to 25 percent) in some hotels and they and their families may be furnished with lodging, meals, parking, laundry and other services.

➤ **KEY CONTACTS:** For information on careers in hotel management contact:

- **The American Hotel and Motel Association:** Information Ctr., 1201 New York Ave. NW, Washington, DC 20005-3931

- **Council on Hotel, Restaurant, and Institutional Educational:** 1200 17th St. NW, Washington, DC 20036-3097, Tel. 202/331-5990

- **The Educational Institute of the American Hotel and Motel Association:** 1407 Harrison Road, 3rd Floor, East Lansing, MI 48823, Tel. 517/353-5500

RESERVATION AND TRANSPORTATION TICKET AGENTS AND TRAVEL CLERKS

➤ **EMPLOYMENT OUTLOOK:** Growing demand for travel services is expected to lead to a faster than average increase in employment. However, applicants can anticipate considerable competition because of the relatively low turnover and large supply of these workers. Jobs are expected to increase from 170,000 in 1998 to 215,000 in 2006.

➤ **NATURE OF WORK:** Reservation and transportation ticket agents and travel clerks facilitate passenger travel by answering questions and offering suggestions on travel arrangements. They make and confirm transportation and hotel reservations, calculate expenses, and write and sell tickets. When passengers are about to embark on their trip, these agents and clerks check their baggage, direct them to the point of departure, and help them to board.

Reservation agents usually work in large central offices answering customer telephone inquiries and booking reservations. Most agents have access to computer terminals and can obtain necessary information or modify the record on the computer. Ticket agents sell tickets, answer inquiries, check baggage, examine passports and visas, ensure passenger seating, and check-in animals.

➤ **WORKING CONDITIONS:** Working conditions vary. Although agents and clerks are found throughout the country, most work in downtown ticket and reservations offices and at large metropolitan transportation terminals, where most passenger business originates. Most work in comfortable well-lit space, some jobs require standing behind ticket counters, most involve working with people—either in person or by telephone. Since reservation facilities often operate 24-hours a day, many positions require working evenings, week-ends or holidays.

➤ **EDUCATION, TRAINING, QUALIFICATIONS:** Training requirements vary, however a high school diploma or its equivalent is usually required. For some jobs, such as airline reservation and ticket agents, some college education is preferred. With the exception of airline reservation and other passenger transportation agents, orientation and training for travel clerks is generally given on the job. Most airline reservation agents learn their skills through formal company programs. After completing classroom instruction, new agents work under supervisors or experienced agents for a short period of time. Automobile clubs train their travel clerks on the job, without formal classes.

➤ **EARNINGS:** In 1998, the median yearly earnings of reservation and transportation ticket agents and travel clerks was $22,500. Reservation and transportation ticket agents and travel clerks receive free or very low cost travel on their company's carriers for themselves and their immediate family.

➤ **KEY CONTACTS:** For information about job opportunities as reservation and transportation ticket agents and travel clerks, write the personnel manager of individual transportation companies. Addresses of airlines are available from:

- **Air Transport Association of America:** 1301 Pennsylvania Ave., NW, Suite 1100, Washington, DC 20004-1707

A brochure describing airlines jobs is available from:

- **Air Line Employees Association:** Job Opportunity Program, 5600 South Central Ave., Chicago, IL 60638-3797

RESTAURANT AND FOOD SERVICE MANAGERS

➤ **EMPLOYMENT OUTLOOK:** Growth in the number of eating and drinking establishments will result in faster than average growth in employment. Jobs are expected to increase from 500,000 in 1998 to 660,000 in 2006. Job opportunities will be especially good for those with a bachelor's or associate degree in restaurant and institutional food service management.

➤ **NATURE OF WORK:** Efficient and profitable operation of restaurants and institutional food service facilities requires that managers and assistant managers select and appropriately price interesting menu items, efficiently use food and other supplies, achieve consistent quality in food preparation and service, recruit and train adequate numbers of workers and supervise their work, and attend to the administrative aspects of the business. In larger establishments, much of the administrative work is delegated to a bookkeeper, but in others the manager must keep accurate records of the hours and wages of employees, prepare the payroll, and do paperwork to comply with licensing laws and reporting requirements of tax, wage and hour, unemployment compensation, and Social Security laws. They must also ensure that accounts with suppliers are paid on a regular basis. Today many managers are able to ease the burden of recordkeeping through the use of computers.

➤ **WORKING CONDITIONS:** Since evenings and weekends are popular dining periods, night and weekend work is common. Many restaurant and food service mangers work 50 hours or more per week. However, some managers of institutional food service facilities work more conventional hours because factory and office cafeterias are often open only on weekdays for breakfast and lunch.

When problems occur it is the responsibility of the manager to resolve them with minimal disruption to customers. The job can be hectic during peak dining hours, and dealing with irate customers or uncooperative employees can be particularly stressful.

➤ **EDUCATION, TRAINING, QUALIFICATIONS:** Many restaurant and food service manager positions are filled by promoting experienced food and beverage preparation and service workers. Waiters, waitresses, chefs, and fast-food workers who have demonstrated their potential for handling increased responsibility sometimes advance to assistant manager or management trainee jobs when openings occur. However, most food service management companies and restaurant chains recruit management trainees from among graduates of 2-year and 4-year college programs. They prefer to hire persons with degrees in restaurant and institutional food service management. A bachelor's degree in restaurant and food service management provides especially strong preparation.

➤ **EARNINGS:** Earnings vary greatly according to the type and size of the establishment. In 1998, restaurant and food service managers earned an average base salary of approximately $32,000 a year, but managers of the largest facilities often had base salaries in excess of $53,000. Besides a salary, most managers received an annual bonus or incentive payment based on their performance. In 1998, these payments ranged between $2,000 and $10,000 a year. Most received free meals.

➤ **KEY CONTACTS:** Career information is available from:

- **Council on Hotel, Restaurant, and Institutional Education:** 1200 17th St. NW, Washington, DC 20036-3097

- **Educational Foundation of the National Restaurant Association:** 250 South Wacker Dr., Suite 1400, Chicago, IL 60606

TRAVEL AGENTS

➤ **EMPLOYMENT OUTLOOK:** Much faster than average employment growth is projected due to the large increases expected in both
vacation and business related travel. Jobs should increase from 145,000
in 1998 to 195,000 in 2006. However, these projections could significantly change should more and more travel commerce, such as making
hotel and airline reservations, be conducted via the Internet. The recent
movement of airlines to reduce commissions to travel agents as well as
the move toward ticketless airline reservations are important signs that
such changes may well erode the traditional role of travel agent.

➤ **NATURE OF WORK:** Depending on the needs of the client, travel
agents give advice on destinations, make arrangements for transportation,
hotel accommodations, car rentals, tours, and recreation, or plan the right
vacation package or business/pleasure trip combination. They may advise
on weather conditions, restaurants, tourist attractions and recreation. For
international travel, agents also provide information on customs regulations, required papers and currency exchange rates. Travel agents may
visit hotels, resorts and restaurants to rate, firsthand, their comfort and
quality.

➤ **WORKING CONDITIONS:** Travel agents spend most of their time
behind a desk conferring with clients, completing paperwork, contacting
airlines and hotels for travel arrangements, and promoting group tours.
They may work under a great deal of pressure during vacation seasons.
Many agents, especially those who are self-employed, frequently work
long hours.

➤ **EDUCATION, TRAINING, QUALIFICATIONS:** Formal or
specialized training is becoming increasingly important for travel agents
since few agencies are willing to train people on the job. Many vocational
schools offer 3- to 12-week full-time training programs, as well as
evening and Saturday programs. Travel courses are also offered in public
adult education programs and in community and 4-year colleges. A few
colleges offer a bachelor's and a master's degree in travel and tourism.
Although few college courses relate directly to the travel industry,
courses in computer science, geography, foreign language and history are
most useful. The American Society of Travel Agents (ASTA) and the

Institute of Certified Travel Agents offer a travel correspondence course. Some people start as reservation clerks or receptionists in travel agencies.

➤ **EARNINGS:** Experience, sales ability, and the size and location of the agency determine the salary of a travel agent. The 1998 annual earnings of travel agents with less than 1 year experience were $17,000; from 1-3 years, $21,000; from 3-5 years, $23,000; from 5-10 years, $27,000; and more than 10 years, $33,000. Earnings of travel agents who own their agencies depend mainly on commissions from airlines and other carriers, cruise lines, tour operators, and lodging establishments. When they travel, agents usually get substantially reduced rates for transportation and accommodations.

➤ **KEY CONTACTS:** For further information on training opportunities contact:

- **American Society of Travel Agents:** 1101 King St., Alexandria, VA 22314, 703/739-2782
  Web site: *http://www.astanet.com*

- **The Institute of Certified Travel Agents:** 148 Linden St., P.O. Box 812059, Wellesley, MA 02181-0012, Tel. 800/542-4282

14

Resolution, Personal Services, and Transportation Careers

I n the final chapter of this section we survey a few careers that should provide numerous job opportunities in the decade ahead. The rate of increase for each of these jobs will be above average.

Given the pervasive and increased use of insurance and credit by both businesses and individuals in American society, we expect job opportunities for claim representatives and bill and account collectors to be excellent in the decade ahead.

Opportunities for animal caretakers will also increase in the coming decade given the growing population of pet owners who require the services of professional animal caretakers. Pet stores and kennels, and veterinary facilities should do an excellent business.

The services of electricians will continue to be in great demand for new construction, replacement of existing wiring, and the use of telecommunications and computer equipment.

One of the fastest growing job fields will be for services sales representatives. Given the highly competitive nature of growing services industries, the services of sales representatives to market a variety of services to both businesses and individuals will be in great demand.

Opportunities for truck drivers will continue to expand in response to overall population growth, businesses expansion, and the continuing turnover of drivers.

ADJUSTERS, INVESTIGATORS, AND COLLECTORS

➤ **EMPLOYMENT OUTLOOK:** Employment is expected to grow faster than average, in line with a growing population and a rising number of business transactions and consumer indebtedness. Growth should be slightly faster for claim representatives and bill and account collectors than for insurance clerks, adjustment clerks, or welfare eligibility workers. Jobs are expected to increase from a total of 1.4 million jobs in 1998 to 1.6 million in 2006.

➤ **NATURE OF WORK:** Handling complaints, interpreting and explaining policies or regulations, resolving billing disputes, collecting delinquent accounts, and determining eligibility for government assistance are tasks that must be handled for many organizations to run smoothly. Insurance companies, department stores, banks and government social services agencies employ adjusters, investigators, and collectors to act as intermediaries with the public in these kinds of situations.

➤ **WORKING CONDITIONS:** Most claim examiners have desk jobs and work a standard 5-day, 40-hour week. Claim examiners may work longer hours during peak periods. They may have to travel occasionally to obtain information by personal interview. Some may visit the scene of a disaster such as a hurricane to work with local adjusters. Adjustment clerks, bill and account collectors, and welfare eligibility workers and interviewers work in offices dealing with clients by telephone or in person. Dealing with upset clients can be stressful and is often part of the daily routine. Adjusters, investigators, and collectors who spend a lot of time working at video display terminals may experience musculoskeletal strain and eyestrain.

➤ **EDUCATION, TRAINING, QUALIFICATIONS:** Most companies prefer to hire college graduates for claim representatives positions.

Persons may be hired without college training, however, if they have specialized experience. For example, persons with knowledge of auto mechanics may qualify as material damage adjusters. Although courses in insurance, economics, or other business subjects are helpful, a degree in almost any field is adequate. Most large insurance companies provide on-the-job training and home-study courses to beginning claims adjusters and examiners.

Because they often work closely with claimants, witnesses, and other insurance professionals, claim representatives must be able to communicate effectively and gain the respect and cooperation of others.

➤ **EARNINGS:** Earnings vary significantly. In 1998, adjusters and investigators earned a median yearly salary of $23,500. The median yearly earnings for records clerks were $21,000. The median yearly earnings for full-time welfare eligibility workers and interviewers were $24,000. Median yearly earnings of full-time bill and account collectors were about $22,000. Some bill and account collectors receive a base salary and work on commission beyond that.

➤ **KEY CONTACTS:** General information about careers as a claim representative is available from the home offices of many life and property and liability insurance companies. Contact:

- **Alliance of American Insurers:** 1501 Woodfield Rd., Suite 400 West, Schaumburg, IL 60173-4980

- **Insurance Institute of America:** 720 Providence Rd., P.O. Box 3016, Malvern, PA 19355-0716

- **Life Office Management Association:** 2300 Windy Ridge Pkwy., Atlanta, GA 30327-4308

Career information on bill and account collectors is available from:

- **American Collectors Association, Inc.:** P.O. Box 39106, Minneapolis, MN 55439-0106
  Web site: *http://www.collector.com/consumer/careers.html*

ELECTRICIANS

➤ **EMPLOYMENT OUTLOOK:** Average employment growth should result from the need to install and maintain electrical wiring in new facilities and replace existing wiring. Increased use of telecommunications and computer equipment also should create job opportunities. The number of jobs should increase from 580,000 in 1998 to 650,000 in 2006.

➤ **NATURE OF WORK:** Electricians install and maintain electrical systems for a variety of purposes, including climate control, security, and communications. They also may install and maintain the electronic controls for machines in business and industry.

➤ **WORKING CONDITIONS:** Electricians' work is sometimes strenuous. They may stand for long periods and frequently work on ladders and scaffolds. They often work in awkward or cramped positions. Electricians risk injury from electrical shock, falls, and cuts. Most work a standard 40-hour week, although overtime may be required.

➤ **EDUCATION, TRAINING, QUALIFICATIONS:** The best way to learn the electrical trade is by completing a 4- or 5-year apprenticeship program. Those who do not enter a formal apprenticeship program can begin to learn the trade informally by working as helpers for experienced electricians. High school courses in mathematics, electricity, electronics, mechanical drawing, science and shop provide a good background. Good color vision is needed because workers must frequently identify electrical wires by color.

➤ **EARNINGS:** Median annual earnings for full-time electricians who were not self-employed were $33,300 in 1998. The highest 10 percent earned more than $53,000 a year.

➤ **KEY CONTACTS:** For general information about the work of electricians contact:

- **Independent Electrical Contractors, Inc.:** 507 Wythe Street, Alexandria, VA 22314, Tel. 703/549-7351

- **National Electrical Contractors Association (NECA):** 3 Metro Center, Suite 1100, Bethesda, MD 20814

- **International Brotherhood of Electrical Workers:** 1125 15th Street, NW, Washington, DC 20005

- **International Society of Certified Electronics Technicians:** 2708 West Berry Street, Suite 3, Fort Worth, TX 76109-2356, Tel. 817/921-9101
  Web site: *http://www.iscet.mainland.cc.tx.os*

SERVICES SALES REPRESENTATIVES

➤ **EMPLOYMENT OUTLOOK:** The continued rapid increase in the demand for services will result in much faster than average employment growth. The number of jobs should increase from 700,000 in 1998 to 820,000 in 2006. Over half of their jobs will continue to be in firms providing business services, including computer and data processing; personnel supply; advertising; mailing, reproduction, and stenographic services; and equipment rental and leasing.

➤ **NATURE OF WORK:** Services sales representatives sell a wide variety of services, from pest control and printing services to advertising services and telephone communication systems. Sales representatives must fully understand and be able to discuss the services their company offers. They must develop lists of potential clients, meet with clients, and try to persuade prospective clients to use their services. If they fail to make a sale with the first contact, they must follow-up with more visits, phone calls or letters.

➤ **WORKING CONDITIONS:** Working conditions vary. Representatives who cover a large territory may spend a great deal of time traveling; those who sell exclusively by telephone will spend all their time in the office. Selling can be stressful work and the constant pressure of making new contacts is difficult for some people.

➤ **EDUCATION, TRAINING, QUALIFICATIONS:** Many employers require that services sales representatives have a college degree, but requirements vary depending on the service that a particular company sells. Employers who market advertising services seek individuals with a college degree in advertising or marketing or master's degree in business administration; companies that market educational services prefer individuals with an advanced degree. Companies that sell computer services prefer sales representatives with a background in computer science or engineering. Some employers hire sales representatives with a high school diploma if they have a proven sales record. This is particularly true for those who sell nontechnical services such as linen supply or exterminating services.

➤ **EARNINGS:** In 1998, median annual earnings of full-time advertising sales representatives were over $29,000. Representatives selling other business services had median earnings of nearly $33,000. Some sales representatives earn well over $100,000 a year and a select few may earn over $200,000. Sales representatives work on different types of compensation plans. Some get a straight salary; others are paid solely on commission; others get a combination of a base salary and commissions.

➤ **KEY CONTACTS:** For details about employment opportunities for services sales representatives, contact employers who sell services in your area or contact:

- **Sales and Marketing Executives International:** 6600 Hidden Lake Trail, Brecksville, OH 44141

TRUCK DRIVERS

➤ **EMPLOYMENT OUTLOOK:** Employment is expected to grow about as fast as average. Job opportunities in this large occupation should be plentiful because of the growing demand for truck transportation services and the need to replace drivers who leave the occupation. Jobs are expected to increase from 3.1 million in 1998 to 3.5 million in 2006.

➤ **NATURE OF WORK:** Work of truck drivers varies. Long-distance drivers may make short "turnaround" hauls where they deliver a load to a nearby city, pick up another loaded trailer and drive back to their home base in one day. Other runs take an entire day or longer and drivers remain away from home overnight. Local truck drivers may pick up a loaded truck in the morning and spend the rest of the day making deliveries or may make several trips between their dispatch point and customers to make deliveries.

➤ **WORKING CONDITIONS:** Truck driving has become less physically demanding because most trucks now have more comfortable seats, better ventilation, and improved cab designs. However, driving for many hours at a stretch, unloading cargo and making deliveries can be tiring. Driving in bad weather, heavy traffic or mountains can be nerve racking. Some self-employed long distance truck drivers who own as well as operate their trucks spend over 240 days a year away from home. Local truck drivers frequently work 48 hours or more a week. Many who handle food for chain grocery stores, produce markets, or bakeries drive at night or early in the morning. Many load and unload their own trucks, which requires considerable lifting, carrying, and walking.

➤ **EDUCATION, TRAINING, QUALIFICATIONS:** Qualifications are established by state and federal regulations. All truck drivers must have a driver's license issued by the state in which they live, and most employers strongly prefer a good driving record. All drivers of trucks designed to carry at least 26,000 pounds are required to obtain a special commercial driver's license. Many firms require that drivers be at least 25 years old, be able to lift heavy objects, and have driven trucks for 3-5 years. Many prefer to hire high school graduates and require annual physical examinations. Since drivers often deal directly with the company's customers, they must get along well with people.

➤ **EARNINGS:** As a rule, local truck drivers are paid by the hour and receive extra pay for working overtime—usually after 40 hours. Long-distance drivers are generally paid by the mile and their rate per mile can vary greatly. In 1998, truck drivers had average straight-time hourly earnings of $14.00. Most long-distance drivers operate tractor-trailers, and their earnings vary from as little as $22,000 annually to over $45,000. Most self-employed truck drivers are primarily engaged in long-distance hauling, and earnings of $23,000 to $28,000 a year are common after deducting living expenses and the costs associated with operating their trucks.

➤ **KEY CONTACTS:** Information on career opportunities in truck driving may be obtained from:

- **American Trucking Associations, Inc.:** 2200 Mill Rd., Alexandria, VA 22314, Tel. 703/838-1700
  Web site: *http://www.cais.com*

- **International Brotherhood of Teamsters, Chauffeurs, Warehousemen, and Helpers of America:** 25 Louisiana Avenue, NW, Washington, DC 20001, Tel. 202/624-6800

- **Professional Truck Driver Institute of America:** 8788 Elk Grove Blvd., Elk Grove, CA 95624, Tel. 916/686-5146

VETERINARY ASSISTANTS AND NONFARM ANIMAL CARETAKERS

➤ **EMPLOYMENT OUTLOOK:** Employment is expected to grow much faster than average, reflecting a growing population and economy. The number of cats and dogs has increased significantly over the last 10 years and is expected to continue to increase from 170,000 jobs in 1998 to 230,000 in 2006

➤ **NATURE OF WORK:** Kennels, animal shelters, pet stores, stables, veterinary facilities, laboratories, and zoological parks all house animals and employ caretakers. Caretakers feed, water, groom, bathe, and exercise animals and clean and repair their cages.

➤ **WORKING CONDITIONS:** People who love animals get satisfaction from working with and helping animals. However, some of the work may be physically demanding and unpleasant. Caretakers have to clean animal cages and lift heavy supplies like bales of hay. The work setting is often noisy. Animal caretakers can be exposed to bites, kicks, and disease from the animals they attend. Caretakers may work outdoors in all kinds of weather. Animals have to be fed every day, so caretakers rotate week-end shifts.

➤ **EDUCATION, TRAINING, QUALIFICATIONS:** Most animal caretakers are trained on the job. Thirty-five states require veterinary technicians to be licensed; this is the only animal caretaker position requiring licensure. Large zoological parks may require their keepers to have a bachelor's degree in biology, animal science or a related field. Requirements for laboratories vary with the position.

➤ **EARNINGS:** In 1998, median annual earnings for full-time animal caretakers were $16,000. The top 10 percent earned $26,000 a year.

➤ **KEY CONTACTS:** For more information write to:

- **Animal Veterinary Medical Association:** 1931 North Meacham Road, Schaumburg, IL 60173-4360

- **The Humane Society of the United States:** 2100 L St., NW, Washington, DC 20037-1598

- **National Animal Control Association:** P.O. Box 480851, Kansas City, MO 64148-0851

Part III

Resources For the 21st Century

Finding Your Best Job For the Future

Numerous resources are available to help you identify the best jobs of the future. These range from government publications to books, articles, computer software, and Web sites. Since the best jobs constantly change in response to changes in the economy, you may want to periodically review these resources.

This final chapter outlines key resources that can provide you with further linkages to the best jobs for the 21st century. We urge you to review many of these useful resources.

Key Directories

The U.S. Department of Labor publishes a wealth of information relating to job trends. We strongly recommend reviewing these publications which are available in most libraries:

➤ *Occupational Outlook Handbook*: Published biannually, this is the "bible" for surveying the top 250 occupations which cover nearly 85 percent of all jobs in the United States. Popularly referred to as the *OOH*, this book is the first place most job seekers should start if they are interested in considering job forecast information in their job search. Includes a wealth of information on outlook education, working conditions, earnings, related occupations, and resources. An interactive version of the OOH is available on the Internet by visiting the U.S. Department of Labor's Web site: *http://stats.bls.gov/oco/oco1000.htm*.

➤ *Dictionary of Occupational Titles*: This huge volume includes descriptive information on over 13,000 occupations. A great place to get an overview of all occupations and job titles. Most recent edition was published in 1991. This system of occupational titles is being phased out as the U.S. Department of Labor introduces its new O*NET (The Occupational Information Network) system of job classification.

➤ *O*NET Dictionary of Occupational Titles:* This is a new directory published by JIST Works but based on the U.S. Department of Labor's new O*NET job classification system which reduces the number of job titles from 13,000, as found in the *Dictionary of Occupational Titles*, to nearly 1,200 job titles. The new system has been designed to more accurately reflect the jobs of the 21st century. It will quickly become the standard by which all jobs in the coming decade will be classified.

➤ *Occupational Outlook Quarterly*: This quarterly magazine includes many informative articles on labor market trends, including the best jobs.

The U.S. Department of Commerce also publishes a useful directory relevant to job seekers:

➤ *U.S. Industrial Outlook*: Similar to the *Occupational Outlook Handbook*, this directory summarizes 350 major industries. It includes brief descriptions, forecasts, market trends, sales projections, and sources of additional information.

Several other directories also help individuals explore a variety of career options. The major ones include:

➤ *Encyclopedia of Careers and Vocational Guidance:* Produced by Ferguson Publishing (Chicago), this popular directory is used extensively in high schools and colleges for career exploration purposes. Published in four volumes, it examines several hundred technical and high-tech occupations in addition to the standard career and job fields. Also available on CD-ROM.

➤ *Specialty Occupational Outlook: Trade and Technical:* Published by Gale Research (Detroit), this directory includes information on 150 high-interest careers that do not require a bachelor's degree and do not appear in the *Occupational Outlook Handbook.*

➤ *Specialty Occupational Outlook: Professional:* Published by Gale Research (Detroit), this directory supplements the *Occupational Outlook Handbook* by providing insight into dozens of careers. Answers common questions in essay style within focused subsections.

➤ *The Complete Guide For Occupational Exploration:* Based on U.S. Department of Labor data and published by JIST Works (Indianapolis). Relates the 12,741 job titles in the *Dictionary of Occupational Titles* to 12 clusters of occupations based on the intersts of job seekers. Divides interest areas into 66 work groups.

➤ *Enhanced Occupational Outlook Handbook:* Based on U.S. Department of Labor data and published by JIST Works. Combines the best features of the *Occupational Outlook Handbook* with the *Dictionary of Occupational Titles.* Includes complete narrative from the OOH and all 7,700 related DOT job titles and job descriptions for the 3,000 most important ones.

➤ *Enhanced Guide For Occupational Exploration:* Based on U.S. Department of Labor data and published by JIST Works. Provides job descriptions for 2,500 of today's most important jobs.

➤ *Vocational Careers Sourcebook:* Published by Gale Research. Profiles 135 careers in the service industries, construction, sales, and other fields. Includes summary of skills and responsibilities, salary levels, and growth potential. Includes descriptions of career guides, associations, test guides, certification agencies, educational programs, scholarships, reference books, periodicals, and meetings.

➤ *Careers Encyclopedia:* Published by NTC Publishing (Lincolnwood, IL) and edited by Craig Norback. Provides information on 200 different careers. Includes job descriptions, employment opportunities, working conditions, qualifications, advancement, and income.

➤ *The Top 100: The Fastest Growing Careers For the 21st Century:* Published by Ferguson Publishing. Identifies and describes the 100 top jobs for the coming decade.

Annual Surveys

Several magazines publish annual surveys of the best or hottest jobs for the year. Many of these articles also make projections for the coming decade. The most popular and widely quoted such surveys are found in:

- *Money* (March issue)
- *U.S. News and World Report* (October issue)
- *Working Women* (July issue)

Since this is such a popular topic for magazines, you will periodically find similar articles in magazines such as *Glamour, Newsweek,* and *Time.*

Future Jobs

As noted in Chapter 4, several authors have published books that outline what they consider to be the best jobs and careers for the 1990s and beyond. A few of these books are published annually whereas others come out irregularly or only once. The major such titles include:

The 100 Best Careers For the 21st Century, Shelly Field (New York: Arco, 1996)

Adams Jobs Almanac 1998 (Holbrook, MA: Adams Media, 1997). Annual publication.

American Almanac of Jobs and Salaries, Jack Wright (New York: Avon, 1996). Irregular—published every two to four years.

The Great Jobs Ahead, Harry S. Dent, Jr. (New York: Hyperion, 1995)

Jobs 1998, Kathryn Ross and George Petras (New York: Simon & Schuster, 1997). Annual publication.

Jobs Rated Almanac, Les Krantz (New York: Wiley, 1995). Irregular—published every two to three years.

Several other books primarily focus on the best employers at present or in the decade ahead:

100 Best Companies to Work For in America, Robert Levering and Milton Moskowitz (New York: Doubleday, 1993)

150 Companies For Liberal Arts Graduates, Cheryl Woodruff (New York: Wiley, 1992)

Almanac of American Employers (Boerne, TX: Corporate Jobs Outlooks, 1994)

America's Fastest Growing Employers, Carter Smith (Holbrook, MA: Adams Media, 1994)

Best Companies For Minorities, Lawrence Otis Graham (New York: Penguin Books, 1993)

The Hidden Job Market 1999 (Princeton, NY: Peterson's, 1998)

Hoover's Hot 250 (Austin, TX: Hoover Publishing, 1997).

Hoover's Masterlist of 2,500 of America's Largest and Fastest Growing Employers (Austin, TX: Ready Reference Press, 1995). This paper directory comes complete with a computer diskette.

The Job Vault, Samer Hamadeh, Mark Oldman, H.S.Hamadeh (New York: Houghton Mifflin Co., 1997)

The JobBank Guide to Computer and High-Tech Companies (Holbrook, MA: Adams Media, 1997)

The JobBank Guide to Health Care Companies (Holbrook, MA: Adams Media, 1998)

Quantum Companies and *Quantum Companies II*, A. David Silver (Princeton, NJ: Peterson's, 1995)

Alternative Jobs and Careers

Several publishers produce series of books on alternative jobs and careers, many of which include the best jobs and employers for the decade ahead. For example, Impact Publications publishes separate volumes on government and international jobs:

- *Alternative Careers in Secret Operations*
- *Complete Guide to International Jobs and Careers*
- *Complete Guide to Public Employment*
- *Directory of Federal Jobs and Employers*
- *Federal Applications That Get Results*
- *Federal Jobs in Law Enforcement*
- *Find a Federal Job Fast!*
- *Guide to Careers in World Affairs*
- *International Jobs Directory*
- *Jobs in Russia and the Newly Independent States*
- *Jobs Worldwide*

NTC Publishing publishes one of the most comprehensive series of books on alternative jobs and careers. Their books now address 170 different job and career fields. Representative titles in their *"Opportunities in..."* series include:

- *Opportunities in Advertising*
- *Opportunities in Airline Careers*
- *Opportunities in Banking*
- *Opportunities in Business Management*
- *Opportunities in Child Care*
- *Opportunities in Craft Careers*
- *Opportunities in Electrical Trades*
- *Opportunities in Eye Care*
- *Opportunities in Interior Design*
- *Opportunities in Laser Technology*
- *Opportunities in Microelectronics*
- *Opportunities in Optometry*
- *Opportunities in Pharmacy*
- *Opportunities in Public Relations*
- *Opportunities in Robotics*
- *Opportunities in Sports and Athletics*
- *Opportunities in Telecommunications*

NTC Publishing also publishes two other useful sets of books in a *"Careers in..."* and a *"Careers For You"* series. The 22 titles in the *"Careers in..."* series include:

- *Careers in Accounting*
- *Careers in Advertising*
- *Careers in Business*
- *Careers in Child Care*
- *Careers in Communications*
- *Careers in Computers*
- *Careers in Education*
- *Careers in Engineering*
- *Careers in Environment*
- *Careers in Finance*
- *Careers in Government*
- *Careers in Health Care*
- *Careers in High Tech*
- *Careers in Horticulture and Botany*
- *Careers in International Business*
- *Careers in Journalism*
- *Careers in Law*

- *Careers in Marketing*
- *Careers in Medicine*
- *Careers in Science*
- *Careers in Social and Rehabilitation Services*
- *Careers in Travel, Tourism, and Hospitality*

You will find 31 books in NTC Publishing's *"Careers For You"* series:

- *Careers For Animal Lovers*
- *Careers For Bookworms*
- *Careers For Car Buffs*
- *Careers For Caring People*
- *Careers For Computer Buffs*
- *Careers For Courageous People*
- *Careers For Crafty People*
- *Careers For Culture Lovers*
- *Careers For Cybersurfers*
- *Careers For Environmental Types*
- *Careers For Fashion Plates*
- *Careers For Film Buffs*
- *Careers For Foreign Language Aficionados*
- *Careers For Good Samaritans*
- *Careers For Gourmets*
- *Careers For Health Nuts*
- *Careers For High Energy People*
- *Careers For History Buffs*
- *Careers For Kids at Heart*
- *Careers For Music Lovers*
- *Careers For Mystery Buffs*
- *Careers For Nature Lovers*
- *Careers For Night Owls*
- *Careers For Number Crunchers*
- *Careers For Plant Lovers*
- *Careers For Self Starters*
- *Careers For Shutterbugs*
- *Careers For Sports Nuts*
- *Careers For Stagestruck*
- *Careers For Travel Buffs*

Peterson's publishes a *"Careers Without College"* series of books. They currently have fourteen books in this growing series:

- *Building*
- *Cars*
- *Computers*
- *Emergencies*
- *Entertainment*
- *Fashion*
- *Fitness*

- *Health Care*
- *Kids*
- *Money*
- *Music*
- *Office*
- *Sports*
- *Travel*

Peterson's also publishes three popular *"Job Opportunities For..."* volumes for college graduates which are revised annually:

- *Job Opportunities For Business Majors*
- *Job Opportunities For Engineering and Computer Science Majors*
- *Job Opportunities in For Health and Science Majors*

Facts on File publishes seven books on alternative jobs and careers in the communication and entertainment industries:

- *Career Opportunities in Advertising and Public Relations*
- *Career Opportunities in Art*
- *Career Opportunities in the Music Industry*
- *Career Opportunities in the Sports Industry*
- *Career Opportunities in Television, Cable, and Video*
- *Career Opportunities in Theater and Performing Arts*
- *Career Opportunities in Writing*

JIST Works also publishes a series of books in their "America's Top Jobs" Series. Most are re-edited versions of the *Occupational Outlook Handbook* and other publications of the U.S. Department of Labor:

- *50 Fastest Growing Jobs*
- *Federal Jobs*
- *Top Jobs For College Graduates*
- *Top Jobs For People Without College*
- *Top 300 Jobs*

- *Top Industries*
- *Top Military Jobs*
- *Top Medical and Human Services Jobs*
- *Top Office, Management, and Sales Jobs*

If you are unable to find these books in your local library or bookstore, you can order most of these titles directly from Impact Publications. Order information is included at the end of this book in the "Career Resources" section. You may also want to visit Impact's online bookstore which includes many of these titles: *http://www.impactpublications.com*

Community Opportunities

Research on different communities can be initiated from your local library or on the World Wide Web. While most of this research will be historical in nature, several resources will provide you with a current profile of various communities. Statistical overviews and comparisons of states and cities are found in the *U.S. Census Data, The Book for the States,* and the *Municipal Yearbook.* Many libraries have a reference section of telephone books on various cities. If this section is weak or absent in your local library, contact your local telephone company. They have a relatively comprehensive library of telephone books. In addition to giving you names, addresses, and telephone numbers, the Yellow Pages are invaluable sources of information on the specialized structures of the public and private sectors of individual communities. The library may also have state and community directories as well as subscriptions to some state and community magazines and city newspapers. Research magazine, journal, and newspaper articles on different communities by consulting references in the *Reader's Guide to Periodical Literature,* the *Social Science and Humanities Index,* the *New York Times Index,* and the *Wall Street Journal Index.*

If you use the World Wide Web, you'll find numerous useful resources on communities. Most cities or local Chambers of Commerce have they own home pages which include linkages to local businesses and organizations. Many local newspapers and telephone directories also can be found on the World Wide Web.

If you are trying to determine the best place to live, you should start with the latest edition of David Savageau's and Richard Boyer's *Places Rated Almanac* (Simon & Schuster). This book ranks cities by various indicators. The new *Moving and Relocation Sourcebook* (Omnigra-phics) profiles the 100 largest metropolitan areas with information on population, education, recreation, arts, media, health care, taxes, transportation, and per capita income.

You should also consult several city job banks that will give you contact information on specific employers in major metropolitan communities. Adams Media (Holbrook, MA) annually publishes *The National JobBank* and *The JobBank Guide to Employment Services* as well as 33 annual job bank guides:

- *The Atlanta JobBank*
- *The Austin/San Antonio JobBank*
- *The Boston JobBank*
- *The Carolina JobBank*
- *The Chicago JobBank*
- *The Cincinnati JobBank*
- *The Cleveland JobBank*
- *The Dallas/Fort Worth JobBank*
- *The Denver JobBank*
- *The Detroit JobBank*
- *The Florida JobBank*
- *The Houston JobBank*
- *The Indianapolis JobBank*
- *The Las Vegas JobBank*
- *The Los Angeles JobBank*
- *The Minneapolis/St. Paul JobBank*
- *The Missouri JobBank*
- *The New Mexico JobBank*
- *The New York JobBank*
- *The North New England JobBank*
- *The Ohio JobBank*
- *The Philadelphia JobBank*
- *The Phoenix JobBank*
- *The Pittsburgh JobBank*
- *The Portland JobBank*
- *The Salt Lake City JobBank*
- *The San Francisco Bay Area JobBank*
- *The Seattle JobBank*

- *The Tennessee JobBank*
- *The Upstate New York JobBank*
- *The Virginia JobBank*
- *The Wisconsin JobBank*
- *The Washington D.C. JobBank*

Surrey Books (Chicago) also publishes a similar job bank series for ten major metropolitan areas:

- *How to Get a Job in Atlanta*
- *How to Get a Job in Chicago*
- *How to Get a Job in New York*
- *How to Get a Job in San Francisco*
- *How to Get a Job in Seattle/Portland*
- *How to Get a Job in Washington, DC*

Electronic Job Resources

You also will find numerous computer software programs, CD-ROM programs, and online services that provide information on the best jobs, employers, and communities. Our *Ultimate Job Source CD-ROM* (Professional Version), for example, includes this book as well as the *Dictionary of Occupational Titles* and *The Occupational Outlook Handbook* along with twelve other books and two hours of videos. Adams Media's CD-ROM entitled *Adams JobBank Fast Resume* provides access to a database of 17,000 companies.

Several resume databases and online career services offer a wealth of information about alternative jobs and employers. While disproportionately used with success by individuals in computer and high-tech fields, these services and sites appeal to individuals outside such technical fields. The major sites worth visiting include:

❑ **America's Job Bank:** *http://www.ajb.dni.us.* Here's the ultimate "public job bank" that could eventually put some private online entrepreneurs out of business. Operated by the U.S. Department of Labor, this is the closest thing to a comprehensive nationwide computerized job bank. Linked to state employment offices, which daily post thousands of new job listings filed by employers with their offices, individuals should soon be able to explore more than a million job vacancies in both the public and private sectors at any time through this service. Since this is your government at work, this service is free. While the jobs listing covers everything from entry-level to professional and managerial positions, expect to find a disproportionate number of jobs requiring less than a college education listed in this job bank. This service is also available at state employment offices as well as at other locations (look for touch screen kiosks in shopping centers and other public places) which are set up for public use. Useful linkages.

❑ **Career City:** *http://www.careercity.com.* Operated by one of the major publishers of career books (Adams Media), this online service includes job listings, discussion forums (conferences, workshops, Q&A sessions), specialized career services, and publications.

❑ **Career Magazine:** *http://www.careermag.com.* Offers a wealth of online information about jobs and employers as well as provides numerous linkages to other important sites. Tel. 303/440-5110.

❑ **CareerPath:** *http://www.careerpath.com.* By visiting this site, you will have access to over 125,000 job openings from major metropolitan areas across the country. Their database includes job openings in a wide array of fields, including technical, accounting, customer service, education, sales, social work, etc. New jobs are added daily. Free service. No registration required. Run by CareerPath; phone: 213/237-6658.

❑ **CareerMosiac:** *http://www.careermosaic.com.* This job service is appropriate for college students and professionals. Includes hundreds of job listings in a large variety of fields, from high-tech to retail, with useful information on each employer and job. Includes a useful feature whereby college students can communicate directly with employers (e-mail) for information and advice—a good opportunity to do "inside" networking.

❑ **CareerWEB:** *http://www.cweb.com.* Operated by Landmark Communications (Norfolk, Virginia) which also publishes several newspapers and operates The Weather Channel, The Travel Channel, and InfiNet, this service is a major recruitment source for hundreds of companies nationwide. Free service for job seekers who can explore hundreds of job listings, many of which are in high-tech fields. Includes company profile pages to learn about a specific company.

❏ **E-Span:** *http://www.espan.com.* This full-service online employment resource includes thousands of job listings in a variety of fields as well as operates a huge database of resumes. Job seekers can send their resumes (e-mail or snail mail) to be included in their database of job listings and search for appropriate job openings through the Interactive Employment Network. Also includes useful career information and resources. If you use commercial online services, E-Span can be accessed through America Online, CompuServe, and GEnie.

❏ **JobTrak:** *http://www.jobtrak.com.* This organization posts over 500 new job openings each day from companies seeking college students and graduates. Includes company profiles, job hunting tips, employment information, and numerous job resources compiled by Margaret Riley. Good source for entry-level positions, including both full-time and part-time positions, and for researching companies. Very popular with college students.

❏ **JobWeb:** *http://www.jobweb.org.* A relatively new and comprehensive online service targeted for the college scene, following the demise of kiNexus and Connexion. Operated by the National Association of Colleges and Universities (formerly the College Placement Council), this service is designed to do everything: compiles information on employers, including salary surveys; lists job openings; provides job search assistance; and maintains a resume database.

❏ **The Monster Board**: *http://www.monster.com.* This site provides job seekers with three primary services—job search, on-line resume building, and employer profiles. The job search provides for intelligent querying of both a U.S. and international job database. *The Employer Profiles* contained information on over 4,000 corporations worldwide.

❏ **National Business Employment Weekly:** *http://www.nbew.com.* The NBEW web site has links to many career-related resources.

Given the reputation and impact of the Wall Street Journal's *National Business Employment Weekly*, we recommend checking out this site. Lots of good employment-related information.

❑ **Online Career Center:** *http://www.occ.com/occ.* This is the grand-daddy of career centers on the Internet. It's basically a resume database and job search service. Individuals send their resume (free if transmitted electronically) which is then included in the database. Individuals also can search for appropriate job openings. Employers pay for using the service. Also available through online commercial services.

For more information on these and hundreds of additional online services and Web sites useful for exploring jobs and employers, we highly recommend the following books:

Adams Electronic Job Search Almanac 1998 (Holbrook, MA: Adams Media, 1998)

The Guide to Internet Job Searching, Margaret Riley, Frances Roehm, Steve Oserman (Lincolnwood, IL: NTC Publishing, 1998)

CareerXroads 1998, Gerry Crispin and Mark Mehler (Kendall Park, NJ: MMC Group, 1998)

Index

A

Accountants, 195-196
Actors, 234-236
Actuaries, 196-197
Adjusters, 263-264
Adult education teachers, 212-213
Advertising managers, 206-207
Age, 75-76
Agriculture, 79
Aircraft pilots, 247-248
Animal caretakers, 269-270
Apprenticeships, 67
Approaches, 37-39
Art careers, 233-246
Artists (see Visual artists)
Audiologists, 167-169
Auditors, 195-196

B

Baby-boomers, 44-45, 56-57, 75-76
Benefits, 66-67
Biological scientists, 182-183
Birth rates, 46-47, 75
Business:
    careers, 194-210
    small, 63

C

California, 62
Camera operators, 239-240
Career
    advancement, 64
    choices, 1
Careering, 9-11, 40-41
Careers, 21, 68, 95
Cashiers, 198-199

Chefs, 248-250
Chemical engineers, 183-184
Chemists, 184-185
Chiropractors, 137-138
Choreographers, 236-237
Cities, 61-62, 113-116
Civil engineers, 185-186
Clinical laboratory technologists
    and technicians, 139-140
Communities:
    declining, 36
    targeting, 109-111
Compensation, 98-106
Compliance officers, 219-220
Computer:
    careers, 171-180
    engineers, 176-177
    programmers, 174-176
    repairers, 173-174
    scientists, 176-177
    systems analysts, 176-177
Consultants, 204-205
Cooks, 248-250
Correctional officers, 213-214
Costs:
    housing, 124
    living, 125
    relocation, 121-123
Counselors, 214-216
Counter clerks, 199-200
Crises, 55

D

Dancers, 236-237
Demographics, 44-49
Dental assistants, 140-141

Dental hygienists, 142-143
Dentists, 143-145
Designers, 237-238
Detectives, 224-226
Dietitians, 145-146
Directors, 234-236
Diversity, 45, 57, 75
Downsizing, 2-3, 63-64
Dreams, 3, 8, 21

E

Economy, 2-4, 13-14, 23-27, 54-55
Editors, 244-245
Education:
   administrators, 221-223
   careers, 211-233
   system, 22, 25
   role of, 2, 59-60
Electrical and electronics engineers,
   186-187
Electricians, 265-266
Electroneurodiagnostic technologists,
   146-147
Electronic cottage, 51, 69-70
Emergency medical technicians,
   147-148
Employers, 116-120
Employment:
   dynamics, 28-30
   increases, 77
   temporary, 58-59
   white-collar, 59
Empowerment, 3, 16-17
Engineering careers, 181-193
Engineers:
   chemical, 183-184
   civil, 185-186
   electrical and electronics, 186-187
   industrial, 188-189
   mechanical, 189-190
Entertainment careers, 233-245
Entrepreneurism, 3

F

Financial managers, 209-210
Flight attendants, 250-251
Food and beverage service, 251-253
Food service managers, 258-259
Future:
   forecasting, 12-13
   planning, 8-9
   predicting, 42-68

G

Geologists, 187-188
Geophysicists, 187-188
Government:
   careers, 211-232
   employment, 77-78
   initiative, 33, 54
Guards, 218-219

H

Health care, 33, 66, 135-170
High school graduates, 110-112
High-tech, 67-68
Hiring practices, 65
Homemaker—home health aides,
   148-149
Hospitality careers, 246-261
Hotel managers, 255-256
Hotel/motel desk clerks, 253-254
Human Resources, 201-203
Human service assistants, 229-231

I

Immigrants, 48, 58
Industrial engineers, 188-189
Information clerks, 203-204
Initiative, 32-33
Inspectors, 219-220
Internet:
   careers, 171-180
   using, 284-287
International, 34, 54-55
Investigators, 263-265

J

Job(s):
   $100,000+, 106
   best, 3-6, 71-97
   creation, 35
   declining, 80
   disappearing, 12-13, 35
   generation, 39, 45
   growth, 74-80
   hopping, 63, 65
   hottest, 66, 79-80
   market, 37-40, 127-128
   new, 56
   opportunities, 72
   satisfaction, 64-65
   search, 37-39, 126-127
   top, 5-6
   transformation, 14-15
   trends, 4

Judges, 221-222

K
Kitchen workers, 248-250

L
Labor:
    relations specialists, 201-202
    shortages, 46,
Lawyers, 221-222
Legal careers, 211-232
Licensed practical nurses, 150-151
Lifestyles, 22
Literacy, 45, 52

M
Management analysts, 204-205
Manufacturing, 53, 78
Marketing managers, 206-207
MBA, 73
Mechanical engineers, 189-190
Media careers, 233-245
Medical:
    assistants, 151-152
    careers, 135-170
    record technicians, 152-154
    scientists, 182-183
Meteorologists, 190-191
Metropolitan areas, 121
Minorities, 45, 47, 57

N
Nurses, 165-166
Nursing aides, 153-154

O
Occupational profiles, 72-74
Occupations:
    declining, 83
    growing, 79-88
    new, 79
O*NET, 96
Operations research analysts, 178-179

P
Paralegals, 223-224
Pay (see Salary)
Pensions, 33
Perceptions, 27
Personal services careers, 262-270
Pharmacists, 156-157
Photographers, 239-240

Physical therapists, 157-158
Physicians, 158-159
Places, 107-132
Podiatrists, 160
Police, 224-226
Positive thinking, 3
Producers, 234-236
Productivity, 23
Property managers, 207-209
Psychiatric aides, 153-154
Psychologists, 226-228
Public policy, 23, 36-37

R
Race (see Diversity)
Radio, 240-242
Radiologic technologists, 162-163
Real estate:
    costs of, 124
    managers, 207-209
Re-careering, 40-41
Recreational therapists, 163-164
Regions, 61-62
Registered nurses, 165-166
Relocation, 39, 65-66, 108-109
Rental clerks, 199-200
Reservation clerks, 256-258
Resolution careers, 262-270
Respiratory therapists, 166-167
Resources, 15-16, 273-298
Restaurant managers, 258-259
Retirement, 57
Retraining, 32-33
Revolution, 7-8

S
Salaries, 4-6, 66, 98-106
School teachers, 228-229
Science:
    careers, 181-193
    technicians, 192-193
Service:
    industries, 77
    sector, 35
Services sales representatives,
    266-267
Social:
    service assistants, 229-231
    workers, 231-232
Special agents, 224-226
Speech-language pathologists,
    167-169
States, 55, 62, 111-113

Suburbs, 61
Success, 2-3

T
Talent, 3-4
Teachers (see School teachers)
Technology, 49-51
Television, 240-242
Temporary workers, 58-59
Third World, 67-68
Training, 201-203
Training managers, 201-203
Transportation careers, 262-270
Travel:
    agents, 260-261
    careers, 246-261
    clerks, 256-258
Truck drivers, 267-269

U
Uncertainty, 11-12
Underwriters, 209-210
Unemployment:
    cyclical, 53-54
    insurance, 23
    rates of, 23, 29
    structural, 31-32, 35-36
Unions, 60-61
Unique events, 12, 26
U.S. Department of Labor, 72-73,
    93-94, 96-97

V
Veterinary assistants, 269-270
Veterinarians, 169-170
Vision, 21
Visual artists, 242-244

W
Webmaster, 179-180
Women, 47, 57, 76
Workforce, 52
Writers, 244-245

Y
Youth, 44, 46, 75

The Authors

Ronald L. Krannich, Ph.D. and Caryl Rae Krannich, Ph.D., operate Development Concepts Inc., a training, consulting, and publishing firm. Ron received his Ph.D. in Political Science from Northern Illinois University. Caryl received her Ph.D. in Speech Communication from Penn State University.

Ron and Caryl are former university professors, high school teachers, management trainers, and consultants. As researchers, trainers, and consultants, they have completed numerous projects on management, career development, local government, population planning, and rural development in the United States and abroad during the past twenty years.

In addition to their extensive public sector work, the Krannichs are two of America's leading career and travel writers. They are authors of 28 career books and 11 travel books. Their career books focus on key job search skills, government jobs, international careers, nonprofit organizations, and career transitions. Their work represents one of today's most extensive and highly praised collections of career writing: *101 Dynamite Answers to Interview Questions, 101 Secrets of Highly Effective Speakers, 201 Dynamite Job Search Letters, Change Your Job Change Your Life, The Complete Guide to International Jobs and Careers, Discover the Best Jobs For You, Dynamite Cover Letters, Dynamite*

Resumes, Dynamite Salary Negotiations, Dynamite Tele-Search, The Educator's Guide to Alternative Jobs and Careers, Find a Federal Job Fast, From Air Force Blue to Corporate Gray, From Army Green to Corporate Gray, From Navy Blue to Corporate Gray, Resumes and Job Search Letters For Transitioning Military Personnel, High Impact Resumes and Letters, International Jobs Directory, Interview For Success, Jobs and Careers With Nonprofit Organizations, Jobs For People Who Love Travel, and *Dynamite Networking For Dynamite Jobs.* Their books are found in most bookstores, libraries, and career centers. Many of their works are available interactively on CD-ROM (*The Ultimate Job Source*).

Ron and Caryl live a double career life. In addition to their extensive career work, they continue to pursue their international interests through their innovative and highly praised *"Treasures and Pleasures...Best of the Best"* travel series which focuses on quality shopping and travel. When they are not found at their home and business in Virginia, they are probably somewhere in Europe, Asia, Africa, the Middle East, the South Pacific, or the Caribbean pursuing their other passion—researching and writing about quality arts and antiques. This is one of *their* best jobs for the 21st century!

Career Resources

C ontact Impact Publications for a free annotated listing of career resources or visit their World Wide Web site for a complete listing of career resources: *http://www.impactpublications.com*. The following career resources, many of which were mentioned in previous chapters, are available directly from Impact Publications. Complete the following form or list the titles, include postage (see formula at the end), enclose payment, and send your order to:

IMPACT PUBLICATIONS
9104-N Manassas Drive
Manassas Park, VA 20111-5211
1-800-361-1055 (orders only)
Tel. 703/361-7300 or Fax 703/335-9486
E-mail address: *impactp@impactpublications.com*

Orders from individuals must be prepaid by check, moneyorder, Visa, MasterCard, or American Express. We accept telephone and fax orders.

Qty.	TITLES	Price	TOTAL
Job Search Strategies and Tactics			
___	Career Chase	$17.95	___
___	Change Your Job, Change Your Life	17.95	___
___	Complete Idiot's Guide to Getting the Job You Want	24.95	___
___	Complete Job Finder's Guide to the 90's	13.95	___
___	Five Secrets to Finding a Job	12.95	___
___	How to Get Interviews From Classified Job Ads	14.95	___
___	How to Succeed Without a Career Path	13.95	___
___	Me, Myself, and I, Inc	17.95	___

___ New Rites of Passage at $100,000+   29.95 ___
___ The Pathfinder   14.00 ___
___ What Color Is Your Parachute?   14.95 ___
___ Who's Running Your Career   14.95 ___

Best Jobs and Employers For the 21st Century

___ 50 Coolest Jobs in Sports   15.95 ___
___ 100 Best Careers For the 21st Century   15.95 ___
___ 100 Jobs in the Environment   14.95 ___
___ 100 Jobs in Social Change   14.95 ___
___ 100 Jobs in Technology   14.95 ___
___ 100 Jobs in Words   14.95 ___
___ Adams Jobs Almanac 1998   15.95 ___
___ American Almanac of Jobs and Salaries   20.00 ___
___ Best Jobs For the 21st Century   19.95 ___
___ Breaking and Entering: Jobs in Film Production   17.95 ___
___ Careers Encyclopedia   39.95 ___
___ Careers in Multi-Media   24.95 ___
___ Great Jobs Ahead   11.95 ___
___ Jobs 1998   15.00 ___
___ Jobs Rated Almanac   16.95 ___
___ Sunshine Jobs   16.95 ___
___ The Top 100   19.95 ___

Key Directories

___ American Salaries and Wages Survey   110.00 ___
___ Business Phone Book USA 1998   148.00 ___
___ Careers Encyclopedia   39.95 ___
___ Complete Guide to Occupational Exploration   39.95 ___
___ Consultants & Consulting Organizations Directory   565.00 ___
___ Dictionary of Occupational Titles   47.95 ___
___ Encyclopedia of American Industries 1998   520.00 ___
___ Encyclopedia of Associations 1998 (all 3 volumes)   1195.00 ___
___ Encyclopedia of Associations 1998 (National only)   470.00 ___
___ Encyclopedia of Careers & Vocational Guidance   149.95 ___
___ Enhanced Guide For Occupational Exploration   34.95 ___
___ Enhanced Occupational Outlook Handbook   34.95 ___
___ Hoover's Hot 250   29.95 ___
___ Job Hunter's Sourcebook   70.00 ___
___ JobBank Guide to Employment Services 1998-1999   200.00 ___
___ National Job Bank 1998   320.00 ___
___ National Trade & Professional Associations 1998   129.00 ___
___ Occupational Outlook Handbook, 1998-99   22.95 ___
___ O*NET Dictionary of Occupational Titles   49.95 ___
___ Professional Careers Sourcebook   99.00 ___
___ Specialty Occupational Outlook: Professions   49.95 ___
___ Specialty Occupational Outlook: Trade & Technical   49.95 ___
___ Vocational Careers Sourcebook   82.00 ___

Education Directories

___ Colleges With Programs For Students With
    Learning Disabilities   32.95 ___
___ Free and Inexpensive Career Materials   19.95 ___
___ Internships 1998   24.95 ___

___	Peterson's Guide to Graduate & Professional Programs	239.95 ___
___	Peterson's Two- and Four-Year Colleges 1998	45.95 ___
___	Scholarships, Fellowships, & Loans 1998	161.00 ___

Electronic Jobs Search

___	Adams Electronic Job Search Almanac 1998	9.95 ___
___	CareerXroads 1998	22.95 ___
___	Guide to Internet Job Search	14.95 ___
___	How to Get Your Dream Job Using the Web	29.99 ___

Best Companies

___	Hidden Job Market 1998	18.95 ___
___	Hoover's Top 2,500 Employers	22.95 ___
___	Job Vault	20.00 ___
___	JobBank Guide to Computer & High-Tech Companies	16.95 ___
___	JobBank Guide to Health Care Companies	16.95 ___
___	Quantum Companies	25.95 ___
___	Quantum Companies II	26.95 ___

Best Places

___	30 Great Cities to Start Out In	17.95 ___
___	Places Rated Almanac	22.95 ___

$100,000+ Jobs

___	The $100,000 Club	25.00 ___
___	100 Winning Resumes For $100,000+ Jobs	24.95 ___
___	201 Winning Cover Letters For $100,000+ Jobs	24.95 ___
___	1500+ KeyWords For $100,000+ Jobs	14.95 ___
___	New Rites of Passage at $100,000+	29.95 ___
___	Six-Figure Consulting	17.95 ___

Finding Great Jobs

___	5 O'Clock Club Job Search Skills Program	43.95 ___
___	100 Best Careers in Casinos and Casino Hotels	15.95 ___
___	101 Ways to Power Up Your Job Search	12.95 ___
___	110 Biggest Mistakes Job Hunters Make	19.95 ___
___	Adams Executive Recruiters Almanac	16.95 ___
___	Alternative Careers in Secret Operations	19.95 ___
___	Back Door Guide to Short-Term Job Adventures	19.95 ___
___	Careers For College Majors	32.95 ___
___	College Grad Job Hunter	14.95 ___
___	Directory of Executive Recruiters 1998	44.95 ___
___	First Job Hunt Survival Guide	11.95 ___
___	Get Ahead! Stay Ahead!	12.95 ___
___	Get a Job You Love!	19.95 ___
___	Get What You Deserve!	23.00 ___
___	Great Jobs For Liberal Arts Majors	11.95 ___
___	How to Get Interviews From Classified Job Ads	14.95 ___
___	In Transition	12.50 ___
___	Job Hunting Made Easy	12.95 ___

___	Job Search: The Total System	14.95	___
___	Job Search 101	12.95	___
___	Job Seekers Guide to Executive Recruiters	34.95	___
___	Job Search Organizer	12.95	___
___	Jobs & Careers With Nonprofit Organizations	15.95	___
___	JobSmart	12.00	___
___	Knock 'Em Dead	12.95	___
___	New Relocating Spouse's Guide to Employment	14.95	___
___	No One Is Unemployable	29.95	___
___	Non-Profits and Education Job Finder	16.95	___
___	Perfect Pitch	13.99	___
___	Professional's Job Finder	18.95	___
___	Strategic Job Jumping	20.00	___
___	Top Career Strategies For the Year 2000 & Beyond	12.00	___
___	What Do I Say Next?	20.00	___
___	What Employers Really Want.	14.95	___
___	Work Happy Live Healthy	14.95	___
___	World Almanac Job Finder's Guide	24.95	___
___	You Can't Play the Game If You Don't Know the Rules	14.95	___

Assessment

___	Discover the Best Jobs For You	14.95	___
___	Discover What You're Best At	12.00	___
___	Do What You Are	16.95	___
___	Finding Your Perfect Work	16.95	___
___	I Could Do Anything If Only I Knew What It Was	19.95	___
___	Richard Bolles Self-Assessment Tool Kit	19.95	___

Inspiration & Empowerment

___	100 Ways to Motivate Yourself	15.99	___
___	Career Busters	10.95	___
___	Chicken Soup For the Soul Series	75.95	___
___	Doing Work You Love	14.95	___
___	Emotional Intelligence	13.95	___
___	Personal Job Power	12.95	___
___	Power of Purpose	20.00	___
___	Seven Habits of Highly Effective People	14.00	___
___	Survival Personality	12.00	___
___	To Build the Life You Want, Create the Work You Love	10.95	___
___	Your Signature Path	24.95	___

Resumes

___	100 Winning Resumes For $100,000+ Jobs	24.95	___
___	101 Best Resumes	10.95	___
___	1500+ KeyWords For $100,000+ Jobs	14.95	___
___	Adams Resumes Almanac & Disk	19.95	___
___	America's Top Resumes For America's Top Jobs	19.95	___
___	Asher's Bible of Executive Resumes	29.95	___
___	Best Resumes For $75,000+ Executive Jobs	14.95	___
___	Better Resumes in Three Easy Steps	12.95	___
___	Complete Idiot's Guide to Writing the Perfect Resume	16.95	___
___	Designing the Perfect Resume	12.95	___
___	Dynamite Resumes	14.95	___
___	Encyclopedia of Job-Winning Resumes	16.95	___

___	Gallery of Best Resumes	16.95 ___
___	Gallery of Best Resumes For Two-Year Degree Grads	14.95 ___
___	Heart and Soul Resumes	15.95 ___
___	High Impact Resumes & Letters	19.95 ___
___	How to Prepare Your Curriculum Vitae	14.95 ___
___	Internet Resumes	14.95 ___
___	Just Resumes	11.95 ___
___	New 90-Minute Resumes	15.95 ___
___	New Perfect Resume	12.00 ___
___	Portfolio Power	14.95 ___
___	Ready-to-Go Resumes	29.95 ___
___	Resume Catalog	15.95 ___
___	Resume Shortcuts	14.95 ___
___	Resumes & Job Search Letters For Transitioning Military Personnel	17.95 ___
___	Resumes For Dummies	12.99 ___
___	Resumes For Re-Entry	10.95 ___
___	Resumes in Cyberspace	14.95 ___
___	Resumes That Knock 'Em Dead	14.95 ___
___	Sure-Hire Resumes	14.95 ___

Cover Letters

___	175 High-Impact Cover Letters	10.95 ___
___	201 Dynamite Job Search Letters	19.95 ___
___	201 Killer Cover Letters	16.95 ___
___	201 Winning Cover Letters For $100,000+ Jobs	24.95 ___
___	Adams Cover Letter Almanac & Disk	19.95 ___
___	Complete Idiot's Guide to the Perfect Cover Letter	14.95 ___
___	Cover Letters For Dummies	12.99 ___
___	Cover Letters That Knock 'Em Dead	10.95 ___
___	Dynamite Cover Letters	14.95 ___

Networking

___	Dynamite Networking For Dynamite Jobs	15.95 ___
___	Dynamite Telesearch	12.95 ___
___	Great Connections	19.95 ___
___	How to Work a Room	11.99 ___
___	People Power	14.95 ___
___	Power Networking	14.95 ___
___	Power Schmoozing	12.95 ___
___	Power to Get In	24.95 ___

Interview & Communication Skills

___	90-Minute Interview Prep Book	15.95 ___
___	101 Dynamite Answers to Interview Questions	12.95 ___
___	101 Dynamite Questions to Ask At Your Job Interview	14.95 ___
___	101 Great Answers to the Toughest Interview Questions	9.99 ___
___	101 Secrets of Highly Effective Speakers	14.95 ___
___	111 Dynamite Ways to Ace Your Job Interview	13.95 ___
___	Complete Idiot's Guide to the Perfect Job Interview	14.95 ___
___	Complete Q & A Job Interview Book	14.95 ___
___	Interview For Success	15.95 ___
___	Interview Power	12.95 ___
___	Job Interview For Dummies	12.99 ___

Salary Negotiations

___	Dynamite Salary Negotiations	15.95 ___
___	Get More Money On Your Next Job (page 4)	14.95 ___
___	Negotiate Your Job Offer	14.95 ___

Government & Law Enforcement Jobs

___	Barron's Guide to Law Enforcement Careers	13.95 ___
___	Complete Guide to Public Employment	19.95 ___
___	Directory of Federal Jobs and Employers	21.95 ___
___	Federal Applications That Get Results	23.95 ___
___	Federal Jobs in Law Enforcement	14.95 ___
___	Government Job Finder	16.95 ___
___	Jobs For Lawyers	14.95 ___
___	Paralegal Career Guide	24.95 ___
___	Post Office Jobs	17.95 ___
___	Quick & Easy Federal Application Kit	49.95 ___

International & Travel

___	Complete Guide to International Jobs & Careers	24.95 ___
___	Great Jobs Abroad	14.95 ___
___	International Jobs Directory	19.95 ___
___	Jobs For People Who Love Travel	15.95 ___
___	Jobs in Paradise	14.95 ___
___	Jobs In Russia & the Newly Independent States	15.95 ___
___	Jobs Worldwide	17.95 ___

Job & Career Series

___	***"AMERICA'S TOP JOBS" SERIES***	**134.95** ___
___	▪ 50 Fastest Growing Jobs	14.95 ___
___	▪ Federal Jobs	14.95 ___
___	▪ Top 300 Jobs	18.95 ___
___	▪ Top Jobs For College Graduates	14.95 ___
___	▪ Top Jobs For People Without College	12.95 ___
___	▪ Top Industries	14.95 ___
___	▪ Top Medical and Human Service Jobs	12.95 ___
___	▪ Top Military Jobs	19.95 ___
___	▪ Top Office, Management & Sales Jobs	12.95 ___
___	***"CAREERS IN..." CAREER GUIDANCE SERIES***	**379.95** ___
___	▪ Accounting ('97)	17.95 ___
___	▪ Advertising ('96)	17.95 ___
___	▪ Business ('91)	17.95 ___
___	▪ Child Care ('94)	17.95 ___
___	▪ Communications ('94)	17.95 ___
___	▪ Computers ('96)	17.95 ___
___	▪ Education ('97)	17.95 ___
___	▪ Engineering ('93)	17.95 ___
___	▪ Environment ('95)	17.95 ___
___	▪ Finance ('93)	17.95 ___
___	▪ Government ('94)	17.95 ___
___	▪ Health Care ('95)	17.95 ___
___	▪ High Tech ('92)	17.95 ___
___	▪ Horticulture & Botany ('97)	17.95 ___

___	• International Business ('96)	17.95 ___
___	• Journalism ('95)	17.95 ___
___	• Law ('97)	17.95 ___
___	• Marketing ('95)	17.95 ___
___	• Medicine ('97)	17.95 ___
___	• Science ('96)	17.95 ___
___	• Social & Rehabilitation Services ('94)	17.95 ___
___	• Travel, Tourism, & Hospitality ('97)	17.95 ___

___	***"CAREERS FOR YOU" SERIES***	**449.95** ___
___	• Animal Lovers ('91)	14.95 ___
___	• Bookworms ('95)	14.95 ___
___	• Car Buffs ('97)	14.95 ___
___	• Caring People ('95)	14.95 ___
___	• Computer Buffs ('93)	14.95 ___
___	• Courageous People ('97)	14.95 ___
___	• Crafty People ('93)	14.95 ___
___	• Culture Lovers ('91)	14.95 ___
___	• Cybersurfers ('97)	14.95 ___
___	• Environmental Types ('93)	14.95 ___
___	• Fashion Plates ('96)	14.95 ___
___	• Film Buffs ('93)	14.95 ___
___	• Foreign Language Aficionados ('92)	14.95 ___
___	• Good Samaritans ('91)	14.95 ___
___	• Gourmets ('93)	14.95 ___
___	• Health Nuts ('96)	14.95 ___
___	• High Energy People ('97)	14.95 ___
___	• History Buffs ('94)	14.95 ___
___	• Kids at Heart ('94)	14.95 ___
___	• Music Lovers ('97)	14.95 ___
___	• Mystery Buffs ('97)	14.95 ___
___	• Nature Lovers ('92)	14.95 ___
___	• Night Owl ('95)	14.95 ___
___	• Numbers Crunchers ('93)	14.95 ___
___	• Plant Lovers ('95)	14.95 ___
___	• Self Starters ('97)	14.95 ___
___	• Shutterbugs ('94)	14.95 ___
___	• Sports Nuts ('91)	14.95 ___
___	• Stagestruck ('97)	14.95 ___
___	• Travel Buffs ('92)	14.95 ___
___	• Writers ('95)	14.95 ___

___	***"OPPORTUNITIES IN..." CAREER SERIES***	**2,199.95** ___
___	• Accounting ('96)	14.95 ___
___	• Acting ('93)	14.95 ___
___	• Advertising ('95)	14.95 ___
___	• Aerospace ('95)	14.95 ___
___	• Airline ('97)	14.95 ___
___	• Animal & Pet Care ('93)	14.95 ___
___	• Architecture ('93)	14.95 ___
___	• Automotive Service ('97)	14.95 ___
___	• Banking ('93)	14.95 ___
___	• Beauty Culture ('96)	14.95 ___
___	• Biological Sciences ('90)	14.95 ___
___	• Biotechnology ('90)	14.95 ___
___	• Book Publishing ('87)	14.95 ___
___	• Broadcasting ('92)	14.95 ___

____	▪ Building Construction Trades ('89)	14.95 ____
____	▪ Business Communications ('87)	14.95 ____
____	▪ Business Management ('91)	14.95 ____
____	▪ Cable Television ('93)	14.95 ____
____	▪ Carpentry ('93)	14.95 ____
____	▪ Chemistry ('97)	14.95 ____
____	▪ Child Care ('95)	14.95 ____
____	▪ Chiropractic Health ('94)	14.95 ____
____	▪ Civil Engineering ('96)	14.95 ____
____	▪ Cleaning Services ('92)	14.95 ____
____	▪ Commercial Art & Graphic Design ('92)	14.95 ____
____	▪ Computer Aided Design & Computer Aided Manufacturing ('93)	14.95 ____
____	▪ Computer Maintenance ('95)	14.95 ____
____	▪ Computer Science ('91)	14.95 ____
____	▪ Computer Systems ('96)	14.95 ____
____	▪ Counseling & Development ('97)	14.95 ____
____	▪ Crafts ('93)	14.95 ____
____	▪ Culinary Careers ('90)	14.95 ____
____	▪ Customer Service ('92)	14.95 ____
____	▪ Data and Word Processing ('96)	14.95 ____
____	▪ Dental Care ('91)	14.95 ____
____	▪ Desktop Publishing ('93)	14.95 ____
____	▪ Direct Marketing ('93)	14.95 ____
____	▪ Drafting ('93)	14.95 ____
____	▪ Electrical Trades ('97)	14.95 ____
____	▪ Electronics Careers ('92)	14.95 ____
____	▪ Energy ('92)	14.95 ____
____	▪ Engineering Careers ('95)	14.95 ____
____	▪ Environmental Careers ('95)	14.95 ____
____	▪ Eye Care Careers ('94)	14.95 ____
____	▪ Farming & Agriculture ('95)	14.95 ____
____	▪ Fashion Careers ('93)	14.95 ____
____	▪ Fast Food ('89)	14.95 ____
____	▪ Federal Government ('92)	14.95 ____
____	▪ Film ('90)	14.95 ____
____	▪ Financial ('91)	14.95 ____
____	▪ Fire Protection ('97)	14.95 ____
____	▪ Fitness Careers ('97)	14.95 ____
____	▪ Food Service ('92)	14.95 ____
____	▪ Foreign Language ('93)	14.95 ____
____	▪ Forestry ('92)	14.95 ____
____	▪ Franchising ('95)	14.95 ____
____	▪ Funeral Services ('97)	14.95 ____
____	▪ Gerontology & Aging Services ('95)	14.95 ____
____	▪ Health & Medical Careers ('91)	14.95 ____
____	▪ Heating, Ventilating, Air Con., Refrigeration ('96)	14.95 ____
____	▪ High-Tech ('95)	14.95 ____
____	▪ Home Economics ('88)	14.95 ____
____	▪ Homecare Services ('93)	14.95 ____
____	▪ Horticulture ('95)	14.95 ____
____	▪ Hospital Administration ('97)	14.95 ____
____	▪ Hotel & Motel Management ('92)	14.95 ____
____	▪ Human Resources Management ('94)	14.95 ____
____	▪ Information Systems ('91)	14.95 ____
____	▪ Installation and Repair ('94)	14.95 ____
____	▪ Insurance ('93)	14.95 ____
____	▪ Interior Design & Decorating ('95)	14.95 ____

___	▪ International Business ('95)	14.95 ___
___	▪ Journalism ('93)	14.95 ___
___	▪ Laser Technology ('89)	14.95 ___
___	▪ Law ('94)	14.95 ___
___	▪ Law Enforcement & Criminal Justice ('96)	14.95 ___
___	▪ Library & Information Science ('96)	14.95 ___
___	▪ Machine Trades ('94)	14.95 ___
___	▪ Magazine Publishing ('92)	14.95 ___
___	▪ Marine & Maritime ('88)	14.95 ___
___	▪ Marketing ('94)	14.95 ___
___	▪ Masonry ('93)	14.95 ___
___	▪ Medical Imaging ('93)	14.95 ___
___	▪ Medical Sales ('97)	14.95 ___
___	▪ Medical Technology ('96)	14.95 ___
___	▪ Mental Health ('95)	14.95 ___
___	▪ Metalworking ('91)	14.95 ___
___	▪ Military Careers ('89)	14.95 ___
___	▪ Modeling ('91)	14.95 ___
___	▪ Museum Careers ('96)	14.95 ___
___	▪ Music ('97)	14.95 ___
___	▪ Newspaper Publishing ('89)	14.95 ___
___	▪ Non-Profit Organizations ('94)	14.95 ___
___	▪ Nursing ('95)	14.95 ___
___	▪ Nutrition Careers ('92)	14.95 ___
___	▪ Occupational Therapy ('95)	14.95 ___
___	▪ Office Occupations ('95)	14.95 ___
___	▪ Paralegal Careers ('90)	14.95 ___
___	▪ Paramedical Careers ('94)	14.95 ___
___	▪ Part-Time & Summer Jobs ('87)	14.95 ___
___	▪ Performing Arts ('91)	14.95 ___
___	▪ Petroleum Careers ('90)	14.95 ___
___	▪ Pharmacy Careers ('90)	14.95 ___
___	▪ Photography Careers ('91)	14.95 ___
___	▪ Physical Therapy Careers ('93)	14.95 ___
___	▪ Physician Assistant ('94)	14.95 ___
___	▪ Physician Careers ('91)	14.95 ___
___	▪ Plastics Careers ('91)	14.95 ___
___	▪ Plumbing & Pipefitting ('95)	14.95 ___
___	▪ Postal Service ('92)	14.95 ___
___	▪ Printing ('92)	14.95 ___
___	▪ Property Management ('90)	14.95 ___
___	▪ Psychology ('94)	14.95 ___
___	▪ Public Health ('95)	14.95 ___
___	▪ Public Relations ('95)	14.95 ___
___	▪ Publishing ('95)	14.95 ___
___	▪ Purchasing ('90)	14.95 ___
___	▪ Real Estate ('97)	14.95 ___
___	▪ Recreation & Leisure ('90)	14.95 ___
___	▪ Religious Service ('88)	14.95 ___
___	▪ Research and Development ('97)	14.95 ___
___	▪ Restaurant Careers ('90)	14.95 ___
___	▪ Retailing Careers ('96)	14.95 ___
___	▪ Robotics ('93)	14.95 ___
___	▪ Sales ('95)	14.95 ___
___	▪ Science Technician ('96)	14.95 ___
___	▪ Secretarial Careers ('92)	14.95 ___
___	▪ Social Science ('97)	14.95 ___
___	▪ Social Work ('96)	14.95 ___

____ ▪ Special Education ('95)   14.95 ____
____ ▪ Speech-Language Pathology ('95)   14.95 ____
____ ▪ Sports & Athletics ('93)   14.95 ____
____ ▪ Sports Medicine ('93)   14.95 ____
____ ▪ State & Local Government ('93)   14.95 ____
____ ▪ Teaching ('93)   14.95 ____
____ ▪ Teaching English to Speakers of Other Languages ('95) 14.95 ____
____ ▪ Technical Writing & Communications ('94)   14.95 ____
____ ▪ Telecommunications ('95)   14.95 ____
____ ▪ Telemarketing ('94)   14.95 ____
____ ▪ Television & Video ('93)   14.95 ____
____ ▪ Tool & Die ('92)   14.95 ____
____ ▪ Training and Development ('97)   14.95 ____
____ ▪ Transportation ('97)   14.95 ____
____ ▪ Travel Careers ('96)   14.95 ____
____ ▪ Trucking ('92)   14.95 ____
____ ▪ Veterinary Medicine ('93)   14.95 ____
____ ▪ Visual Arts ('93)   14.95 ____
____ ▪ Vocational & Technical ('92)   14.95 ____
____ ▪ Warehousing ('93)   14.95 ____
____ ▪ Waste Management ('93)   14.95 ____
____ ▪ Welding ('97)   14.95 ____
____ ▪ Word Processing ('91)   14.95 ____
____ ▪ Writing ('89)   14.95 ____
____ ▪ Your Own Service Business ('85)   14.95 ____

City/State Job Guides

____ **CITY & STATE JOB FINDERS FOR 1998**   699.95 ____

Adams Media's "Jobs Banks to..."

____ ▪ Atlanta   16.95 ____
____ ▪ Austin/San Antonio   16.95 ____
____ ▪ Boston   16.95 ____
____ ▪ Carolina   16.95 ____
____ ▪ Chicago   16.95 ____
____ ▪ Cincinnati   16.95 ____
____ ▪ Cleveland   16.95 ____
____ ▪ Dallas/Fort Worth   16.95 ____
____ ▪ Denver   16.95 ____
____ ▪ Detroit   16.95 ____
____ ▪ Florida   16.95 ____
____ ▪ Houston   16.95 ____
____ ▪ Indianapolis   16.95 ____
____ ▪ Las Vegas   16.95 ____
____ ▪ Los Angeles   16.95 ____
____ ▪ Minneapolis/St. Paul   16.95 ____
____ ▪ Missouri   15.95 ____
____ ▪ New Mexico   16.95 ____
____ ▪ New York   16.95 ____
____ ▪ North New England   16.95 ____
____ ▪ Ohio   16.95 ____
____ ▪ Philadelphia   16.95 ____
____ ▪ Phoenix   15.95 ____
____ ▪ Pittsburgh   16.95 ____
____ ▪ Portland   16.95 ____
____ ▪ Salt Lake City   16.95 ____

___	▪ San Francisco Bay Area	16.95	___
___	▪ Seattle	16.95	___
___	▪ Tennessee	15.95	___
___	▪ Upstate New York	16.95	___
___	▪ Virginia	16.95	___
___	▪ Wisconsin	16.95	___
___	▪ Washington	16.95	___

City Job Source Guides

___	▪ Baltimore Job Source	15.95	___
___	▪ Miami Job Source	15.95	___
___	▪ Pittsburgh Job Source	15.95	___
___	▪ Washington Job Source	16.95	___

Insider's "How to Get a Job In..."

___	▪ Atlanta	16.95	___
___	▪ Chicago	16.95	___
___	▪ New York	16.95	___
___	▪ San Francisco	16.95	___
___	▪ Seattle/Portland	16.95	___
___	▪ Southern California	16.95	___

SUBTOTAL   _____

Virginia residents add 4½% sales tax   _____

POSTAGE/HANDLING ($5 for first
product and 8% of SUBTOTAL over $30) $5.00

8% of SUBTOTAL over $30 -------------------------- _____

TOTAL ENCLOSED ------------------------- _____

NAME _____

ADDRESS _____

_____

_____

❏ I enclose check/moneyorder for $ _____ made payable to
IMPACT PUBLICATIONS.

❏ Please charge $ _____ to my credit card:
❏ Visa   ❏ MasterCard   ❏ American Express   ❏ Discover

Card # _____

Expiration date: _____/_____

Signature _____

The On-Line Superstore & Warehouse

*Hundreds of Terrific Career Resources Conveniently Available
On the World Wide Web 24-Hours a Day, 365 Days a Year!*

Ever wanted to know what are the newest and best books, directories, newsletters, wall charts, training programs, videos, CD-ROMs, computer software, and kits available to help you land a job, negotiate a higher salary, or start your own business? What about finding a job in Asia or relocating to San Francisco? Are you curious about how to find a job 24-hours a day by using the Internet or what you'll be doing five years from now? Trying to keep up-to-date on the latest career resources but not able to find the latest catalogs, brochures, or newsletters on today's "best of the best" resources?

Welcome to the first virtual career bookstore on the Internet. Now you're only a "click" away with Impact Publication's electronic solution to the resource challenge. Impact Publications, one of the nation's leading publishers and distributors of career resources, has launched its comprehensive "Career Superstore and Warehouse" on the Internet. The bookstore is jam-packed with the latest job and career resources on:

- Alternative jobs and careers
- Self-assessment
- Career planning and job search
- Employers
- Relocation and cities
- Resumes
- Cover Letters
- Dress, image, and etiquette
- Education
- Telephone
- Military
- Salaries
- Interviewing
- Nonprofits
- Empowerment
- Self-esteem
- Goal setting
- Executive recruiters
- Entrepreneurship
- Government
- Networking
- Electronic job search
- International jobs
- Travel
- Law
- Training and presentations
- Minorities
- Physically challenged

The bookstore also includes a new "Military Career Transition Center" and "School-to-Work Center."

"This is more than just a bookstore offering lots of product," say Drs. Ron and Caryl Krannich, two of the nation's leading career experts and authors and developers of this on-line bookstore. *"We're an important resource center for libraries, corporations, government, educators, trainers, and career counselors who are constantly defining and redefining this dynamic field. Of the thousands of career resources we review each year, we only select the 'best of the best.'"*

Visit this rich site and you'll quickly discover just about everything you ever wanted to know about finding jobs, changing careers, and starting your own business—including many useful resources that are difficult to find in local bookstores and libraries. The site also includes what's new and hot, tips for job search success, and monthly specials. Impact's Web address is:

http://www.impactpublications.com